FOLK*of*LORE
NORTHAMPTONSHIRE

NORTHAMPTONSHIRE

LINCOLNSHIRE

RUTLAND

• Collyweston

Kingscliffe
•

LEICESTERSHIRE

Corby •

Oundle •

• Rothwell

Kettering •

CAMBRIDGESH

WARWICKSHIRE

Wellingborough •

Daventry •

● Northampton

BEDFORDSHIRE

Towcester •

BUCKINGHAMSHIRE

Brackley •

Kings •
Sutton

OXFORDSHIRE

FOLK*of*LORE
NORTHAMPTONSHIRE

PETER HILL

The
History
Press

Frontispiece: The county of Northamptonshire as it is today. At one time, part of Stamford, and the Soke of Peterborough, were within its boundaries. Changes have been made since the nineteenth century, the last being those which took place in the 1970s. It is still unique in being surrounded by eight other counties.

First published 2005
This edition first published 2009
Reprinted 2012

The History Press
The Mill, Brimscombe Port,
Stroud, Gloucestershire, GL5 2QG
www.thehistorypress.co.uk

British Library Cataloguing in Publication Data.
A catalogue record for this book is available from the British Library.

ISBN 978 0 7524 3522 0

Typesetting and origination by The History Press
Printed in Great Britain

Contents

ACKNOWLEDGEMENTS

I am grateful to the many people who have helped in getting the material for this book. In addition to those named in context for answering my many questions, allowing me access to various archives, private correspondence, diaries, research notes and information intended for publication which never made the final hurdle, I wish to thank Rachel Watson, Sue Groves, Sarah Bridges and the other archivists at the County Record Office for their assistance over the years; the Public Record Office; the Law Society; the staff at Northampton Museum and Peterborough Museum; Rothwell Heritage Centre and Wellingborough Heritage Centre. A word of special thanks is given to Terry Bracher and Colin Eaton of the Local Studies Collection at Central Library, Northampton for access to relevant parts of the John Clare collection and permission to use extracts from the manuscripts; Jo Langley at Corby Library; the staff at Daventry, Brackley, Towcester and Oundle Libraries; Oundle Museum; Manor House Museum at Kettering; Cambridgeshire Record Office; Leicestershire Record Office; and my former associates at the University of East Anglia.

The work of John Clare, Anne Elizabeth Baker, Thomas Sternberg, Christopher Markham and John Askham, all of whom recorded vital aspects of folklore and life, both current and fast disappearing at the time they were writing, is also duly recognised.

I would like to express a particular word of thanks to the following individuals for their help past and present: Gareth Fitzpatrick on behalf of the Duke of Buccleuch, Hugh de Capell Brooke, Gertrude Bagshaw, Jack Bailey, Harold Bazely, Annie Beaver, Burl Bellamy, Mia Butler, Rose Clark, John Clarke, Flo Colyer, George Deacon, Colin Elliott, Frank Ellis, Edna Essex, Norah Field, Alan Fookes, Maurice Goodwin,

John Green, Dorothy Grimes, Jim Harker, Elsie Harrison, Audrey Harwood, John and Gwen Hay, Carl Hector, Robin and Hilary Hillman, Judy Hopkins, Elizabeth Jordan, Pat Kimmons, Matthew Kirk, R.C. Lambeth, Adela Lock, Lance Lock, Mavis Maltby, Norman Mason, Bob Mears, Ron Mears, Alan Milton, Robert Newman, C.J. Ough, David Pain, Edith Palmer, Tom and Jane Parker, Sue Payne, Charles Peach, Connie Pickford, Marian Pipe, Mary Pittam, Harry Pywell, Monica Raine, Bill Richardson, Paul and Yasmin Rogers, Peter Rowney, Elvin Royall of the Rothwell Spoken Archive, Mabel Sculthorp, Beryl and Bill Simon, Audrey Singlehurst, Michael Smith, Reg Sutton, Commander Michael Saunders Watson, Alice Thomas and Mervyn Wilson.

I would like to mark my appreciation and admiration for the unknown photographers and illustrators of the past whom I have been unable to contact, who in many cases recorded something which has long since vanished. My gratitude also goes to Ron Mears, R. Lambeth, Carl Hector, Charles Herbert, Monica Raine and others whose work I have used in this book, and to the British Museum and the Mary Evans Picture Library for woodcut illustrations.

A debt of gratitude is also owed to the many local history societies around the county for whom I have given lectures, and the students on my courses who have given imput from their own experiences, family memoirs and other sources.

A special mention must be given to the many people I have interviewed over the years, most of whom were open and warm in their recollections to someone they hardly knew at first meeting, especially those who were in their eighties and nineties (though even in their time, much had already disappeared), and in particular to one special lady, who was born in the 1870s and died in 1969, who many years ago inspired my interest in folklore and history when I was very young. They were the last links with a world we have lost and it was a special privilege to share those priceless memories with them and to record their experiences, which might never have been written down and would have remained irretrievable. In some cases, they were inspired to personally write down their memoirs for members of their family both present and future, a task that in some ways rolled back the years, and gave them a chance to relive their youth.

Last but not least, my sincere thanks to Katherine Burton of Tempus Publishing for her interest in getting this, my fourth book for the company, into print; and to my family for their patience and understanding while I turned the home into a press office until the project came to fruition.

INTRODUCTION

If such an appliance as a time machine existed and we could go back to the past and see the county as it was 100, 200 or more years ago, most visitors would find it hard to come to terms with what they saw, heard and experienced. Accustomed to having a wide variety of consumables to choose from and the ability to afford them, having a substantial home with a range of utilities and a personal means of travelling from place to place as and when they want, it would not be an exaggeration to say they would be unable to tolerate or survive the life-style of our ancestors. Equally, if our ancestors could visit our world, they would also be shocked, not so much at the way the world has changed visually and made progress in science, medicine and technology, but by seeing the modern emphasis on money and success, the number of cars and the fast, stressful pace of life. They worked hard but they played hard too – they were survivors – and they had a vivid, colourful vocabulary, a superstitious mind and a range of customs, all of which helped them through the good and bad times of life.

Northamptonshire lies almost in the centre of England, stretching north-east to south-west, its shape likened variously to an oak leaf or a deflated balloon. Being surrounded by eight other counties has left it open to so many influences, which have affected its vocabulary and folklore. It is a county of contrasts, with miles of green and well-watered rolling countryside and river valleys punctuating the landscape, making it an attractive proposition for settlement ever since mankind came on the scene. Two of the county's rivers rise in the Naseby area: the Nene, which flows eastwards into The Wash, and the Avon, which meanders westwards through Shakespeare country and beyond. The older dwellings in the county have been constructed either with golden or honeycomb-coloured ironstone or the more durable grey Jurassic limestone, celebrated also for its use in the construction of the original St Paul's Cathedral and King's College Chapel in Cambridge, among other great buildings.

Events of early history within the county's boundaries have left an indelible mark, giving it such a distinctive character – it has been said that no other English county has so much contrast as Northamptonshire (Cox, 1933). Its division in the ninth century and the establishment of the Danelaw over nearly two-thirds of its area initiated the shaping of its character. Much of the county has been devastated in the past: Northampton was destroyed by King Sweyn of Denmark in 1010 and in 1065 the county suffered in the rebellion of Morcar, who swept down from Northumberland to assert his rights as its earl, meeting the King's emissary at Northampton but destroying county settlements en route. Northamptonshire was also one of the last counties to succumb to industrialisation; even today it seems to resist change and retain its rural character, despite the threats to the countryside posed by the need to accommodate new roads, housing and places of work and commerce.

The county has made a great contribution to English literature. The list of Northamptonshire writers is headed by poet John Clare, followed by dramatist and Poet Laureate John Dryden, metaphysical poet Thomas Randolph, novelist H.E. Bates, country life author Denys Watkins-Pitchford (known as BB) and, to a lesser degree, author Charles Kingsley, who spent six years of his early life at Barnack. To the list must also be added a literary figure, now almost forgotten, who had considerable influence on contemporary writers. This was Thomas Percy, who was vicar of St Peter and St Paul at Easton Maudit from 1753 to 1782, during which time he compiled *Reliques* (published in 1765), one of the best-selling literary works of the century. This collection of 195 ancient ballads is, in some ways, of major significance in the field of folklore and encouraged writers like Sir Walter Scott and Robert Burns to refashion old ballads into their own poetry, and inspired John Clare.

Of John Clare, little needs to be said. So much has been written about the great man and his wonderful nature poetry, which evokes all the sights, sounds, scents and activities of the countryside he loved, expressed in local dialect and using a rich vocabulary, much of which has long been obsolete. However, his poetic achievements overshadow his other activities as a collector of folk songs and dances and recorder of customs and games. There are brief glimpses of these features of life in the county in his poems and he described them in some detail in three very important sources for students of folklore: part of the introduction to *The Village Minstrel*, his autobiographical *The Cottage Festival* and a letter to William Hone, a London antiquarian and editor of *The Every-day Book*. These were brought together, with Clare's songs and tunes, by George Deacon in *John Clare and the Folk Tradition* (1983), from manuscripts held at Northampton Central Library, Peterborough Museum and the Carl H. Pforzheimer Library in New York.

We are indebted to other early pioneers in recording the county's folklore, such as the Northampton antiquarian and musician Thomas Sternberg, whose *The Dialect and Folklore of Northamptonshire,* published in 1851, was followed by Anne Elizabeth Baker's *Glossary of Northamptonshire Words and Phrases* (1854). Baker was given generous help and information by John Clare when he was at the asylum in Northampton. In many ways, John Askham of Wellingborough (1825-1894) continued the work of Clare, with wonderfully evocative nature poetry and glimpses of life past and present. Something of a Thomas Hardy-like character in his reaction against the changes around him, his *Sketches in Poems and Verse* (1893) were a milestone in the literature of the county. He also produced several other volumes of verse between 1863 and 1893, including a tribute to Clare.

Charles Montagu-Douglas-Scott published a collection of legends in *Northamptonshire Songs* (1904/1906), which was followed several years later by *Tales of Old Northamptonshire* (1936), which focused on legends from the north of the county in ballad form. Christopher Markham (d.1937) brought out a collection of sayings from around the county in *The Proverbs of Northamptonshire* (1897). More recently, the late Dorothy Grimes of Northampton brought out the first modern overview of past Northamptonshire life and lore in her privately published book, *Like Dew Before The Sun* (1991), which contains a wealth of material gleaned from a variety of sources around the county.

Although Northamptonshire is a county that has surprised and entranced visitors for generations, not all comments have been favourable. In a UK travel survey in the 1990s, Northamptonshire was placed in the lower reaches of a table of counties worth visiting, causing considerable outrage among locals, who rightly asserted that detractors have either not made a proper exploration and discovered its many charms, or have never been to the county and so do not know what they are missing! In some ways, this is due to the county having been bypassed in modern times, with the M1 on its western boundary and the A1 to the east.

In the past, however, some renowned visitors have been scathing. In 1763, author Horace Walpole, the son of Prime Minister Robert Walpole, stayed at the White Swan in Wellingbrough and wrote:

> Never stay in Wellingborough, the beastliest inn on earth is there...We were carried into a vast bed chamber which I suppose is the club room, for it stank of tobacco, like a Justice of the Peace! I desired some boiling water for tea – they brought me a sugar dish of hot water on a pewter plate.

Charles Dickens, as a young reporter for the *Morning Chronicle,* also had one traumatic visit in December 1835, when he stayed at the White Hart Hotel while covering a by-election in Kettering. In a letter to his wife, Kate, he described the chaos he experienced:

The noise and confusion here in Kettering this morning – the first day of polling here – is going to my head. The voters here are drinking and guzzling, howling and roaring, in every house of entertainment ... such a ruthless set of bloody-minded villains have I never set eyes on in my life ... they were perfect savages ... if a foreigner was brought here on his first visit to England I am quite satisfied he would never set foot in England again.

This was obviously a one-off view, for, like the majority of other visitors, he was entranced by what he saw in the county and was later inspired to use locations within it for his famous books. He used the Saracen's Head at Towcester in *The Pickwick Papers* and the local landscape and grounds of Rockingham Castle, the home of Richard and Lavinia Watson, were the inspiration for *Bleak House*. He stayed at Rockingham Castle on several occasions and he wrote and produced his playlets in the Long Gallery for small gatherings. He also dedicated *David Copperfield* to the family.

Every county has its own folklore and Northamptonshire is especially rich in traditions, dialect and vocabulary, legends and wondrous stories that have come down to us through the ages. Much has either vanished or has been ignored, hidden away in different places, awaiting rediscovery. This book sets out to redress the balance.

Peter Hill
January 2005

One of the many colourful village signs that can be seen in Northamptonshire. Most of these were designed and erected in preparation for the Millennium.

one

ROSE OF THE SHIRES

Northamptonshire is an apple without a core to be cut out, or a rind to be pared away.

These words by one of the county's renowned literary sons, Thomas Fuller of Aldwincle, in his 1662 book, *The Worthies of England*, sum up the affection and protectiveness felt by Northamptonshire folk over the centuries, a process that still continues relentlessly today. And yet, as each year goes by, so much of our everyday way of life – because of its very familiarity – has not been considered important, something to be valued, and has not been properly documented for future generations. Roy Paine of Rushden, whose family ancestry in the county stretches far back into the mists of time, sums up the attitude of many folk:

> This county is thickly clad in the vestments of the ages, and we locals wear the dialects, lore, deeds and happenings, like a comfortable suit of clothes. We know where to go to walk with the shades of the past ... you could say we have taken it all for granted.

Until recently, only a few interested individuals or local history societies were recording or researching the heritage of their communities. With the dawn of the new millennium, all this has changed and the county now has a fine network of enthusiasts and websites. Allied to this is the growth of interest in Northamptonshire's folklore.

So what is folklore? It is a study of the traditional beliefs, stories, events and customs of the common people. It is a never-ending process, as this store of traditions from the past is still being added to today, for as time goes on what is a normal part of life for us will gradually change and be forgotten, or become a distant memory. In other words, something that is modern now will, within a relatively short time, be seen as old-fashioned. Our way of life will join that of our ancestors as part of antiquity as new ideas and advances change the world.

Events that have determined the course of England's history in some way have taken place in the county, giving rise to certain connections and colourful, if fanciful, traditions that have become part of folklore. Thomas à Becket's Well in Northampton is where he is said to have paused to slake his thirst and rest during his flight from the town after his trial at the castle in 1164 for the misappropriation of funds and breach of Constitutions of the Realm. The Queen's Oak in Salcey Forest is said to be the tree where Edward IV met his future wife and consort, Elizabeth Woodville, whom he later secretly married at Grafton Regis, her family home, in May 1464. The tree was described in an early account as 'an oak so hollow, huge and old, it look'd a tower of ruin'd masonwork'.

Earlier, a crucial battle of the War of the Roses had taken place in the rain-drenched meadows at Delapré in Northampton in July 1460, which saw Yorkist forces defeat the Lancastrians, inflicting heavy losses (around 500 men) and taking Henry VI prisoner. The conditions and bloody carnage led to the field 'turning red' and the ghosts of the slain were said to have been seen and heard for many years afterwards.

The Tudor and Stuart periods would give rise to more fanciful legends. In 1585, Queen Elizabeth I is said to have visited Kirby Hall, which lies in isolation near Gretton. Kirby Hall was the newly acquired home of her chancellor and favourite dancing partner, Sir Christopher Hatton, a member of a distinguished county family. The esteem in which she held him was mentioned, if somewhat humorously, by Richard Barham in *The Ingoldsby Legends* (1837):

> So what with his form and what with his face,
> And what with his velvet coat guarded with lace,
> And what with his elegant dancing and grace,
> His dress and address so tickled Queen Bess
> That her Majesty gave him a very snug place;
> And seeing, moreover, at one single peep, her
> Advisers were, few of them, sharper or deeper,
> (Old Burleigh excepted) she made him Lord Keeper.

It is said that on certain nights of the year, a banquet given by Hatton in her honour is re-enacted at Kirby Hall, with flickering lights and shadowy figures seen dancing in the long-uninhabited building. Although there is no evidence that Elizabeth I did stay there, another tradition says that while in the area, she fell from her horse into a treacherous bog during a hunt and was rescued by men from nearby Corby. In gratitude, she issued a charter commanding that all men and tenants of the village be given certain rights and concessions around the kingdom:

> to be quit from such toll, pannage, murage and passage to be paid on accounts of their goods and things throughout our whole realm aforesaid ... Also that you do not place the same men and tenants of the same manor in any assizes, juries or recognisances to be held out of the Court of the Manor.

Fotheringhay is also the site of several traditions. In 1387, Edmund of Langley, the first Duke of York, acquired the castle which was in a ruinous state, rebuilding and enlarging it to grand proportions, as befitted such an illustrious family. The village became a hive of activity, with more accommodation being built outside the castle to cater for the number of important guests arriving for feasts and tournaments. Three members of the family who were slain on the battlefield were eventually buried there: Edward, the second Duke of York, who died at Agincourt in 1415; Edward IV's father, Richard, the third Duke of York; and brother Edmund, who

A costumed re-enactment at Kirby Hall, as part of an English Heritage Living History event.

were both slain at Wakefield. The future Richard III was born at Fotheringhay in October 1482, with one biased chronicler writing:

> ...he was suppressed in his mother's womb for two years, emerging with teeth and shoulder length hair.

Long after the demise of the castle, many local people insisted they could hear 'strange music' from drums and trumpets coming from the earthworks of the former castle, including one well-documented case in the 1950s of a policeman from Oundle who went to investigate but was unable to find or see anything tangible. A similar situation has also occurred on occasion in the now truncated church, the missing portion being part of an attached chantry college which disappeared in the years following the Dissolution. There have been cases of medieval funeral music being heard from within, but when the door has been opened to investigate, everything goes silent.

Mary Queen of Scots, who was seen as a threat to Elizabeth I, was imprisoned and ultimately beheaded at Fotheringhay Castle. On the way to her final destination, she is said to have uttered the word 'Perio!' as she sighted the village in the distance. The word was incorrectly taken to mean 'I perish!', when in fact she was passing through the former settlement called Perio and the road on which she was journeying was known as Perio Lane.

An engraving of the execution of Mary Queen of Scots at Fotheringhay Castle.

On 31 January 1587, eight days before her execution, a strange incident took place, for an hour from midnight, when a flame of bright fire appeared from nowhere and hovered outside the window of the queen's chamber, lighting up the room. It disappeared then returned twice more to act in the same manner. It was not visible anywhere else at the castle; only the guards, frightened out of their wits, were witnesses.

Mary's beheading took two blows of the axe and, after a final severing with a knife, the head was held up by the executioner. It became detached from the wig in the process and fell to the floor. An eyewitness, Robert Wynfield, wrote an account of the execution to Chief Minister Burghley, which included a description of a remarkable sight following the beheading:

> one of the executioners pulling of her garments espied her little dogge which was under her clothes, which could not be gotten forth but by force, and afterwards would not depart from its dead companion, but came and laid betweene her head and shulders.

After Mary's death, her apparition was said to follow an underground passage from the castle to the oratory at nearby Southwick Hall, her footsteps sounding on the stone steps leading up to the door and pausing before she entered the small room, holding a rosary, to pray. A tradition was also passed down through the centuries that when Mary's son, James VI of Scotland, became James I of England, he had the walls of the castle torn down as an act of retribution for his mother's execution. However, history proves otherwise, since the castle survived for many

The only surviving fragment of the keep of Fotheringhay Castle and the mound on which it formerly stood. The church in the background is where members of the York family were buried.

years, at one stage being used as an armaments store, until the mid–1630s when its stonework was used for the building or repair of local dwellings, walls and, in one case, a chapel at Fineshade. A visitor in the castle's final days is said to have found graffiti scratched on a window sill by Mary's diamond ring with the words:

From the top of all my trust, mishap hath laid me in the dust.

Robert Catesby, the charismatic leader and instigator of the Gunpowder Plot, was associated with the county, being based at Ashby St Ledgers. Two other conspirators, also associated with the county, were the last to join the plot: Sir Everard Digby of Gayton and, more reluctantly, Catesby's cousin and boyhood companion, Francis Tresham of Rushton, 'a wyld and unstayed man'. Significantly, two places where the conspirators are said to have met in secret to hatch the plot were the gatehouse of Catesby's home and the Triangular Lodge at Rushton Hall. It is Tresham who is credited with revealing the plot by secretly delivering a letter to his brother-in-law, Lord Monteagle, in London, urging him not to attend the opening of Parliament. It began:

My Lord, out of love I bear to some of your friends, I have care of your preservation. Therefore I would advise you, as you tender your life, to devise some excuse to shift of your attendance at this Parliament.

The letter was taken to the Chief Minister and acted upon. It may well have been a forgery, planted by ministers who knew about the plot but waited to watch its development before doing anything, but this did not prevent Tresham from being implicated and he died in painful circumstances in the Tower on 23 December 1605, possibly from a urinary infection, although some say he was poisoned. Innocent or not, he was beheaded after his death. His body was thrown into a hole in the vicinity and his head was sent to Northampton, where it was put on public display.

Monteagle became a national hero for saving King and Country and another high-ranking county man, Sir Edward Montagu of Boughton House, introduced a Bill in Parliament proposing an annual day of rejoicing on the anniversary of the plot's discovery, which was the origin of Bonfire Night. Initially, 5 November was a day of bell-ringing and church attendance for prayers of thanksgiving. The prayers were later dropped and by 1625, bonfires began to be a regular feature, these being combined with firework displays by 1662.

In later years, a popular rhyme or 'catch' chanted by children around the county as they went from house to house on Bonfire Night was:

Guy Fawkes and his companions did the plot contrive,
To blow up the king and parliament and people all up alive.
By God's providence they were cotch'd,

Above and right: Two of the supposed meeting places of the conspirators the Gunpowder Plot: the gatehouse at Ashby St Ledgers (above) and Rushton Triangular Lodge (right).

With a dark lantern and a lighted match.

['cotch'd' means 'caught']

Northamptonshire was the scene of much action during the Civil War. The county was mainly Parliamentarian in allegiance and it was difficult to be in the Royalist faction. Many of the leading aristocracy were either taken prisoner or went into exile and their great houses were plundered, such as that at Deene where a valuable local history collection was ransacked and depleted, or at Rockingham where the castle was left virtually as a shell, with the church, almshouses and much of the village destroyed. Some Royalists did hold their ground, however, such as the daring Dr Michael Hudson, rector of Kingscliffe and chaplain to Charles I, whom he accompanied from Oxford to Newark. Hudson was constantly trying to recruit men for the Royalist cause and legends abound about how he managed to escape the clutches of Parliamentarian troops three times, on one occasion with a basket of apples on his head. In anger, the Parliamentarians used the church as stables and caused damage to its spire. Finally, on 6 June 1648, they pursued Hudson to Woodcroft Castle, on the county border near Elton. Hudson hung on to a parapet while they hacked at his fingers, causing him to fall to his death in the moat below. The incident was used by Sir Walter Scott in his novel *Woodstock*.

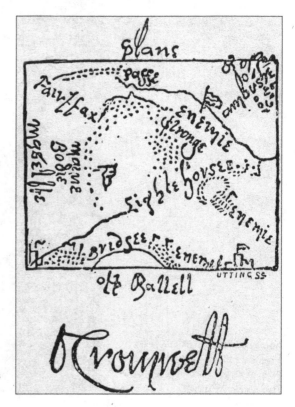

A pen-and-ink sketch, said to be by Oliver Cromwell, of the 'Plane of Batell' at Naseby, showing the positions of the opposing armies.

The decisive battle of the war took place in the county, at Naseby. On 14 June 1645, 14,000 Parliamentary troops under Fairfax and Cromwell routed the 10,000-strong Royalist forces commanded by Prince Rupert. In the aftermath, 4,000 bodies lay on the field and for many years afterwards, on the anniversary, the battle was said to have been re-enacted in the sky above. There were also eyewitness accounts of regular ghostly combat on the field itself. According to widely held belief, Cromwell's body was taken back to the scene of his victory after his death in 1658 and his ghost was said to roam in the fields. Today, anyone visiting that bleak isolated spot, where a memorial overlooks the site, cannot fail to picture the scene of such carnage.

The slaughter continued as Royalist survivors fled the scene. Cromwell wrote about the aftermath in a letter shortly after the victory:

> We pursued them from three miles short of Harborough to nine beyond
> even to sight of Leicester, whither the King fled.

Years later, an elderly eyewitness gave an account of the battle and its aftermath, reporting that even women accompanying the defeated troops were cut and slashed in the face or nose, some with the comment: 'Remember Cromwell, you whores!'

Part of the battlefield, as seen from the memorial at Naseby.

At Marston Trussell, a group of Royalists were trapped in an enclosed field known as Pudding End, close to the church, and were massacred, their bodies buried in a shallow pit, long afterwards known as Cavaliers' Grave, giving rise to yet another haunted location in the county.

Tradition also says that Oliver Cromwell and some of his men stayed in the Hind Hotel in Wellingborough on the eve of the battle, although this has been proved impossible. However, true or not, a room named after him exists there today. Similarly, a table in the church at Naseby is where Royalists were dining when they were interrupted by the unexpected arrival of Cromwell's men.

These events are just some of many that have given rise to all kinds of speculation over the centuries, contributing to the vast body of folklore of Northamptonshire, Rose of the Shires. Let us now enter that fascinating world, go along some of its paths and explore the rich landscape within.

An idyllic scene evoking a lost era: the former watermill, now Conygar Farm, at Woodnewton.

two

WHAT'S IN A NAME?

If you could travel back in time to old Northamptonshire, you would encounter many familiar words such as holt, stag, hog, crab stick, twang, budget, stickers, shorts, take away, tight, great, hike, fridge, fashion, broad cast and drop out, to name but a few. The problem is that these words had a different meaning then. That process of change in our language continues unabated today, as our way of life changes. In spelling, vocabulary, grammar and usage, new words are coming in, others going out of fashion and some (e.g. gay, pad, coke) undergoing a change of meaning. Many of these words can be found in the Glossary section of this book.

Our county ancestors had a whole host of local words and expressions (folk rhymes), some of which were used by one community to describe a neighbouring one, mainly alluding to some characteristic of the topography or reputation of the inhabitants, justified or invented by inter-village rivalry or harmless ribaldry, the origins of which have often been lost or distorted long ago. There have been occasions when rivalry has been apparent in some form (usually a form of superiority) between the adjoining villages of Cottingham and Middleton, as well as between Wilbarston and neighbouring Stoke Albany, Rothwell and Desborough, and Corby and Kettering. A case in point was the discovery of a saying marked on a wall of a demolished pub in Corby some years ago:

> Rockingham on the hill, Oakley in the vale
> Kettering for silly b-----s, Corby for ale!

The same saying occurred elsewhere for many years in the north of the county towards Leicestershire and other parts of the Midlands, as any villages or towns could be substituted in the rhyme at will. Here it may have reflected the one-time strong feelings and rivalry between the two towns, with Corby feeling that Kettering gladly accepted the generous employment prospects offered by their large steelworks, but looked down on them as coarse and uneducated.

Some expressions are a complete mystery and may be some form of underhand insult about those living in a certain place, such as that for Raunds: 'Go to Ranse to see the dogs dance'. There may be an insult – or a compliment, depending how you see it – about the quality of the local water supply at Warkworth, on the edge of the county near Banbury, in the expression: 'Cattle that drink Warkworth water, never come back'. For Corby, which perhaps suffered greater poverty than elsewhere when the weaving industry collapsed in the first years of the nineteenth century, there may be sympathy for the plight of the inhabitants in the expression, 'Where do you come from? Corby, God bless you!'

The supposed quality of a village's bells often led to neighbourly derision or bragging in the form of a taunting rhyme. Aynho boasted that its bells were better than those in Souldern just over the boundary in Oxfordshire: 'Aynho, bell metal; Souldern, tin kettle'. Among other villages that were mocked for their poverty were Rockingham and Naseby: 'poor people, one bell, wooden steeple'.

Little Bowden was also mocked for having 'poor people, one bell, wooden steeple' and Great Houghton had 'wicked people' who 'sold their bells to buy a steeple'. However, taunt and response was the case with two other neighbouring villages: Cotterstock would chant, 'Who rings best, who rings best?' to which Tansor would reply, 'We do! we do!'

Reciprocation would also take place between the males of the neighbouring villages of Piddington and Hackleton, one of them taunting the other about their aloofness and manliness. If the former shouted, 'Hackleton bolshen, shut up in a den. Don't come out to Piddington men', the rhyme would be shouted back with the names of the villages reversed!

Two places in the county, Brackley and Yardley Gobion, seem to have had more than their fair share of taunting, neither being held in high estimation by their neighbours, who considered them to be of low intelligence. One expression was: 'Half sharp and hardly, like the folk of Yardley'. Another was: 'Yardley skegs come to Pury, to suck eggs', a taunt used by the boys of Pury End when those from the neighbouring village went there. This is in fact a very clever play on the two words 'suck' and 'eggs', in which letters were taken out to form 'skegs'. A skeg was a name for the wild plum or bullace but it also meant 'a foolish person' and to suck eggs, of course, means to tell someone something he or she already knows.

Brackley was given a similar form of insult by Evenley in the expression: 'Brackley skegs come t'Imley ta et th'addled eggs', with the implication that they ate rotten or empty eggs. Brackley was also the target of another saying. At one time its people were said to be the most bad-mannered in the county and the village had a considerably large number of poor and unemployed people. This gave rise to the expression: 'Brackley breed, better to hang than to feed'.

The village of Little Houghton was apparently happy with its lowly status and made the most of what it had, at the same time having a swipe at Brayfield which it thought was affluent and artificial:

> Houghton for pride and poverty, Brayfield for money and muck.

However, Brayfield retaliates in another rhyme, adding a second neighbour to the argument. Perhaps there is an undercurrent of three-way rivalry in the saying, in which Brayfield tries to show it is smarter, adding a touch of bravado as its shows the weaknesses of the other two:

> Denton folk don't know when they're told,
> Houghton folk know before they're told,
> Brayfield folk know when they're told.

A whole group of villages in the Nene valley are given various attributes in the following rhyme which goes back to at least the first decade of the nineteenth century and appeared in an edition of the *Northampton County Magazine* in the 1920s:

> Thorpe and Achurch stand in a row,
> Lilford and Pilton and peevish Wadenhoe,
> Onicle the Chronicle stands by the waterside, Islip is
> nothing but malice and pride,
> Thrapston, Whitehorse; Titchmarsh, the Cross;
> Clapton, the Clay, Barnwell, King's Highway,
> Armston, On the hill, Polebrook, In the hole,
> Ashton, Blows the bellows, Oundle, Burns the coal.

'Thorpe' is Thorpe Waterville and 'Onicle' is the old pronunciation of Aldwincle. Even today, Wadenhoe folk cannot account for why their village was called 'peevish' – in any of the word's meanings of foolish, bad-tempered, obstinate or mischievous – and the residents of Islip would definitely say they are not haughty!

Sometimes the joke was at the expense of those who used the expression against another village. Grendon men were called 'moonrakers' after a legend sprang up that a group of locals were said to have once seen the reflection of the full moon in a pond and tried to rake it out, thinking it was a giant cheese. This was based on the more renowned Wiltshire legend, in which local men were engaged in retrieving smuggled casks of brandy hidden in the water of a pond and pretended to be idiots by raking out the moon's reflection in a pond when they saw revenue men coming their way. The revenue men were the real fools for believing them, and missed their chance of catching the criminals. Grendon would have used the legend for themselves as a means of attention seeking and one-upmanship, like the 'penning in the cuckoo' or treacle mines (q.v.), the joke boomeranging back on anyone who believes or says it.

Other sayings are of a much more complimentary nature. Around England, a famous saying about the county is 'Northamptonshire for spires and squires'. This is certainly justified, as the county was at one time the country seat of over 100 squires – some of them, such as the Montagus, Cecils, and Hattons, holding high positions in the nation – and has a similar number of spires on its churches, many of which have been built in the fine, durable local limestone.

One rhyme describes stand-out features of a particular settlement: 'Doddington dovecote, Wilby hen, Arthlingborough ploughboys, Wellingborough men'. Another village, Holdenby, once had a fine hall, most of which was replaced by the present building in 1887. One can imagine its grandeur on a sunny day, as shown in the saying: 'It shines like Holmby'.

The epithet 'Naseby children' was applied to the old people of that village, many of whom were noted for having full control of their mental abilities, even powers of physical regeneration at an advanced age. One villager who died at the age of ninety-four is said to have cut a new set of teeth after reaching the age of seventy. No one has ever worked out the secret of such a phenomenon, though some sources put it down to the water!

Four villages lying close together on the Nene are grouped together in a complimentary rhyme about their picturesque appearance: 'Chelveston cum Caldecot, Stanwick little none, pretty little Denford, and fine Addington'. However, it is King's Sutton that takes some beating for a description of its qualities. If the saying is correct even now, then it would certainly be a successful public relations exercise and a persuasive advertisement for coming to the village:

> King's Sutton is a pretty town, and lies all in a valley,
> It has a pretty ring of bells, besides a bowling alley,
> Wine and liquor in good store, pretty maidens plenty,
> Can a man deserve more? There ain't such a town in twenty!

Another rhyme is of much more ancient origin and, according to tradition, was uttered by the Danes fighting King Alfred at Danesmoor in the ninth century, as they swept across the region. It refers to Padwell, which is a spring at Edgcote, and the stone is a boundary marker on the Warwickshire border:

> If we can Padwell overgoe, and Horestone we can see,
> Then Lords of England we shall be.

Interestingly, a similar saying is associated with the Rollright Stones a few miles away on the Warwickshire and Oxfordshire border, where a mythical king with aspirations to extend his power was told by a local witch:

> If Long Compton thou canst see,
> The King of England thou shalt be.

It was also customary in many communities around the county to give certain people names according to their appearance, habit, personality, or occupation. This was useful, especially among males, as several often had the same Christian name such as Bob or Bill; however, it was important in other ways. Gertrude Watkins of Brixwoth wrote in 1881:

> It was rather necessary to be acquainted with the nicknames of some people. Frequently on enquiry for a person by his real name, the only answer would be a blank stare, when yet the nickname elicited an immediate response.

Around the county, Stump would be a common name for a person walking on one leg, Sexy for a sexton and Toby was not unknown for anyone with a face like the jug of that name! Later, Hobbs or a similar well-known name would be given to a particularly avid cricket fan. Other one-time common names were Nipper, Stubby, Mossy, Sammy Rags, Wagger, Dripping, Dribbler, Goggy, Hedgehog, Spider, Monkey, Ferret, Donkey, Whoppy, Bodger, Bobby Noddles, Fiddler, Fidgit, Doshy, Spot, Fleshy, Pudden, Porky, Giant, Snobby and Spud. An unusual county version of the common expression 'like father, like son', was 'such words, such chips'.

A famous deer stealer active in Rockingham Forest in the seventeenth century was Jack o'Lantern of Kingscliffe. Another, active around Gretton, was Jumping Jack. At Brixworth, there were two brothers with the same first name who were known according to their occupations: Chip Bob was a carpenter and Dough Bob a baker. At Higham Ferrers, there was a poor couple known as Lord and Lady Higham. Watercress Harry was the name given to a Kettering inspector of milestones, who plied his wares in the area. In early Victorian times, lads named Albert were given the epithet Prince, in honour of the Prince Consort.

Field Names

Life, Lunch, Wormstalls, Deadman's Grave, Grimble White, Ankers, Cobra, Jack Arthur, Wounds, Easter Hill – the names conjure up all kinds of images – are just a few of the many colourful descriptions of landscape features around Northamptonshire that have come down through the ages, a rich vocabulary applied to the type, status or nature of a particular field, pasture, meadow, wood, hill or spring. But their names are often not what they seem. Many of these are either regional or national. Most are no longer known by their original fanciful names – names that would have changed in pronunciation and spelling over the years and have now become part of folklore. So why were they given such interesting names, making our modern-day imagination work overtime, trying to guess their meaning?

Unlike place names, field names are often more difficult to trace, firstly because written records before the thirteenth century do not usually mention them, so we have to rely on their Middle English (medieval) or later names, many of which have been changed etymologically, in spelling or in pronunciation. In this chapter and in the Glossary, the following codes are used for the three language sources: OE (Old English), ON (Old Norse), and ME (Middle English).

In some exceptional cases, there may be a hidden or implicit meaning, using sarcasm, irony or humour. For example, Van Dieman's Land, a name usually applied to a distant working field, may be a play on the word 'demon', implying that it is land that the Devil own, i.e. hard to plough. The name also had criminal connotations current at the time the field was named, as criminals were transported to Van Dieman's Land on the other side of the world; in this case the name implies that the field would be the ideal location for certain elements of society meeting under dubious circumstances, e.g. poachers!

More straightforward is Dedequene Moor, near Towcester. In 1907, a thirteenth-century document was discovered detailing a grant of land by Edward I at 'Dedequenemor', leading to speculation that the name referred to a dead queen, probably Boudicca. For centuries, the exact location of Boudicca's burial site has been a source of intrigue and one of the supposed sites was off Watling Street, near where the fatal British tribal battle took place with the Romans, and where the queen is said to have taken poison in defeat. The field is in the right region, albeit further south of the struggle. Unfortunately, any speculation by county people must be dashed, since the word 'quene' was the Old English word for 'lady'; today it is still found in the Danish 'kvinde' and Swedish 'kvinna', where 'kv' is the equivalent of our 'qu'. Blatherwycke, at the other end of the county, also laid a claim to having Boudicca's remains, as two separate stone coffins containing the upper and lower parts of a very tall female skeleton were once discovered. Being so tall of course would be a mark of distinction – not just physically but also in status!

Before the days of treated sewage and public toilets, human waste had to be deposited somewhere, often being scattered across fields, in midden heaps or at some discreet location. However, one could not help but notice where these functions took place and appropriate names were given to these places. There was a Shitten Alley at Finedon, a Mickstead – meaning 'dungheap' – at Desborough, Fish Alley at Bozeat and Dinge Lane, from the OE 'dycge' meaning manure, at Polebrook. One survivor is Jericho at Oundle, an enclosed narrow cul-de-sac just

Above and below: Two curious street names in Oundle: Blackpot Lane recalls the hostelry that stood in the vicinity, itself named after a type of drinking vessel used in olden times; Jericho refers to a secluded place for emptying the bladder.

off the old marketplace. The name comes from 'jerry', an old word for a chamber pot. With dozens of public houses at one time in the vicinity, it was vital to have some kind of watering place nearby!

Daglin Lane at Harringworth and Dag Lane at Corby, Stanion, Deene and Cottingham are references to the muck that accumulated on the underside of sheep as they passed through. Lumbertubs Lane at Moulton was so-called after being used at one time by local shopkeepers disposing of their rubbish. 'Lumber' meant articles of no further use and 'tubs' were presumably the containers for butter and other commodities. Ramshackle houses or an area infested with rats would be referred to as Rats Hall, as at Wadenhoe and elsewhere, or Rotten Row, as at Rushden, Oundle, Geddington and Kettering. In the latter town, the name was given to a row of twelve shops facing the north of Market Place, which were 'very irregularly Built and all Thatch'. The upper floors were accommodation for the poor and very disagreeable to the people that occupied the shops or lived near them.

In modern times, niceties have crept in and names have undergone a change. Northampton's Cow Meadow was renamed because the Ladies' Bowling Club was based there and they would have objected to the bovine connection! Shutlanger was the new name for the village of Shitlanger, for obvious reasons. Boothville replaced the name Buttocks End.

Other names are far from what they might seem in their meaning. Hell's Yard at Aynho has no unpleasant connection but is simply a corruption of the surname Hill, referring to a family who once lived and farmed on the site. An alternative name for Gartree Road, a Roman road running from Huntingon via Thrapston and Corby into Leicestershire, was the Via Devana. However, it is misleading to think this is an original name, for it was invented by scholars in the eighteenth century solely to give it a classical feel. Scotgate at Harringworth comes from the Old Norse 'skog gata', meaning a woodland road, and nearby Turtle Bridge is a corruption of the surname of Ralph Turcle (ON: Thorkill), who owned land here in 1277. Therefore it is not a reference to turtles swimming in the River Welland below!

Little London, despite fanciful interpretations of its meaning, was a jocular village name. In the nineteenth century, as the population began to rise again after emigration and newcomers began to arrive, some villages began to expand and any extra dwellings would have given a sense of overcrowding in an area previously unspoilt or uninhabited. Change is anathema to human nature! Among villages hosting this name past and present are Gretton, Yardley Gobion, Passenham, Silverstone and Earls Barton.

Another jocular name was given to the dominant street of Middleton by locals in the nineteenth century: a plaque on the front of The Maltings in Main Street is inscribed 'Birmingham Street', since that was the name of the largest town in the region at the time, and the road – with diversions – would eventually lead to it!

The Folly at Rothwell was a local name for Shotwell Mill Lane, stemming from the fact that a builder erected two cottages at a site which at the time was so distant from the town that folk said, 'What a folly to build so far out!' and the name stuck.

Many streets have 'pudding' in their names. In some cases it is a description of the sticky surface, as in Pudding Lane, Wadenhoe and Plum Pudding Lane, Titchmarsh. Featherbed Lane at Little Oakley got its name for similar reasons. Pudding End, Braybrooke; Pudding Bag, Sibbertoft and Pudding Bag Lane in

A tablet on the wall of a house in Middleton, with a jocular alternative name for the street in which it stands.

Kettering, Bozeat and Paulerpury were so-called because there was no way out of them, like a cloth-covered steamed pudding. These roads were a dead-end as a public right of way, although there was often private land beyond, and access would in some cases have been tantamount to trespass.

More curious names include Polopit at Titchmarsh, which derives from an earlier name, Puddle Pit, where the villagers got stone, gravel or sand for roads or their own use. Derngate at Northampton originates from the Celtic 'dubras', meaning water, hence its meaning is 'watergate'. The same element gives rise to the name Derwent. Hatchdoyle Lane at Stoke Doyle refers to a 'dole', which was the name formerly applied to a portion of the common fields, and came to mean 'gateway to the field', the name later corrupted to Doyle after the name of the village.

Jordan Bridge, spanning the River Jordan at Braybrooke. The name derives from the local Baptist church who used its water in their services.

The names of the county's villages are more straightforward and well-documented, though there are some that need more research. Interesting examples are Maidford and Maidwell, meaning 'ford where the maidens gathered' and 'spring where the maidens gathered' respectively. While one can imagine the younger women collecting water at such sites, there are other possible origins, for the prefix, with spelling variations in older names, can mean either 'folk', 'meadow' or 'stone', all of which are plausible. Place names have always been of great interest to county folk, with such a variety of colourful names within its boundaries, but we can discount an etymological list which appeared in the 1920s in the *Northampton County Magazine*, under the giveaway name of the compiler, L.E.G. Puller! For example:

> *Hanging Houghton*: It was the custom to hang beggars as soon as they were seen.
> *Sywell*: There was a famous well here to which lovers used to repair to plight their troth; the ceremony, for which there was no charge, was necessarily accompanied by many a sigh and so Sigh-well.
> *Isham*: Literally 'home of the ice' but actually 'home of the Ise' as called because the river when first seen was frozen, and it was called Ice, but the Saxons, no more than the Danes, ever could spell.
> *Sulgrave*: From Sol, the sun. At a suitable place to the east at the vernal equinox, the sun appears to sink into the earth at Sulgrave, to go into its grave as it were, thus Sul-grave.

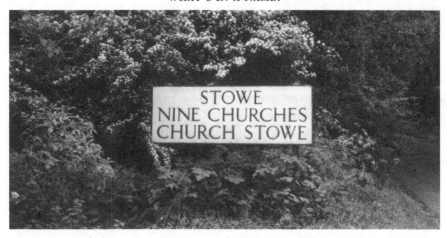

Above and below: Two of the more unusual place names to be found in the county: Stowe Nine Churches, named after the number of attempts at building the church, or alternatively the number of churches visible from the site; and Luddington in the Brook, named after the proximity of its original location, before realignment in the mid-1800s.

Epitaphs

At Bozeat there is an inscription on a mid-nineteenth century gravestone to John and Mary Partridge which ends with a warning to would-be desecrators that today's vandals would do well to heed: 'May all the afflictions of Job be the lot that disturbs the remains of those that repose below'. At Weedon Bec is a stone to Alice Old, who honoured her name by living 'through six reigns', from Charles I through the Commonwealth to William and Mary. Beneath the carpet in the nave of the church of St John the Baptist at Harringworth is a floor memorial to one of its former vicars, Matthew Palmer, who died in 1752 at the remarkable age of 110 years. At Weedon Lois, there is a weatherworn tombstone depicting a woman handing a cup of poison to her husband. According to tradition, she was the last person to be burned at the stake in England. This is erroneous of course, as burning was only for heresy not murder. At Welton, facing the roadside, there is a poignant inscription to a six-year-old boy found starved to death.

The chancel of the partially ruined church of All Saints in Barnwell has an elaborate wall memorial with a tall obelisk decorated with texts, water symbols and coloured panelling. It stands behind shutters which, on opening, reveal pictures of a christening robe and hearse mantle. It is that of the infant son of Henry Montagu, lord of the manor, who drowned before his third birthday. The inscription reads:

> Thursday 16 May 1622 Borne
> Much rain falling Aprill 1625 filled a pond
> Wet with a scoopet, lieing by way
> Supposedly ye occasion of his end
> Thus Ascension Day Christened,
> Thus 28 Aprill 1625 dyed.

In the peaceful, isolated churchyard of Holy Trinity at Blatherwycke, there is something of a mystery, for which an answer has never been forthcoming: one

The poignant inscription on a gravestone in the churchyard at Welton.

of the tombstones has its inscribed side facing the boundary wall away from the church, making it difficult to read. It marks the resting place of a black servant, Anthony Williams, who had worked at the Hall and who had drowned in the lake in 1836 while trying to save his master, who had fallen from a boat while fishing. The inscription contains a piece of poetry:

> Here a poor wanderer hath found a grave
> Who death embraced while struggling with a wave.
> His home far off in the broad Indian main
> He left to rid himself of slavery's chain.
> Friendless and comfortless, he passed the sea
> On Albion's shores to seek for liberty.
> Yet vain his search for aye with toiling brow
> He never found his freedom until now.

Another curiosity lies along the road between Gretton and Harringworth, set back from the verge and now almost lost in the undergrowth. Fanny Blaydes, the wife of the vicar of Harringworth, was returning home with friends in a horse and carriage after a visit to Gretton one Sunday afternoon in 1884, when the horse took fright on a downward slope, the shafts going up as high as the animal's

The Blaydes Stone beside the Gretton–
Harringworth road, a monument
marking the site of an untimely death.

head causing it to panic. As this happened, Mrs Blaydes jumped off and fell onto a grass verge, the impact knocking her unconscious. She died shortly afterwards and at a later date her husband erected a stone in her memory on the spot where she had died, with the inscription: 'Sudden Death, Sudden Glory'.

Lying alongside a bridleway between Brigstock and Weldon is a commemoration stone from the time of Charles I, known as the Bocase Stone. It records the site of a large oak tree blown down by a gale early in the seventeenth century. The inscription reads: 'In This Plaes Grew Bocase Tree.' Speculation has always been rife as to the meaning of its name, with suggestions ranging from the corruption of the surname of a local huntsman to Robin Hood or others using the tree to hide their bows and arrows! It is more likely, however, to come from the French 'bocage', meaning a wood adjoining a field.

The Bocase Stone, near Brigstock, whose name and purpose have been the subject of much speculation.

three

A CORNUCOPIA OF CUSTOMS

We can categorise customs under four headings: those connected with the agricultural year, those of the church calendar – these two were often intertwined – those of a secular nature, and superstitious rituals. At one time, at least sixty holidays would have been taken annually and countless others performed when the occasion demanded, such as fundraising events – known as 'ales' – for the needy, many of which helped to consolidate social bonds and community charity. The feast days were subsequently reduced to twenty-five during the Reformation, in an Act passed in 1552, and by 1834 there were only four, which were now known as Bank Holidays. Today we have eight.

If a community felt let down by the behaviour of an individual or group, a common way of showing disapproval and dealing with the problem was to put on a unified front by making a lot of noise and using guising. Such a custom had its roots in ancient times, when any form of social deviance was believed to have a potentially harmful effect on the growth of the crops or the harmony of the community; however, these roots had long been forgotten when the custom was performed in later times. This custom was known variously around the county as lewbelling (in the southern part), lowbelling, rough music, tin-canning, tin-kettling, nagging-out or banging-out (around Piddington). It would often be accompanied by 'riding the stang', in which someone impersonating the offender by wearing similar clothes and using their mannerisms would be carried around on a pole or in a cart, or by the parading of an effigy of the offender(s) which would then be burned, like the guy on Bonfire Night. This would be aimed at anyone who had strayed from the norm by lapsing into some form of immorality, like wife-beating, nagging, malicious gossiping, rumour-mongering, adultery or incest.

The custom was particularly common in the nineteenth century and was carried on into the early 1900s. Several records exist in contemporary newpapers and in the memoirs of county people. Blisworth in particular was far from tolerant on several occasions and often fell foul of the law. In 1895, two policemen confronted and stopped 200 demonstrators who had gathered outside the house of an unmarried couple with tin cans and kettles and effigies of the offenders. The last case was recorded there in 1936.

Members of the Broughton Tin Can Band in the 1920s.

In 1909, at Middleton Cheney, a procession passed along the street banging washtubs and carrying an effigy of a person who had caused offence, which was later burnt on the village green. The marked house was surrounded in order to make the culprit come out. At Shutlanger in the 1930s, lowbellers gathered to create pandemonium outside the home of a man who had been having an affair with a married woman. Their methods worked, for the culprit moved away from the village shortly afterwards.

The custom still survives in one place, albeit only for fun. At Broughton, during the second week of December, a procession known as the Tin Can Band takes to the streets in the early hours of the morning, making as much noise as possible with pots, pans, lids, drums and so on, starting from the church gates at midnight. It is said to have originated during the 1920s in order to scare off a group of gypsies who had encamped in the village precincts but earlier versions exist, with a leader being chaired round directing the noisy proceedings.

In November 1929, the parish council, being of the opinion that the custom was stupid and antisocial, put up warning notices in the village stating that 'the practice of the Beating of Tin Kettles and the noise created thereby' would not be allowed to take place that year, and threatened police action against anyone doing so. The notice was issued despite the village being overwhelmingly in favour of the custom. The police were duly called in but found themselves swept up in the festivities. They finally had to do their duty in getting the names and addresses of those who had caused trouble. Fines were later given to the fifty-four revellers found breaching the peace, but these were paid for by a dance put on especially to raise money for the fines. Response was generous, with folk coming from Kettering and nearby villages, with the result that there was enough money left over for a day out for the elderly. The custom took place again the following year, with less police involvement and fewer charges, and has continued ever since, a rare and perhaps precarious survival of the once widespread practice of 'rough music'.

Another unique custom, but one which has long disappeared, was 'Auction by Pin and Candle', a tradition known to date back to the seventeenth century, in which a piece of land – often belonging to the Church or a charity – was let for a set period. In Northamptonshire it had become almost defunct by the end of the nineteenth century and was considered to be noteworthy on the rare occasions it was still carried out. At Corby in 1892, the custom was considered to be worth mentioning in the following notice of the letting of the Charity and Town Lands in South Wood:

A curious and ancient custom has just been observed at the village of Corby near Kettering, where the land belonging to the parish charities has been let by the interesting custom of a burning candle. A pin was inserted in the candle a short distance from the light and the bidding advanced until the pin dropped ... watched and attended by many of the parishioners. When the heat dislodged the pin, the last bidder found that he had the land on lease for eight years.

Bidding in progress during a pin and candle auction at Corby, *c.* 1918.

Nether Heyford appears to have been the last to let out grazing rights for the following twelve months on its big village green – one of the largest in England, at just over two hectares – the custom continuing until 1924. However, at Raunds the same system was used but for a different purpose: selling property. The last recorded occasion was in 1889 when 'Mr William Hills, according to ancient custom, put three old tenements up for sale in Rotton Row'.

The hobby horse was originally a fertility symbol, ridden by a person with a stang, or pole, between the legs like a witch's broom, covered in a skirted frame. At street pageants and festivals, the hobby horse would look out for the young women in a crowd and chase them, enveloping them under its skirts, theoretically to ensure they would later conceive but in reality to impart good luck. According to churchwardens' accounts, this custom was fairly common in the county at one time but slowly vanished. It survived for a time at Culworth where the hobby horse was specially painted on 1 January for the village's Hobby Horse Night. An original hobby horse is now kept in the museum at Northampton. However, in the summer of 1995, the horse made a welcome return to the county, appearing at Barnwell Country Park along with a giant Green Man, as part of the Common Ground Apple Day festivities.

The Hobby Horse makes a welcome reappearance after a long absence in the county, at Barnwell Country Park, 1995.

On the third Monday after Twelfth Night, the beginning of the ploughing season was originally marked with the blessing of the plough in church. By the fifteenth century, however, the plough had begun to be drawn round the streets from house to house to raise money for the good of the parish. By the end of the eighteenth century, this practice had degenerated into a fun activity for personal gain, in which participants known in the county as 'plough moggers' or 'plough witches' would dress up as various characters or wear special clothes. They would then either whiten their faces or blacken them with soot or blacklead and then go around the houses, performing a short play and demanding money from the occupants. At Raunds, one of the participants in the 1890s was Matthew Kirk, who recalled how he and several other plough witches, including a squaw and a character called Old Pat, blackened their faces and wore grotesque garb in preparation for the ritual. He wore an inverted chimneypot hat and others had hunches on their backs, with a knave of hearts sewn on, which gave rise to the name 'red jacks'. As they made their way round the streets, carrying besoms, many a door would be hastily locked at their approach. This was not unusual, since many folk did not consider it harmless fun. For example, Norah Field recalled her childhood memories of this custom in Rothwell:

Every year a possy [sic] of them with blackened faces shouting and banging on tin cans, came round begging for money. Plough Moggers they were called. As a little one they scared me to death, and I think Mother as well, for I remember one dark night they swarmed up to the back gate shouting and making a terrific din, and being alone, we hid in the pantry.

At Weldon, Florence Colyer had a similar experience as a four-year old child, when a group of moggers, using features of the mummers' plays, walked into her house. She vividly remembered the occasion:

I remember four or five men, with their faces blackened or reddened and wearing extraordinary garb, bursting through the front door calling out: 'In comes I, I never bin before, three merry actors at your door!' They then proceeded to dance around, asking if they could perform their play. I was so frightened, being only about four years old that I hid under the table. My grandmother produced a coin or two and said, 'You'll have to go, this child is terrified'.

Some kind of threat when asking for money was not unusual. For example, at Brigstock the use of red sheep-dip was the usual form of intimidation: 'Tinker, tinker, poor ploughboy, if you don't give anything I'll raddle your face!' A refusal in some cases led to the ground outside the dwelling being ploughed! Sometimes the response could be at the moggers' expense: on one occasion in Northampton, the moggers were told by the householder to wait while he went to get some money; he subsequently returned not with cash but with a dog, which he promptly set loose on them. More humorously, at Althorp House, a mogger whose face was made up half black and half white was told by the butler who opened the door that he did not like him because he was two-faced!

St Valentine's Day was a special day in the county, not just for lovers but for children who would get together in groups for the custom of Gwain Valentinin – going from house to house, like trick or treating at Halloween, in the hope of being given apples or a few pence to share out among themselves, after offering a rhyme. At Ecton it was: 'Morrow, morrow, Valentine, empty your purse and fill mine!' At many other places, the rhyme – given here in a dialect version – was:

Good morrow, Valentine. Plazt to give me Valentine
I be yourn, if ye'l be mine. Good morrow, Valentine.

At Kislingbury, St Valentine's Day was a day for the girls to play pranks by going around the streets throwing Valentines at people's doors and then running away. In the villages around Northampton, special sweet plum Valentine Buns were baked by godparents to give to their godchildren on the Sunday before and the Sunday after St Valentine's Day. Elsewhere, 'catching' was a common feature of the day for young people, who would get up early in the morning in order to be the first to say, 'Good morrow, Valentine' to their parents or any elder relatives. By doing this before the adults had a chance to answer or before the adults spoke to them, they were rewarded with a present.

On Shrove Tuesday, the Pancake Bell was rung, preceded by a shriving bell at ten o'clock or earlier for people to come and confess. Bells were still rung in the county as late as 1850, though no longer for confession. The Pancake Bell was usually rung at eleven o'clock for an hour. At Daventry, where it was called the Panburn Bell, and Staverton, one side of the bell was 'buffed', meaning muffled with leather, while at Blakesley and Oundle, two bells were thought to sound as if they were saying 'Pan On'. Ringing did not last long up at Stamford Baron, where each bell was 'tolled for a short while'. At five villages – Islip, Lowick, Higham Ferrers, Stanwick and Aldwincle St Peter – the young were allowed to 'jangle the bells', while at Sudborough it was an occasion for the women to have a go and at Thrapston it was the turn of the boys. There was an added attraction to the occasion at the church of All Hallows in Wellingborough: while the sixth bell, called Old Pancake, was rung, pancakes were thrown from the tower windows. One wonders if they were caught or landed on anyone! In some villages, special rhymes were chanted by children on the day. At Geddington, the rhyme was identical to that chanted on Tander Day at Spratton: 'If you don't give us a holiday, we'll run away'.

For adults, there were other ways of celebrating. There may perhaps have been a traditional game of football in which, before rules were laid down in the mid-1800s, was a case of anything goes, with no set number of players, no teams, no passing, only kicking, pushing and hacking down, in order to keep the ball in one's possession! The day was less dangerous and exhausting at Harpole, where a clay-pipe-smoking competition took place in which the contestants were allowed to light up only once, with the one who smoked the longest being declared the winner.

On Palm Sunday, real palms were rarely carried in procession; their substitute being pieces of a tree called sallow or grey willow, which flowers just before Easter – earlier than most other plants. This practice would be normal for a county then under the Diocese of Lincoln, whereas some other dioceses used yew. In his poetry, Clare describes how 'gold stamened catkins stand out, rich strains of sunny gold show where the sallows bloom.'

An associated Palm Sunday custom, which was unique to the county, was the eating of figs at teatime. The market at Northampton always had extra supplies delivered on the Saturday before for purchase by people of all social classes. Until fairly recently, the custom was still being honoured at Peterborough, Weldon and other villages in the north of the county.

It was commonly believed that Good Friday was a lucky day to bake cakes and bread. It was said that items baked on this day would never to go mouldy and could avert calamities. However, during the eighteenth century, the opposite view appears to have been taken in Northamptonshire, at least in some areas, as there was a well-known saying:

> He who bakes or brews on Good Friday will have his house burnt down before the end of the year.

This was probably due to some lingering superstition or religious fervour – declaring the day unlucky as it was when Christ was crucified – or a combination of both. Whatever the case, the nineteenth century saw many a hot cross bun and fresh ale consumed over the Easter period in the county.

May Day

No other season of the year can evoke as much happiness among people as spring. After the dark, cold days of winter, the return of spring – with the anaemic sun gaining in strength and warmth and bringing lighter, longer days, the Earth rewakening after her long sleep with the birth and blooming of new life, and birdsong and the sounds of insects filling the air – was a time for joy and celebration.

The first day of May signalled the custom of 'bringing in the may', which lasted from the medieval era until the seventeenth century and involved young people spending much of the night and the early part of the morning searching for flowering branches, or 'knotts', of may to bring home around sunrise. This would be a time of freedom and temptation for many of the young gatherers and it was an activity scorned by Puritans, one of whom by the name of Featherton wrote: 'of tenne maydens which went to fetch May, nine of them came home with childe'. It was also common for girls to wash their faces in the dew, as it would supposedly add fairness to their complexions, eradicate any blemishes in the skin and perhaps improve eyesight. It was even supposed to bring them a husband within a year!

Once the branches were gathered, the young people returned to the village, singing May carols. A branch of the tree – later a garland – would then be taken from cottage to cottage. In some villages in the county, the branches were either left on the doorstep or protruding from a chimney of certain houses, perhaps the home of a popular girl, which had been determined beforehand by the Mayers. For anyone who was not held in such esteem, this would be substituted with blackthorn, thistles, nettles or wrinkled crab apples left over from the autumn, depending on how she was regarded!

Eventually the branch of may was replaced by a specially made garland, which was taken round the houses by a procession of people singing a special May song.

The may blossom and foliage would have been used for the garland, together with other flowers, commonly bluebells (referred to as wild hyacinths), cowslips, buttercups, daisies, sweet violets and dog violets, wild pansies and wood anemone. Dolls representing the Queen of May, or even the Virgin Mary, were added to the decorations. Hone's *Every-Day Book* (1824) has the earliest description of a Northamptonshire garland, as it was made at Kingsthorpe:

> The skeleton of the garland is formed of two hoops of osier or hazel crossing each other at right angles, affixed to a staff, about five feet long, by which it is carried; the holes are twined with flowers and ribbons so that part of them is visible. In the centre is placed one, two, or three dolls according to the size of the garland and the means of the youthful exhibitors; great emulation is excited among them [the makers] and they vie with each other in collecting the choicest flowers and adorning the dolls in the gayest attire; ribbon streamers of all the varied colours of the rainbow, the lacemakers adding their spangled bobbins, decorate the whole.

A sketch of a Northamptonshire May garland from William Hone's *Every-Day Book*, 1824.

Taking the garland from house to house could have a remarkable effect on the occupants of each home visited. H. Bazely wrote about his experiences of May Day at Ecton in 1883, when he and his elder brother were woken by their father coming up the stairs with a large garland made of hawthorn branches tied in hoops decked with dolls, flowers, and ribbons, one doll larger and more beautiful than the others, as the centrepiece. They went downstairs and returned it to the 'sweet golden-haired Queen of May with the lovely eyes' and her attendants with shining happy faces waiting below. They then gave a verse of their May song:

> This is the first of May, the bright time of the year
> And if I live to tarry here, I'll call another year.

Anne Baker, in 1854, mentions that in some of the villages around Northampton a garlanded doll was carried round from place to place concealed in a large cloth and occupants were asked: 'Would you like to see the Queen of May?' If the reply was in the affirmative they would chant simple ditties and conclude with wishes for a joyful May. This accords with what a resident of Rothwell, Norah Field, said of her May Day experiences in the town in the early part of the twentieth century:

> All the girls at that time used to decorate a washing basket with flowers, a doll or dolls and a money box in the middle. They would come and ask for flowers the day before and then come in pairs on May Day, the basket covered with a sheet to see if the householder wanted to 'see the May Garland'. If they said 'yes' then the sheet would come off. One lady always insisted they sing the May Song before putting money in the box.

Going round from house to house, the children would sing a special May song; either one written by someone in the village or the standard May song, which had lyrical variations depending on where it was sung in the county. These variations are discussed in Chapter Ten.

Some villages had a formal May Queen crowning ceremony. A pretty girl was elected as May Queen and, in some cases, a May King would also be chosen, who would give the queen a kiss and swear allegiance to her. A rare copy of a script for one of these ceremonies has come down to us, with a slight variation in that the May King has been substituted with a Captain of the Guard. The script is from Woodnewton and dates from the first decade of the twentieth century:

> Presenter of the Garland:
> You are the Queen of May, as May throws over the land
> Bright garlands of beauty. My loyal duty is thus with loving hand,
> To put this Garland green, over the neck of our Queen.

The May Queen, Bessie Palmer, with her retinue and the maypole outside the National School in Oundle, *c.* 1910.

May Queen (on receiving the garland):
For your loyal hand to deck, low I bend my royal neck,
Lovely is your garland gay, that adorns your Queen of May.

Presenter of the Crown (the crowning):
Spring is the Queen of the year, and May is the Queen of Spring,
You are the Queen of May most dear, and so your crown I bring.
Bend your pretty head, I pray, that I may crown you Queen of May.

May Queen (on receiving the crown):
Brighter far than gold or gem, is this flowery diadem,
I wear upon my brow today, that does crown your Queen of May.

Presenter of the Sceptre:
Gentle is your royal mien, rule as gently, lovely Queen,
Now your flowery sceptre hold, bright with gems of green and gold.

May Queen (on receiving the sceptre):
Sceptre, bright with leaf and flower, token of my queenly power,
Love shall guide its royal sway, while I rule as queen of May.

Captain of the May Queen's Guard:
I am the Captain of the May Queen's Guard,
If anyone harms her, I shall fight him hard.

Men of the Guard:
So shall we!

Captain of the May Queen's Guard:
And that no danger shall come upon her,
I pledge my life and my sacred honour!

Men of the Guard:
So do we!

Captain of the Queen's Guard:
And now I bravely take my stand,
The May Queen's Guard at the Queen's right hand.

Men of the guard:
So do we!

May celebrations in Castle Fields, Wellingborough, *c.* 1910.

At one time, cottages in the north of the county had their own unique way of celebrating May. A native of Fotheringhay, Charles Peach, reminisced about his childhood in the village and described a custom which existed for many years until the beginning of the nineteenth century. A long branch of a tree, with haw-thorn being the most esteemed and symbolic, was ceremoniously planted in a specially made hole at the front of the house and made to look as if it was grow-ing. Known as the May Bush, it would be decorated like a Christmas tree, which was introduced into the country many years later. It was garnished with cowslips, bluebells, primroses and other spring flowers. Apart from its attractiveness, there was an underlying notion of spring being honoured and the spirit of the season bestowing its beneficial power on the household.

There was also another custom unique to the north of the county, which involved a rope being strung across the street from chimney to chimney, from which garlands were suspended close to the centre. At Fotheringhay and Polebrook, children would compete with each other by attempting to successfully throw small balls through the centre of the hoop of the garland. At Nassington, the Mayers would dance beneath the rope and there would also be a game known as Duck under Water, in which the young people ran in pairs under a handkerchief held aloft by two persons standing on either side with extended arms.

Nassington also had a strange custom which took place at Sulehay, an extra-parochial area of meadowland between Nassington and Yarwell. On May Eve, a barrier was placed across entrance to a particular field by local lads. There was a lot of rivalry among them, so much so that they watched through the night until the break of dawn, when the girls came along with the cows. Then they would see which cow could leap over the barrier first, the successful animal being led round village in the afternoon, its horns decorated with ribbons. The least successful one was decked with nettles, elder and thistles as a token of its failure, accompa-nied by the jibes and jeers of onlookers. No doubt there were sour grapes and a confused cow.

In the 1790s, a new character appeared in the May ceremonies and soon became popular: Jack-in-the-Green, a man covered in a frame of foliage who would be led round a village or town to the accompaniment of music and dancing. Chimney sweeps, a symbol of the new industrial age, had adopted May Day as their holiday and festival. It replaced an older festival in which dairymaids, their heads crowned with flowers, danced in the streets with their pails and garlands, for money. Together with Jack-in-the-Green, the other participants would usu-ally be a fiddler and drummer, a Lord and Lady or King and Queen of May and sometimes a fool. The Jack may well be based on an earlier figure of the May celebrations known in the sixteenth century as Jack-in-the-Bush and in the sev-enteenth century as George-a-Green. The custom of having a Jack-in-the-Green was popular throughout the nineteenth century but had virtually disappeared by the 1920s. There is an interesting glimpse of the old custom recorded by the late Dorothy Grimes in an interview with Rose Clark of Barton Seagrave, recalling her younger days at Broughton:

> In the blacksmith's garden at Broughton was a plant we always used to wait for. It was the Crown Imperial, a lily-like plant that was always ready for May Day. It would be placed on top of the green man's face and frame and used to nod as he bowed in time to the singing. It was never picked till the green man needed it ...Two boys used to walk with the Jack o' the Green, one each side, ready to lift off the frame by the handles when Jack got tired ...The other name for him was 'the Old Man of the Woods'.

In another part of the county, at Boughton, Charles E. Kimbell recalled his younger days in the village in a book *Boughton in the 1880s*. He describes how, prior to May Day, a wicker frame would be covered with spring flowers, especially tulips, primroses, ladslove, sweetbriar and flowering redcurrant. When it was finished:

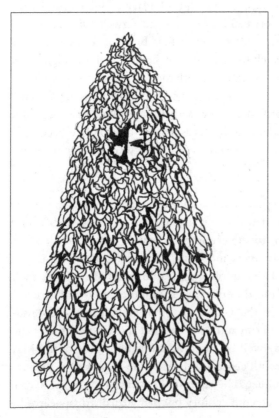

Jack-in-the-Green. A chimney sweep with blackened face would be enclosed in a frame covered in leaves and led around the streets on 1 May.

The Jack had a charming appearance and delightful combination of scents ... [it] enveloped the one appointed to carry it, and unable to see, he was guided around by companions ... the honour to bear him was eagerly sought by the bigger lads at the start, but gradually the lot fell to the younger, weaker ones until eventually no one volunteered.

Although a youngster in terms of folklore and custom, the figure's association with spring and rebirth is rooted way back in the mists of time. In 1996 a local folk musician, Paul Rogers, wrote a song which perfectly encapsulates the spirit and deeper symbolism of the Jack-of-the-Green, the lyrics bringing the figure and his world of nature to life:

> Over the hills and into the woodlands, out past the trees and into the glade
> Catchers catch can, but you'll never find me, I am the sun to banish your shade.

> Bury me deep in my snowy white blanket, you may forget me and think that I've gone
> I will rise up to colour the springtime, follow the circle and lead the bells on.

> *(Chorus)*
> Up in the morning, gone without warning, there lies the spirit that you'll never see,
> Lord of the harvest, king of the woodlands, I am forever Jack-in-the-Green!

> Hear my laughter deep in the forest, Oak and Ash will bow as I pass,
> I am the flames that leap in your fireplace, I am the barley that fills up
> your glass.

> Many's the name I've had since my coming, some call me Robin, and
> some the Green Man,
> I've seen your birth and I'll see your dying, so join in the Wild Hunt, and catchers catch can.

After 1660, on 29 May it was a tradition in Northampton for families to put a large branch of oak over the doorways of homes or on balconies, and later to cover a statue of the King with oak boughs to commemorate the Restoration. By the 1850s, however, the custom had virtually disappeared, though the corporation still had a procession to the church of All Saints in which boys and girls of the town's charity shools participated, each wearing an oak sprig or a gilt oak apple pinned to the front of their clothes. Some villages around the town also decorated their houses with oak branches or the children carried sprigs of oak around with them; anyone not wearing one was beaten with nettles. The custom survived longer in Northampton than elsewhere as the town was still expressing its gratitude to the king for giving large quantities of timber from Whittlebury to help rebuild the town after the great fire of 1675, and for exemption from the crippling chimney tax for seven years.

Perhaps the most highly awaited festival of the year was that of Whit-tide, which got its name from the white clothing worn by the newly baptised. It was traditionally celebrated fifty days after Easter, somewhere between mid-May and 13 June, and was originally a week-long holiday. This was later reduced to Whit Sunday and Whit Monday; the latter is known today as the spring Bank Holiday.

In the county, two men were chosen before the festival to be churchwardens, their first task being to bake cakes and brew a special Whit ale. Another election was then held for a Lord and Lady of the Ale to preside over the festivities on Whit Monday in a decorated barn or a specially constructed bower in the churchyard, to which everyone would make their way, dressed in their best clothes, to join in the merrymaking and enjoy the food and drink.

For opulence and innovation, however, it would be hard to beat Greatworth, where until 1785 the overseer for the occasion was not a lord but a specially designated house steward with his lady as Queen of May and a local lad acting as their son. The court was similar to that at Kings Sutton with the addition of a constable and the 'fool fiddler' replaced by a different fool, dressed in colourful clothing with a gridiron depicted on his back and holding a stick to which a bladder and calf's tail were attached. In addition to the barn, the festivities spilled over outside, where a garlanded maypole was erected for the dancers. A unique feature of the celebrations was a rigorously enforced law against anyone misbehaving, the penalty in the first instance being 'to ride a wooden horse'. If they persisted in being unruly, they were put into the stocks, a sentence humorously referred to as 'being my lord's organist'.

Treading the maze

Boughton Maze was first mentioned in 1364 in the charter for Boughton Fair granted by Edward III. It lay in a large enclosed area on the green and was known as the Shepherd's Race. It was made up of a series of grass verges 1ft in width, with 4in trenches on either side, spiralling to the centre and back to a single entrance.

A sketch of Boughton Maze as it was before its final destruction, resulting from troop movements during the First World War.

Originally it would have been used in village games by the young people of the area, who walked to the centre for amusement and back out again. On other occasions, the maze was used for games in which young people could potentially win a partner; one version of the game involved an attractive unattached girl standing in the centre while each young man took turns racing to where she stood, keeping to the pathway without falling off or changing track, at the penalty of being disqualified. Each competitor would be counted and the fastest was deemed the winner and won a kiss from his prize, whom he duly led slowly back to the entrance. Whether the pair went their separate ways on coming out or stayed together is unknown.

This was a secular version of the religious custom of crawling on hand and knees to the centre of a maze on the floor of the church or cathedral as a form of penance, losing any sins and weaknesses en route and coming out reborn, spiritually cleansed. It also acted as a form of pilgrimage for those unable to travel far.

By the time Boughton Fair had expanded and changed in nature, the maze was no longer used. This was true of many other mazes around the country, several of which had disappeared during the Reformation. Boughton Maze was finally ploughed up by troops during an exercise in 1916.

Another maze existed at Maze Green, Woodford and it is highly probable that there were others in the county but, as is normally the case, there are no records, crop marks or other signs as evidence. Today, only eight survive out of over 200 known examples in England; two lie close to the border of the county at Wing in Rutland and Hinton in Cambridgeshire.

Village feasts and special occasions

Village feasts were originally an annual week-long affair in honour of the dedication of the local church but over the centuries they were whittled down to a single day and many died out during the nineteenth century.

By the turn of the twentieth century, church feast days often involved gardens being tidied, hedges trimmed, hams boiled, special cakes – especially cheese cakes – baked, cowslip wine made, sports events held and the community packing the church. A new feature of the day, especially in the north of the county, was decorated bicycles: children adorned their bikes with flowers, foliage, ribbons and flags and the most attractive designs won prizes. It began as a feature of the celebrations for the Coronation of Edward VII in 1902. The custom was particularly popular at Nassington and Geddington and lingered on in some parts of the county until the 1940s.

Some of the feasts were eagerly awaited events, as in Aynho where the event centred around the annual summer flower show. Until recent years, the village was probably the last place in the county to indulge in a form of the old custom of pig running, which took place during wakes and other festivities, in which the tail of a large pig was well soaped and the pig let loose in the street to be chased

Two girls proudly pose for the camera in the grounds of the Rectory at Geddington, during a Decorated Bicycle event, *c.* 1910.

by males of all ages. The person catching the animal – and keeping hold of it – would receive a prize. The Aynho game of Greasing the Pig was similar but took place in a confined area in which contestants attempted to catch a specially greased young pig without using gloves or wiping off the fat.

As was the case elsewhere around the realm, the Golden and Diamond Jubilees of Queen Victoria, in 1887 and 1897 respectively, were celebrated with street parties and concerts and the decoration of homes. Earlier, in 1839, parts of Northamptonshire had welcomed the arrival of the young Queen and her consort Albert, who were passing through the county en route to Burghley House for a christening. Arriving at Weedon by train, the couple disembarked and travelled the rest of the way via Northampton by horse-drawn carriage. This account comes from Vic Lawrence of Kettering:

> Triumphal arches were erected and houses and streets were specially festooned for the occasion in those towns and villages along the route the royal couple were passing. At Kettering, flags, foliage, and flowers could be seen everywhere, some in the form of crowns and hearts, and there were four arches formed of greenery and lettering spanning the roads, which were crowded with people, including 1,100 Sunday school children, some standing in wagons, and who later enjoyed a 'grand tea' in some of the town's school buildings. The bells of the parish church were rung, as the royal couple passed through the cheering masses, to the Market Place, where, to the strains of the national anthem, they alighted at The White Hart for refreshment and a change of horses. [The inn was later renamed The Royal] Accompanied by a troop of the Northamptonshire Yeomanry, they proceeded on their way, with more villagers lining the route, waving flags as the procession passed through Weekley, past Boughton House, Geddington, Little Oakley, Stanion, and on to Weldon where the horses were changed again, at the Kings Arms. They rode on past Deene Park through Bulwick and past Fineshade where the troop left the cortège to return to Kettering. A little way on, at Duddington, they changed horses again for the final leg, and after passing Collyweston and Easton, reached their destination, Stamford.

Another special occasion was Empire Day, which was first celebrated on 24 May 1902 at the end of the Boer War, in recognition of the achievements of the British Empire. Not so much a celebration for adults, it was relished by schoolchildren who had the opportunity to dress up in all kinds of patriotic or fanciful costume.

The end of harvesting was another great reason for celebration, as the last of the crop was loaded onto the cart. In many of the villages around the county, the cart would be decorated with boughs of ash and oak, and the men riding on it would sing a favourite rhyme:

Above: Children dressed in suitable garb for Empire Day at Oundle, *c.* 1910.

Left: A sketch of the Harvest Home ceremony in Northamptonshire, 1824.

Harvest home! Harvest home! Harvest home!
We've plough'd, we've sow'd, we've ripp'd, we've mown,
Harvest home, harvest home, we want water and kaint get nun!

They would get their wish as the cart would be pursued by playful young women carrying bowls of water and, on the last line of song, the contents would be thrown over the thirsty crew. At Ecton, there was a variation of the custom: the prettiest girl in the village would be hoisted to the top of the cart as it made its way to the stock-yard, accompanied by the men on foot. Some of the smaller communities, however, replaced the cart ceremony with the making of a corn dolly.

A corn dolly was made from the last sheaf and after the harvest feast would usually be kept in the farmhouse kitchen until the spring sowing, when it was either laid in a furrow to restore the fertility of the earth, mixed with the new seed or kept until the crop from the next harvest had been gathered successfully. The spirit of the corn was believed to have protective power.

Northamptonshire had two versions of the corn dolly, neither of which were in human form. One type was twisted and plaited in the form of a yoke and placed over the heads of the horses pulling the cart with the last sheaves. This was popular in the north of the county, in villages like Little Oakley, and was basically a variety of the corn dolly known as the Essex Terret, a term used for the loop or ring on a horse's harness, through which the reins were passed. More common around the county was the other type of dolly, fashioned in the form of a pair of pointed horns like those of the ox that once dragged the plough over the fields.

The traditional Northamptonshire corn dolly, in the form of two pointed horns (illustration by R.S. Lambeth).

To modern minds, some county customs and games of the past may seem to have had a cruel streak, particularly those that took place during St Martin's Eve on 10 November. This was a time for jokes, tales and general merriment. John Clare gives a vivid description of the revelry in *The Cottage Festival*, a work that remained unpublished until 1983:

> Beside the fire large apples lay to roast, and in a huge brown pitcher, creamy ale,
> Was warming seasoned with a nutmeg toast, the merry groups of gossips to regale,
> Around her feet the glad cat curled her tail, listening the crickets' song with
>   half shut eyes
> While in the chimney top loud roared the gale, its blustering howl of out door
>   symphonies
> That round the cottage hearth bade happier moods arise.

He then goes on to describe some of the malicious tricks played on gullible victims. In one game a participant closes his eyes, whereupon ashes are placed in his open mouth. In another, a volunteer is blindfolded and seeks to retrieve three knives that have been hidden around the room, one of which has been heated in the fire. Pranks were played on anyone, young or old.

Two festivals of a similar nature and celebrated within days of each other were St Catherine's Day, known as Catterns, and St Andrew's Day, known as Tander Day. Catterns, the lacemakers' holiday, was held on 25 November in the north of the county and got its name from a fusion between two different Catherines: St Catherine, the patron saint of unmarried girls who was martyred on this date, and Catherine of Aragon, who was, incorrectly, said to have introduced bobbin lace into this country while living in Bedfordshire and to have developed the spread of lacemaking as a cottage industry.

Catterns was a time for family gatherings, communal feasting and merriment, with firework displays – including catherine wheels – and games like leap candle and a form of apple bobbing in which blindfolded participants, using only their mouths, had to retrieve pieces of apple which were attached to two points of a bobbin winder, somehow avoiding the pieces of candle stuck on the other two points. The main drink was warm beer with eggs and rum, and food included rabbit casserole, ham and carrots, frumenty and Cattern cakes. At Kettering, Catterns revellers had a special rhyme that they chanted for these cakes:

> Rise, maids, rise,
> Bake your Cattern pies,
> Bake enough and bake no waste
> And let the bellman have a taste.

According to Ann Baker, in the extreme north of the county around Peterborough, girls from the workhouse, whose main occupation was spinning, wore white dresses decorated with coloured ribbons, with an emphasis on scarlet. The girls had a specially elected queen, usually the tallest girl, with a crown and sceptre and went in procession round the town, calling at the homes of the more affluent begging money and singing a special song about Queen Catherine. One of the verses went:

> If we set a-spinning, we will either work or play
> But if we set a-spinning we can earn a crown a day:
> And a-spinning we will go, will go, will go,
> And a-spinning we will go.

Tander Day, also a lacemakers' holiday, was celebrated all round the county and was a more riotous occasion than Catterns. Thomas Sternberg, writing in 1851, stated that it was the only traditional custom which had survived to his time 'in anything like its pristine character'. The special drink for the occasion was elderberry wine, usually drunk in vast quantities. The drinking was followed later in the day and well into the evening by cross dressing, with men dressing as women and women dressing as men, flaunting themselves around the streets. On one occasion in Peterborough in the 1920s, the police were called in as the event got out of control – and it was banned.

At Blisworth, to go tandering involved the children visiting a lacemaker's house where they would receive sweets and gifts, according to Mona Clinch who wrote in 1939 about her early life. At other villages such as Spratton, children had their own unique custom known as barring out, in which they would not permit their teacher to enter the school, strongly resisting any attempt he or she might make at entry, until they were given a holiday. They did this to the following chant:

> Pardon, mistress, pardon, master,
> Pardon for a sin.
> If you won't give us a holiday,
> We will not let you in.

Every autumn, on the Friday following St Michael's Day on 29 September, farm and domestic workers would be present at hiring fairs, or statutes, where they put themselves up for hire in the coming year. They would be recognised by the tools or symbols of their occupation: shepherds with their crooks or wearing a lock of wool, dairymaids with their pails, housemaids with mops, farmers with a scythe or sickle. Would-be employers set the pay and conditions of service and, on acceptance, sealed the bargain with a handshake and the giving of a coin.

Until 1846 a curious ritual, said to have derived from the Hiring Fair, was the Mop and Pail Day held at Rushden on 12 May. On the evening before this day, mops and pails were collected by the young and taken in wheelbarrows and carts, or anything else that moved, and placed in a great heap on the village green for the next morning's sport. At an early hour, the girls and women attempted to retrieve their belongings from the heap, to the accompaniment of a fiddler. Half a dozen would tug away, barging, scrambling and scrapping with their rivals.

Just before Christmas, on the Eve of St Thomas on 21 December, poor or elderly women would go begging – known in the county variously as a-gooding, a-mumping and a-Thomasing – at the homes of the more fortunate in the community, for gifts or money. In some villages, a two-handled pot known as a pad or gossiping pot was carried round for a donation of frumenty wheat with which to make the popular dish of that name. Many years ago, Flo Colyer, who grew up in Weldon in the early years of the twentieth century, wrote down her memories of the occasion and its underlying purpose:

> I well remember seeing the women sitting around the cottage kitchen apparently just gossiping, but the real reason for their being there was to gather a few pence for their Christmas fare. The parish charities provided gifts at Christmas [and still do] for widowers and spinsters, but widows were not catered for, so they toured the village to collect for themselves. They were usually given tea, sugar, jam or money.

County customs that have survived

Perhaps the most unusual of the annual May ceremonies in the county and one that still survives, albeit in a modified form, is the Bread and Bun Dole at Geddington. Originally dispensed by a former Lady Montagu of Boughton House, this was intended to ensure that the poor folk in the village, who normally lived on low-grade rye or barley bread, should enjoy at least one 'white wheaten loaf' a year. On May Day, at the start of the dole, a bell would ring and people would make their way to the church porch, and later outside the bakehouse, where the bread would be distributed. As the population began to increase and it became difficult to sort out who was genuinely poor, a chunk of bread was given instead.

The Pole Fair at Corby is one of the two fairs granted by Henry III to Henry de Braibroc, the lord of the manor, in 1226. However, for a reason that has proved impossible to explain, the fair is only held every twenty years, on Whit Monday in May. It starts with a reading of a charter – which does not mention the fair – granted by Elizabeth I in 1585 and reconfirmed later by Charles II, exempting the

The Bread and Bun Dole outside the bakery at Geddington in the 1930s.

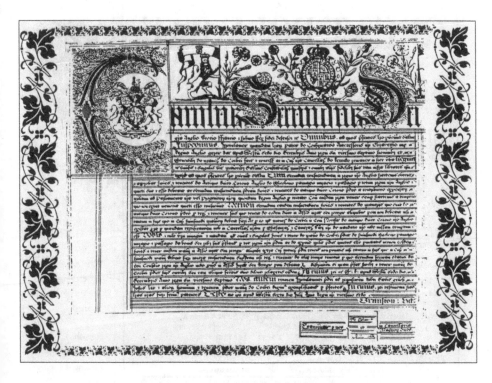

The Charter originally granted by Elizabeth I, as reaffirmed by Charles II.

villagers from various tolls and levies. The charter had probably been purchased by her chancellor, court favourite and dancing partner, Sir Christopher Hatton, who was lord of the manor. A similar situation had occurred at Northampton, which gained its own rights of freedom. Also of interest is the fact that the Queen regarded herself as ruler not just of England but of Scotland, France and Ireland, and this incorrect assertion duly appeared on the charter in Latin and in its later English translation! The original was later lost during the Civil War at the home of the Brudenell family at Deene Park, where Parliament destroyed valuable documents, among which were local historical research papers.

However, there is another twist to the saga, this time concerning the reconfirmation of the charter by Charles II in 1670, written on the document as being the twenty-second year of the King's reign. Charles II dated his reign from the death of his father in 1648 rather than from the Restoration in 1660. However, 1682 mistakenly appeared on banners at the Pole Fair!

Left: A poster advertising the 1902 Pole Fair at Corby.

Opposite: 'Chairing' and 'riding the stang' at the 1902 Pole Fair.

Beginning at 6 a.m, the charter is read at the four main entrances to the village – in Church Street, at the junction of the High Street and Cottingham Road, in The Jamb and, until recently, Rockingham Road near the railway bridge – where triumphal arches and banners of welcome and hope for a successful fair are placed. Formerly, the giving of the charter was also re-enacted in a special pageant performed in costume by schoolchildren in the village, as part of the occasion.

Three people are chaired round to each of the reading points – in recent times these have been the rector, the chairman of the council and the oldest person in the village – and they are the first of many people to end up in the stocks placed originally at the appropiately named Stocks Lane. Other people wanting to come into the village then have to pay a 'coin of the realm' to gain access; if a male person refuses to pay up, he is made to 'ride the stang', being placed on a pole and taken to the stocks. The word 'stang' is an example of the Danish influence in the county, as it is the Danish word for a pole. If a female person refuses, a chair is used for the same purpose. The stocks used for this are unusual in that they have five holes for the feet, instead of the traditional two or four. Various explanations have been given for this – including a suggestion that they were specially made for one-legged tipplers! – but they were most likely made to hold one foot of

The 'toll of the stocks' at the 1902 Pole Fair.

each person, with the bench accommodating three people. Once in the stocks, there is no chance of being released until you give in and pay! For this you receive a ticket, which many folk in the past placed on display in their hats. Sometimes a glass of beer was given to the offenders in the stocks – it must have been thirsty work, just sitting there!

The fair itself is an occasion for merriment, games, feasting and general entertainment. Amos Bell of Great Easton wrote about the event in 1862:

> Many hundred people were present, and a great many went through the ceremony. Stalls, shooting galleries, shows, and a large portable theatre went up as if by magic, flags and banners floated in the air, and the greatest hilarity prevailed. Parish officers, constables, and policemen went through the ceremony, no person being excused ... All the villagers tried to vie with each other in decorating their houses with devices, etc.

On the last five occasions, features of the fair have included climbing a greasy pole, a giant ox-roast, a tug of war and a carnival. The most recent fair was held on 6 May 2002 and attracted hundreds of people from far and wide, eager to soak up the atmosphere of this unique, if somewhat infrequent, custom.

(After opening the Fair. 1900)

Halberdiers standing with the Bailiff stand outside the church in Rothwell, after the opening of the Rothwell Fair, May 1900.

A week after Whit Monday, a five-day Charter Fair takes place at Rothwell, after the reading of a charter by the Bailiff outside the church and at the town's hostelries, declaring the fair open. The charter was given by King John in 1204 for 'a yearly fair at Rowell at the Feast of the Holy Trinity, and on that day, and for the three following days, so nevertheless that such a fair will not be to the hurt of neighbouring fairs'. In fact, the fair lasted for five days. Four centuries later, during the reign of James I, it started a little earlier, on the day after Trinity Sunday, under a new charter.

In the past, it has been a colourful occasion, with the Bailiff riding around the town on horseback, accompanied by six halberdiers carrying a pole – they originally carried a halberd, a weapon which is half-pike, half-axe. At each existing hostelry where the charter is read, it is customary for the reader and halberdiers to receive a drink of rum and milk – an intoxicating experience by the time they reach the end, although by then the Bailiff has given others the opportunity to have a tot and is replaced by whoever has a halberd in his hand during each reading, which could be anybody!

As can be imagined, the charter reading was always a rowdy affair. For many years, young folk would walk around throwing eggs and flour at anybody or

The Charter Fair procession marching through the streets of Rothwell, June 2004.

anything and, if any vehicles dared to come through, they were grabbed and given a violent rocking. The halberdiers – who had longer pikes on their weapons than today – were also a target and efforts were made to obstruct them by linking arms across the road. As one resident says:

> It was quite a shock to anyone passing through who did not know what was going on – and in those days the police kept out of it.

Now of course, like other crowd events, there is a mass police presence to ensure nothing gets out of hand!

After the reading is complete, the hostelries open to serve breakfast, including rum and milk, and remain open all day for the duration of the Fair. Today the fair in its original form as a trading event has been replaced by one for amusement only and is a modern funfair, sprawled out on the original site outside the Market House. Another tradition that has long been defunct is the ancient custom that allowed any townsperson to brew and sell beer for the week by setting up a 'bough house' – putting a tree branch above the door of a dwelling – for the duration of the fair. Another change is the timing of the fair, which now begins at 2 p.m. on the Saturday afternoon before Holy Trinity and lasts until the following Saturday, opening only in the evening on weekdays.

There have been other changes as well. Until quite recently, when the first day was a statutory holiday, houses in the town were inundated with relatives. Special food was made for the occasion, such as Rowell Fair Ham and Rowell Fair curd tarts, and new clothes and bonnets were worn. It was a common sight to see children with popguns and water pistols. On one occasion, a group of boys played a prank on the local bobby who was considered by them to be a miserable individual, as recounted by Norman Mason:

> We had got some fire extinguishers, which we filled with water and set one off over the top of the fairground stalls. On the other side was the constable keeping an eye on the events and he held out his hand and said: 'Oh God, it's raining!' but he was the only one to get wet. It was all part of the fun.

For many years, the children had their own kind of festival after the fair, known as a Fote Fair – 'fote' being the name for a cigarette card. These were given instead of money to go on the various attractions and stalls the children had set up. The fair ran for a week after school and on the following Saturday. Ann Rowlett who still lives in the town recalls:

> There was darts, card games and all sorts of things; my dad made a wooden game for me where coins were rolled down a board with numbered holes.

In 2004, the Charter Fair celebrated its 800th anniversary in style, slightly later than usual, in June. Special sausages were made for the occasion by a local butcher, and there was a competition to see who could make the best Rothwell tarts, a recipe for which can be found in Chapter Nine.

An old custom that has appeared in the county for the first time reflects the demographic changes that have taken place in modern times: Burns Night has become popular in Corby, with its large Scottish contingent. It is an occasion for

John Lobb Douglas about to perform the Burns Night ritual in Corby by reciting the poet's verse over the haggis.

which local supermarkets have plenty of haggis delivered. In the pubs, a kilted Scot enters the room with a steaming haggis on a tray with tatties and neeps – potatoes and turnips – and addresses the dish with a verse of Burns' poetry before piercing it with his dirk. This is duly completed with a wee dram of whisky.

Finally, a youngster that looks set to be around for a few more years yet involves that time-honoured pastime of conkers. In the autumn of 1964 at Ashton, near Oundle, four local anglers had to cancel a fishing trip. After a drink or two in the Chequered Skipper, the pub facing the village green, they wandered outside and picked up some of the many conkers lying in the vicinity and decided to amuse themselves with a custom from their boyhood – playing conkers. They found some string and began playing enthusiastically until there was an outright win-ner left triumphantly holding his battle-scarred, though still intact, 'conqueror'. They enjoyed themselves so much that they returned with other companions the following year and the Ashton Conker Club was formed, with a committee of eighteen setting out rules for a contest to be held annually on the second Sunday in October. The World Conker Championships were born.

King Conker about to open the
proceedings for the fortieth (ruby)
anniversary of the Ashton World Conker
Championships, October 2004.

Two competitors in action at the
championships.

The contest is presided over by its own Conker King, holding a bell and crook and wearing a Union Jack bowler, with strings of conkers adorning his shoulders. The club pre-selects the finest conkers it can find, grades them according to size and strings them on leather bootlaces for opponents to use – a fresh one for every round played. Each group of players, known as a panchion, plays a round or 'shel-thred', and opponents take three successive strikes until a conker is demolished, the competitor with the intact conker going on to the next round. The custom has now become so popular that contestants come from all over the world to participate. Entertainment on the periphery includes morris and molly dancers.

four

STRANGER THAN FICTION

I have climbed the decaying wooden stairs of the old mill and looked for treasures that children search for, but I never knew the mill in its active days. I experienced a certain silence of mystery that made me wonder what noises and grindings once issued from its now ruined remains.

This quotation from the family memoirs of Gertrude Bagshaw, about her childhood in the 1880s in Great Oakley, gives an evocative picture of the past, something we can still experience ourselves at various sites around the county, if we are willing to negotiate brambles, undergrowth and other obstacles. Many sites stand in glorious isolation and can be rewarding to visit at any time of the year.

At least twenty-six churches have been lost in the county, mainly due to parish mergers or as the result of a settlement being deserted. However, the remains of some may still be found. The church of St Peter originally stood near the stable block of Lilford Hall, which was demolished in 1778. Attempts were made to resite the building away fom the Hall but they were unsuccessful, so it was decided to relocate parts of the fabric at a completely different location, a decision which was probably influenced by the eighteenth-century fashion for follies. Masonry was precariously carted to The Linches at Achurch, where some of the pillars and stone blocks, each piece marked and numbered for exact replication of the original construction, were reassembled overlooking the River Nene. The three arches and walls of the nave stand today virtually hidden among woodland in an evocative scene reminiscent of the Romantic landscape paintings of the German artist Caspar David Friedrich.

St John's at Boughton Green also forms a picturesque scene, with its crumbling walls covered in ivy, proudly resisting any further ravages by nature or human hand. The last wedding to take place there was in 1708, and by 1719 it was described as being in ruins and roofless. The steeple and tower fell down in 1780 and most of the stonework was transported to the village about half a mile away, for its new church. Only part of the east wall and various fragments still stand today.

North-east of the churchyard at Blatherwycke, attached to the old stable block, could recently be seen the ruins of a chapel. A story as to why this should exist virtually next door to the church has been passed down. Between 1876 and 1890, a new incumbent at the church was a zealous convert to the ways of the Oxford Movement, the early and ostentatious expression of Anglo-Catholicism, which advocated continuity of the Church of England with the pre-Reformation Catholic Church and its emphasis on elaborate ornamentation and ritual. This would have been anathema to the manorial O'Brien family, who were staunch adherents to the traditional Anglican way of worship. It is believed that they decided to opt for something more acceptable and the chapel was therefore set up for their own form of service for a period of time, certainly for the duration of the village priest's incumbency.

Left: The relocated remains of the church of St Peter (Lilford) standing in The Linches at Thorpe Achurch.

Opposite left: The ruined chapel attached to the stable block of the former manor house at Blatherwycke.

Opposite right: The strange stone built into the churchyard wall at Loddington.

In the west wall of the churchyard of St Leonard's at Loddington, shaded by yew trees, is a large boulder carved with three Roman crosses. It is said to have been a dedication stone from the original stone tower before it was renovated. Before that, however, it may have one of the glacial stones deposited around the county and used for special purposes, in this case marking the sacred site that the church later took over. When this happened, it is possible that it was Christianised, with the crosses of Calvary being engraved on the façade. However, there is something of a mystery, for it is said that in the 1830s five crosses were visible.

Other sites are more accessible, none more so than follies that were originally intended to stand out and catch the eye. They proliferated in the eighteenth century as a new fashionable craze taken up the wealthy, with no practical purpose other than acting as a landmark. Many were bizarre in design, some potentially dangerous, and all were partly inspired by the architecture seen by the young and affluent during their European grand tours to Rome, and by the fashionable taste for the Gothic instigated by Horace Walpole, novelist and pioneer of that genre. However, Northamptonshire can claim to be the home of the father of folly-building, long before the fashion took off.

In 1577, Thomas Tresham (pronounced 'Traysham') began the building of Rothwell Cross, now known as the Market House, at Rothwell. At this time he was veering towards conversion to Catholicism, a dangerous thing to do in

Elizabethan England. He finally converted in 1580 and spent a total of fifteen years out of the next twenty-five years of his life in prison for his beliefs. While incarcerated, he meticulously made plans for buildings which would symbolically reflect his faith, decorating his prison walls with drawings, figures and texts in Hebrew, which unsuspecting visitors were unlikely to understand.

The Rothwell Cross was begun before Tresham was imprisoned and was originally intended to have seven arches, gables and windows – the number of days of the Creation. This never materialised but the building is certainly unique, with ninety heraldic shields and coats of arms of local landowning families depicted on the exterior walls. For some unknown reason, the building was left unroofed until 1895 when a roof was added by a local architect, John Gotch, using plans for the building found in a secret cupboard discovered at Rushton Hall. The building has had several uses over the years, such as council offices, a library, a shop and a 'pensioners' parliament'. According to Lewis Stanley, a Rothwell historian:

> It has also served as a jail, and it is said that one Saturday night during the Victorian era, the parish constable arrested a man for being drunk and disorderly in the street, who was unable to find his way home. He was put in the 'roundhouse' until sober. On awakening, he found himself locked up and not knowing where he was, decided to break out by forcing the bars in the door, but was too fat to get through, so he took all clothes off and was thereby able to squeeze though. Finding his clothes were still inside, he threw caution to the wind and ran home through the early Sunday morning streets, hoping that no prying eyes would spot him. It has been said that he may well have been the county's first streaker!

Tresham's next building was to symbolise the Holy Trinity. Known today as the Triangular Lodge, it was begun in 1595 in the grounds of his home at Rushton Hall, facing the road to Desborough, and was completed in 1595. Ostensibly built for the estate rabbit catcher, it was known variously as Connergerie Lodge, Warryner's Lodge, Three Square Lodge and Trinity House. It was built in the shape of an equilateral triangle, with everything in sets or multiples of three: it is just over 33ft long, is three storeys high and has three triangular windows on all the three sides, each topped with three gables. Each of the exterior wall panels has a Christian motto or symbol.

Nothing remains today, however, of Hawkfield Lodge, begun in 1596 and meant to be a companion building for the Triangular Lodge. Its exact whereabouts are a matter of conjecture, one theory being that it lies on the opposite side of the grounds, facing the road to Rothwell. It was probably built purely for ornamental purposes but, even so, a drawing that exists of the lodge shows it to have been of remarkable appearance, a multi-sided structure with a vaulted roof, central supporting pillar, two porches and three doors. The lodge was built but it is not known if the stone ball shown on the plans was added to the top of the building.

Opposite: Rothwell Cross, later renamed the Market House.

Right: A drawing showing the now lost Hawking Tower in the grounds of Rushton Hall. It is believed to have been built as a companion to the nearby Triangular Lodge.

Lyveden New Bield was the last of the Tresham follies to be built; it was left incomplete on his death. It is now maintained by the National Trust.

Bunkers Hill Farm, near Boughton Green.

Tresham's final folly, Lyveden New Bield, lies off the Brigstock to Oundle road and was built to symbolise the Passion. The Garden House, as it was known, was officially built as a hunting lodge and summer house with landscaped gardens. It is cruciform in design, with many carvings connected with the crucifixion. Tresham, however, died before the building was completed and it was never finished.

Between 1764 and 1780, an extraordinary series of follies were built at Boughton by the Earl of Strafford, William Wentworth. He was a friend of Horace Walpole, who certainly encouraged him to add Gothic battlements and towers to his home at Boughton Hall – now demolished – and grottos, temples and artificial ruins in the grounds, which have also since disappeared. Some of the follies around Boughton Park have survived, however, and have been documented by a local writer, Simon Scott.

The castellated buildings which appeared around the Wentworth estate during the 1770s were Bunkers Hill Farm, named after the site of a major British victory during the American War of Independence and still visible today; New Park Barn, now Fox Covert Hall; and a crenellated archway known as the Spectacle, which was erected as an eyecatcher in 1770, standing a short distance away from the main Boughton to Moulton road, in what is now known as Spectacle Lane. In 1764, a gigantic obelisk with an inscribed plaque hed been erected in memory of Wentworth's friend, the Duke of Devonshire. A farmer on whose land the monument stood grew tired of his crops being trampled by the many inquisitive visitors that it attracted and erased much of the inscription on the plaque. It still stands today, some might say precariously, next to a housing estate and can be seen from a great distance, though curiously it is not visible in the immediate vicinity, until you are almost approaching it.

Below left: The tall obelisk erected in memory of the Duke of Devonshire, a friend of the Earl of Strafford of Boughton Hall.

Below right: The Spectacles, an eyecatcher, situated between Moulton and Boughton.

A member of the Jeyes family, Philadelphus, was so intrigued by the Spectacle that he copied the design for the frontage of his house, Holly Lodge, which was built on the nearby main road between 1857 and 1861. A remarkable additional feature a few metres away was a farm implement gate, which incorporated twelve different tools in its design, including a scythe, flail, spade, and shepherd's crook. The Jeyes family owned a chemist's in Northampton and John, a younger brother of Philadelphus, took out patents on twenty-one sanitary products, including the famed Jeyes Cleaning Fluid.

The follies of Boughton were matched by two related men who lived at different times in Finedon Hall. Sir English Dolben (1750–1837) began his folly-building with the 'medievalisation' of his property and newly erected outbuildings

One of the Jeyes Gates fronting the grounds of Holly Lodge on the Moulton-Boughton road. Various farming implements have been incorporated into its design.

and the construction of a spike-crowned monument known as the Edith Cross which appeared in the hall grounds. It was named after Queen Edith, wife of Edward the Confessor, who was lady of the manor in the pre-Conquest era. It no longer exists, having been vandalised by local boys in 1930. In 1789, Dolben erected what later became known as the Finedon Obelisk as a waymarker at the crossroads of the town. Legend has it that it was put up in that year to commemorate George III's recovery from a long bout of madness, an occasion which was marked by bell-ringing and fireworks in the town, but also to celebrate the beginning of the French Revolution with the storming of the Bastille; the inauguration of George Washington as the first US president; and two family matters: the birth of his fifth daughter and his father's second marriage.

The commemorative obelisk erected as a waymarker at Finedon crossroads.

Dolben's daughter, Frances, married William Mackworth, who added the Dolben surname to his own. Like his father-in-law, he embarked on a spate of folly-building, adding Gothic arches, gargoyles and grottos to the family home and grounds and a four-storey ice tower. In 1860, he converted and crenellated a former windmill just outside the town into a dwelling, now known as Exmill Cottage, which can still be seen today on the road to Harrowden. On the opposite side of the road, heading back towards the town, he built the Volta Tower as a memorial to his son, who had died when the ship of that name capsized off the coast of West Africa in 1863. The building became a dwelling but fell down in September 1951, killing one of the occupants.

In 1869, the uneven flagstones of the floor in the chancel of the church of All Saints at Rushton were being removed in order to level the surface. While levering up one of the uninscribed stones, workmen found a large cavity filled with powdered charcoal. Curiosity getting the better of them, they disturbed the contents and found the perfectly preserved body of a female with all its features intact. Within a few moments of being exposed to the air, however, everything disintegrated. The identity of the woman and the date of her burial have remained a mystery ever since.

Exmill Cottage, a castellated windmill now converted into a home.

The Volta Tower before its collapse in 1951. It was built as a memorial to a son of William Mackworth Dolben who drowned while on active naval service.

In Spring 1866, workmen were engaged in restoration work in St Mary's church at Woodford when a beam was removed from a transitional arch in the nave and a broken stone recess was discovered, which contained a circular bamboo box covered in coarse cloth. It was subsequently found to contain an embalmed heart, believed to be that of Roger de Kirketon, a knight who died in 1280. It can be seen today behind a glass panel near the top of a pillar in the south aisle. Another heart can be found in the church at Yaxley, just outside the county near Peterborough.

The crusader's heart concealed in the stonework of a pillar at the church of St Mary in Woodford.

In 1790, a lock of woman's hair was found in the churchyard, in a perfectly preserved state. Probably Anglo-Saxon, it was a yard in length, flaxen in colour and plaited. For many years, it was kept in the vestry but over time its length gradually diminished to 2ft, probably as a result of people wanting a keepsake. Its whereabouts today are unknown – if indeed anything ever survived the actions of souvenir hunters or the fingers of the superstitious!

On the north wall of the nave of the now redundant church of Holy Trinity at Blatherwycke hangs an unusual benefactors' board, a seventeenth-century bequest by two prosperous villagers for the provision of a plum pudding annually on Christmas Day for the oldest poor males in the village. The plum pudding would not have been the kind eaten today, being a combination of spiced gruel and prunes or other dried fruit.

If you walk around the earthworks of the long-vanished Cistercian abbey at Pipewell, you might be lucky to find an interesting memorial. When the site was excavated in 1909, little was found as all the structure above ground had long been taken away for building purposes, and what little was underground probably plundered over the years. However, a stone tablet was laid with the inscription 'Abbas RIP'. It is still in situ, marking the abbot's grave, but is usually overgrown with grass.

There are also some interesting faces carved in stone on churches. On the south side of the chancel of Holy Trinity at Rothwell is the Rothwell Imp, which has been likened to that at Lincoln Cathedral. It is probably a fertility or apotropaic (having the power to avert evil or bad luck) figure, or possibly the whim of a stonemason or his apprentice active at the time. On the outside of the church of St Botolph at Stoke

BENJAMIN HEALY,
left the Intereſt of One
hundred Pounds depoſited
in the O'BRIEN's hands,
for the uſe of the Poor,
and THOMAS COLES
who died in the Year 1684
left a Cloſe in the Pariſh of
Cliffe,for ever: to buy
ſix of the oldeſt poor men in
the Pariſh,a Plum Pudding
on Chriſtmas Day.

Whoſo giveth to the Poor
Lendeth to the Lord.

A stone benefactor's tablet in the church of Holy Trinity, Blatherwycke.

An inscribed stone placed on the site of Pipewell Abbey during excavations in 1907.

The Rothwell Imp in the choir at the church of the Holy Sepulchre, Rothwell.

The bespectacled image of a former incumbent, Canon Frank Scuffham, on the church at Stoke Albany.

Albany is a stone corbel of a head wearing spectacles – a modern idea also seen in the county at St Peter's in Oundle. This particular figure is that of Frank Scuffham, a former rector. More bizarre are the fifty-one heads of men, women and grotesques on the corbel table forming a frieze around the exterior of the church of St Peter at Stanion. One story is that they represent the number of villagers living at the time of carving, though one wonders about the grotesques!

Three of the fifty-one heads on the exterior of St Peter's church at Stanion. The heads are believed to represent the people living in the village at the time of carving.

One figure that is partly apotropaic and part fertility-inducing is the so-called Green Man. With the exception perhaps of Yorkshire, the county has more Green Men figures than anywhere else in the British Isles – over 360 can be seen on and in religious and secular buildings. The fact that so many figures are still in existence is attributable in the north of the county to the durable limestone that has been prized for other buldings of stature around the realm. It is also due to the determination of the people themselves. At Finedon, the village seems to have been particularly fond of its church furnishings during the period of iconoclasm that began during the Reformation and flared up again during the Civil War. Therefore it took special measures to ensure their preservation: the font was plastered and then encased in wood, painted and used for a long period as a horse trough, while a plainer substitute was used. However, it is the remarkable set of elaborate carvings on the pillars of the chancel and nave that merit special attention. When the church was being restored between 1846 and 1848, layers of plaster were stripped away and there, in pristine condition and looking the same as when they were carved in the fourteenth century, were a fine group of Green Men. Breathing out masses of luxuriant foliage, they now live once again, fulfilling their symbolic roles of regeneration and life. They are among the best figures to be seen in the whole country.

One of the county's finest Green Men, dating from the fourteenth century, at Chichele College, Higham Ferrers.

Running the length of the ceiling in the nave of the church of St Mary the Virgin at Warmington is a well-preserved set of wooden Green Men depicting all the standard forms, including a tongue poker, a figure framed with foliage and others with foliage emanating from the nose, eye or mouth.

Often positioned at the vulnerable points of a church – especially the windows, doors and roof – the Green Man figure would repel any evil forces attempting to enter the sacred precincts. The combination of face and foliage acted as a spur to the medieval churchgoer to flourish in life – and death – by following the true path, with some of the more bestial figures acting as a warning to those who might stray, for evil too can flourish.

During the eighteenth century, a gravedigger working in the churchyard of Holy Trinity at Rothwell felt the ground cracking beneath his spade and feet and this led to the discovery of a small dark room under the ground, full of bones and skulls. It was later estimated that it contained the remains of 1,500 people, subsequently believed to be either victims of the Black Death or casualties of the Battle of Naseby. Later research revealed them to be mainly medieval in date, and they were probably the remains of townspeople who had died from natural causes. One theory is that they were placed in the crypt from other parts of the graveyard

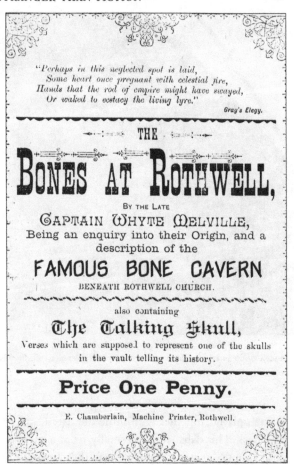

"Perhaps in this neglected spot is laid,
Some heart once pregnant with celestial fire,
Hands that the rod of empire might have swayed,
Or waked to ecstacy the living lyre."

Gray's Elegy.

THE
BONES AT ROTHWELL,

By the Late

Captain Whyte Melville,

Being an enquiry into their Origin, and a
description of the

FAMOUS BONE CAVERN

BENEATH ROTHWELL CHURCH.

also containing

The Talking Skull,

Verses which are supposed to represent one of the skulls
in the vault telling its history.

Price One Penny.

E. Chamberlain, Machine Printer, Rothwell.

The cover of a treatise on the
origins of the bone crypt at
Rothwell, 1880.

to make room for the building of the nearby Jesus Hospital in 1585. Today they
are neatly stacked in piles and can be seen whenever the bone crypt is open to the
public, currently on Sunday afternoons during the summer.

Edna Essex, who grew up in the town, recalls her class being taken down into
the crypt in the days before electricity was laid on. Every second or third child
was given a candle to hold as they made their way down the gloomy steps. When
they reached the bottom:

> The verger blew them out so we were in total darkness for a while, until someone
> lit them all up again. All the children yelled of course ... There was one [skull] there
> that really smiled and had all its teeth, the grinning skull.

In Corby village, when a row of three houses in Church Street was demolished
during the 1960s, six stone slabs that had been inserted in the stonework at various places were saved and removed to the Civic Offices in the town, where they

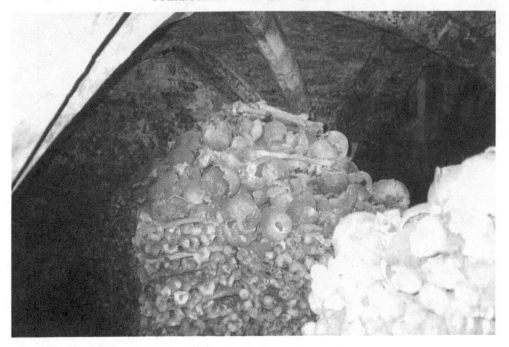

A view of the interior of the bone crypt discovered by a gravedigger at Rothwell in the eighteenth century.

were displayed, together with some old datestones, on the wall behind the reception desk. The slabs were originally from a memorial tablet in the church but until recently it was a mystery how they came to be used for the houses, or to whom they belonged. The mystery has now been partially solved: the connection was with John Twickten, incumbent of the village church from 1614 until 1657, whose daughter Bridgit died tragically early at the age of nineteen in 1638. Before he himself died, Twickten requested in his will, which was proved in 1657, that he wished to be buried 'either in the grave of my deare daughter or close to the grave of my sonne'. There were only three memorials to the family set in the chancel floor: Twickten's memorial stone lay alongside those of his son and wife. It could be that Dr Twickten was buried in his daughter's grave and that is the reason why her memorial stone came to be discarded.

Bulwick may have the tallest tombstone in the county. Set high up in the spire of the church of St Nicholas is an irregularly shaped piece of masonry with a worn inscription. Its provenance is of great interest: in the nineteenth century, a local stonemason needed a slab of a certain size to repair the spire. He thought hard, not having such a piece to hand, and began to look around the churchyard. Eventually his eyes alighted on just what he was looking for: a broken tombstone, said to be of a female relative, Hannah Ireson, who had died in 1724. This was duly inserted into the appropiate place and is still there today!

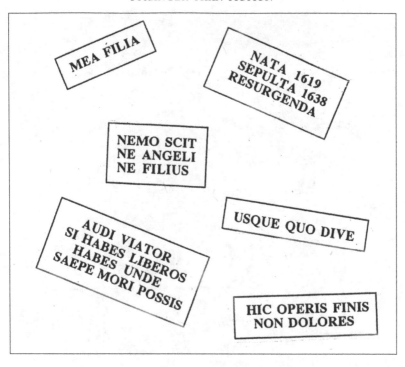

A sketch of parts of a tombstone originally inserted into the walls of a row of now demolished cottages in Church Street, Corby village.

The highest tombstone in the land: a slab used for the repair of the church steeple at Bulwick.

The lantern tower of the church of St Mary at Weldon.

Another complete fabrication in the county is that the lantern tower on the church of St Mary at Weldon was lit up as a beacon to guide travellers through the dark woods of Rockingham Forest. Nothing in the thirteenth-century perambulations or early maps describe or depict any vast stretches of tree-covered land, most of it being ploughland or pasture. Also, the church originally had a spire, as shown on maps of 1585 and 1630. Lightning struck the spire in 1700 and it was not replaced. Instead, a miniature octagonal tower was inserted within the confines of the larger main tower and this in turn was superseded in the nineteenth century by the present lighthouse tower.

The tower is significant because the church has a double association with Horatio Nelson. Firstly, Dr John Clark, a ship's surgeon in service during the Battle of Trafalgar in 1805, retired shortly after the Napoleonic Wars and settled in the village. Probably impressed with the larger lantern towers he had noticed at nearby Lowick and Fotheringhay, he may have paid for the present tower with its unusual lighthouse design to remind him of the years he had at sea. He certainly

The unusual clock face at Whilton.

gave a window to the church in 1860, with an inscription referring to his service at Trafalgar. The second connection with Nelson is another window, made of six-teenth-century Flemish glass and depicting the Adoration of the Magi, which was given by Nelson to Sir William Hamilton, husband of Nelson's mistress, Emma. It was given to the church in 1897 by the Reverend William Finch Hatton, whose father had inherited many of Hamilton's effects.

The clock face on the exterior of the church of St Mary at Whilton has only four minutes between each digit instead of five, which in theory means that time should pass more quickly in the village than elsewhere! Other unusual clocks can be seen at Raunds, where there is a rare fifteenth-century clock adorned with angels and benefactors but with no numbers on the dial, and at the church of St Mary at Wappenham, where there is a one-handed clock dating from the reign of Elizabeth I.

In the north wall of the chancel of St Botolph's at Stoke Albany is a low arch that, until 1790, housed an ornate fifteenth-century monument depicting Johannes de Ros, whose family were lords of the manor from 1285 until the death of Edmund, Lord Ros, early in the sixteenth century. Johannes was the son of William de Ros, who had been Lord High Admiral to Edward II and Edward III. The monument showed him as a recumbent figure dressed in armour, with his hands clasped in prayer and his feet resting on a dog – a common form of funerary design in the Middle Ages. There was an inscription: 'Hic jacet Johannes de Ros le bon compagnon'. The 'bon compagnon' appellation was given by Edward III for his faithfulness and loyalty, particularly in his opposition to Hugh Despenser, an unpopular, greedy and ambitious member of the King's Council whom many wished to remove. It is said that on one occasion a brawl, involving fists and drawn swords, took place in Parliament, at Lincoln Cathedral, between Johannes and one of the Despenser faction, in front of the King, who promptly separated the two parties. Johannes was made Steward of the King's Household and was one of twelve guards or advisors to the monarch. He later fell on hard times, however, for when he died in the village in 1377, he is said to have been so poor that the King was asked for – and gave – 200 marks (approximately £134) for his burial. The present tower is said to have been his gift during more prosperous times.

The monument was removed in 1790 because the minister at the time felt it looked 'black and hideous'. However, it is said that the real reason for this was the constant complaint by a clergyman's wife who felt unsettled by its presence whenever she was in church! First of all, the effigy was overturned and used as a seat, before being broken up and buried under 'an adjoining brick pavement'! The only remaining clue to the monument's original presence is the Ros family coat of arms of three water bougets, which can be seen at the top of the arch.

If you visit Great Oakley, there is a huge mound beside the village hall, the height of which stretches for several metres above the houses. It is covered in conifers and, if you look carefully, you will see a set of worn steps leading to the summit. It has always been a talking point in the area as to why it was constructed.

Arthur Tomblin (1838-1911) was educated at Cambridge and came to the village in 1859, at the age of twenty-one, as curate of the church of St Michael, becoming rector five years later. He soon integrated himself into the village way of life and the front garden of the rectory became a famed attraction in the north of the county, where his prize roses were greatly envied. He was a man of many talents, among which was as an opening batsman in the village cricket team: it was said he could easily have played for the county. He was also an expert marksman with the rifle or pistol, often inviting the young men to take part in a shooting contest, issuing them with revolvers and challenging them to 'cut the candles in two' in a passage under the building.

Arthur Tomblin, rector of Great Oakley, in his
early days, *c.* 1870.

One of Tomblin's favourite pastimes was to walk up Harper's Brook on stilts and he would frequently offer a penny to any child who could walk the farthest without falling in. Years later, John Smith, one of the boys who had taken up the challenge, recalled his own participation and how the rector laughed when he fell in. Another boy, Fred Campion, one day decided to play a prank on the rector, who had a habit of leaving an upstairs window open whenever he had a shave. A few years later, in 1915, John Smith, who was with Fred, reminisced about the incident:

> Fred crept up behind the garden wall, and aimed a shot with his catapult from the gateway, and only missed him by a very small margin. Mr Tomblin straightaway got his revolver and threatened to shoot Fred. Not even a hare ever ran away from the scene as quickly as we did!

In around 1886, however, a sudden change came over the rector. He began to build a huge mound of earth and rubble and invited village children to help him, paying them between a halfpenny and sixpence, according to what they brought. The mound slowly got higher, no doubt with the addition of his prize rose bushes and parts of the rectory roof and walls which he had torn down.

A view of the delapidated rectory, parts of which were used by Revd Tomblin for the giant mound in the 1890s.

For many years afterwards, there was much local gossip as to why he had built the mound – for he never gave his secret away. There were many rumours, guesses and assertions: people suggested that he was trying to recreate Mount Ararat; that he wanted the village to have a landmark in its centre; or that he would stand on the top with a powerful brass telescope to see what people were having for breakfast! The most persistent gossip was that he had been snubbed by the patron of the village Sir Richard de Capell Brooke after asking for the hand of the youngest of his three daughters, though there was an age gap of around thirty years between them. The family only visited the village on occasions, preferring to live at Woodford, where a street is now named after them. What is more likely however is that the two men were not kindly disposed towards one another and Tom decided to show his contempt in some form.

In church, Tomblin's sermons became offensive, with weird ramblings and comments, and he was eventually prevented from performing services and allowed only to officiate at births, deaths and marriages. In 1892, he wrote an epitaph for his *bête noire*, the last two lines of which were: 'and if he's gone to a lower level, let's all commiserate with the Devil'! He was removed from the rectory in 1900 after its condition was condemned by a health inspector, and went to live in a house on the road to Corby, provided for him by Lady Cardigan of Deene Park, where he built a smaller mound of packing cases and rubble. Passers-by would be offered refreshment in the form of sweet pea wine!

On a lighter note, some witty literature has survived which has caused consider-able amusement and amazement since its redicovery. It became fashionable in the latter years of the eighteenth century for town traders to attract wider attention to the range of wares they offered for purchase and thereby increase their prof-its. One way of doing this was the rhyming advertisement, which could reach extraordinary proportions in length. Some may well have been mass-produced by a particular printer. What is incredible is how one of these was used for drumming up trade in a small Northamptonshire community. John Chaney of Naseby, who advertised himself as 'a tea dealer, draper, druggist and auctioneer', used a lengthy 128-line advertisement for the incredibly wide range of services and goods he had to offer, many unheard of today. He offered edible, household, medicinal, surgical and decorative goods, and clothing – not bad for a village business. The following is a short extract from the advertisement of around 1775, which was reproduced in the *Northampton County Magazine*:

> Then let me inform you in what things I trade
> I've flour to make Bread of, and Bread ready made;
> Good Butter and Cheese, that each palate may please,
> Fat Bacon well cur'd and good Boiling Peas,
> With Coffee, and Chocolate, Coco's and Teas,
> I've Sugar, and Raisins, and Currants likewise,
> With which you may sweeten your Puddings and Pies.
> I have Pepper and Salt, I have Oatmeal and Rice,
> I have Hops, I have Treacle and Nutmegs for Spice;
> I have Oranges, Lemons or candied or not,
> Anchovy's rich Essence I Likewise have got;
> And to relish the taste of your juvenile Gluttons
> I have Ginger-bread Cakes, and Ginger-bread Buttons;
> Spanish-juice, Sugar-candy, warm Peppermint Drops,
> And sugar-plums such as you'll find in few Shops.
> To chear up your spirits and to keep you from gripes,
> I have at your service Tobacco and Pipes.
> I have Cinammon, Cloves, fine Mace and Salt-fish,
> And good things to furnish a gentleman's dish

Much shorter, though no less witty, was a trade advertisement formulated and printed by Alan Jones, who was landlord of the Cardigan Arms in the quiet hamlet of Deenethorpe in the 1920s and '30s. The hostelry has long since been demolished but a rare copy of the advertisement offering a 'Free Pass' still exists, as a snapshot of a colourful chapter in the life of the community many years ago. It was in the form of a notice attached to the wall, stating that anyone who could perform a set of impossible tasks and would promise to patronise that particular hostelry and keep to its ten commandments would be issued with the free pass. The notice began with 'essential information' and ended with a jolly verse:

A man is kept engaged in the yard to do all Cursing, Swearing and Bad Language that is required in the Establishment. A dog is kept to do all the barking. Our pot-man (or Chucker Out) has won 75 prizes and is an excellent shot with a revolver. An undertaker calls every morning for orders.

Here's to the working man, who fears no master's frown
May his Beef and Beer increase and wages never go down.
May his dear homely wife be the joy of his life
Never kick up a racket, but love and respect the jolly old man
Who wears a workman's jacket.

five

Natural or Supernatural?

One can imagine the awe our ancestors felt towards trees, with their immense stature and girth, plugged into the depths of the earth and stretching up towards the sky, linking three different worlds. Some of the trees seemed to be of great age, with the ability to withstand the ravages of time and the weather. Some even appear to have human facial features (simulacra) or other illusory formations, all carved by Nature's hand, when observed from certain angles, or depending on lighting conditions, a good example of which can be seen outside the churchyard at Croughton. It is no wonder that trees were associated with the supernatural; one belief was that a nature spirit or elemental often lived in a tree with the ability to animate it – or even be the tree itself – therefore it could share any suffering, or die if harmed. If humans posed a threat, the results could be unpredictable.

A woodman once went into Salcey Forest to fell a tree. As he was about to strike the trunk of an old oak, a fairy jumped out and begged him not to hurt the tree. Moved by fright and surprise, he obliged. As a reward, the fairy granted him three wishes that he could make at any time. He made his way home as dusk fell to tell his wife of his encounter but, for some unknown reason, all memory of the fairy had vanished by the evening. While they were dozing in front of the hearth, the man licked his lips and muttered that he fancied a bit of hog's pudding. No sooner had he said this when there was a rustling in the chimney and a link of sausage landed at his feet. As this happened, he suddenly remembered his earlier

This pollarded beech in Wakerley Woods is one of many fine ancient trees surviving in the county. It is one of three trees planted around 1620 to mark various parish boundaries in the area.

The old tree outside the chuchyard of Croughton. The variety of shapes and images carved by nature catch the eye and stir the imagination.

encounter and told his wife, who called him a fool for his forgetfulness. While chastising him, she muttered: 'I wish em wer atte noäse!', which means 'I wish they were on your nose' and the link of sausages duly attached themselves, stubbornly resisting all attempts by the man to remove them. He hastily wished for the cursed things to go away, whereupon they instantly did so and all the wishes were used up.

Many of our outstanding oak trees with immense girths have been lost in time, so much so that legends have grown up around them. The Lowick Oak, which stood in a field in the south of the village until it fell down in 1968, had a girth of 25ft and a height of 90ft. These measurements were reported by locals, some of whom are still alive, and verified in media coverage. A photograph was taken of a table laid for dinner inside the trunk. Stephen's Oak stood in the vicinity of Stephen's Oak Riding, which lies near Fermyn Woods between Brigstock and Lyveden. According to tradition, it was large enough to hold thirty boys from Brigstock quite comfortably!

Northamptonshire has an excellent network of waterways, including many wells and springs, as place names such as Sywell, Twywell, Pipewell, Scaldwell, Yarwell, Hollowell and so on testify. Three areas were particularly rich in springs. In Cottingham parish even today you can see the remains of at least six pumps, a well-head at adjoining Middleton and evidence of water constantly overflowing into some of the lanes in the vicinity of the church. The area around Boughton was also noted for its springs, in particular St John's Spring which still exists by the walls of the ruined church, and a fine spring at Grotto Spinney, which has some of the purest water found anywhere. In Aynho parish, a strong limestone area, there are numerous springs, the names of which have gradually disappeared over the years. Mentioned in the mid-1800s were Town Well, Friars Well, Painters Well – a petrifying spring – and Puckwell, whose name has a supernatural connection and is a rare example of a name that hadn't undergone Christianisation.

Some wells were believed to have supernatural powers to predict the future. The Drumming Well at Oundle, now long filled in, was said to have a drumming sound 'like a march' coming from its depths whenever a catastrophe was about to befall the land. One observer in the seventeenth century noted that:

> ...it beat for a fortnight at the latter end of the month and the beginning of this month. It was heard in the same manner before the King's death and the death of Cromwell, the King's coming in and the Fire of London.

In later years, a leading geologist explained that the noise was caused by air being expelled from rock crevices into the well through a 'water seal which was periodically in bubbles'.

A domed well in Boughton Spinney, one of the many springs in the county. A similar structure can be seen near Pytchley.

St John's Spring outside the ruins of the church at Boughton Green.

Another particularly interesting spring was mentioned by Morton in *The Natural History of Northamptonshire*. This was Marvelsike Spring in Boughton Field, close to Brampton Bridge and the Kingsthorpe road. He stated that: .

> ...it never runs but in mighty gluts of wet and whenever it does is thought ominous by the country people who from the breaking out of that spring are wont to prognosticate death, the death of some great personage or very troublesome times. It did not run when I was there on Oct 22, 1703 but the forgoing winter it did and had not run before for two years.

A supernatural element may be implicit in the name of Mother Redcap's Well at Harlestone. The name was a common appellation for an alewife: in other words, any local woman brewing and selling ale. There was a public house of that name in Northampton until the end of the nineteenth century and a slogan could be seen above the doorway:

Please to step in and taste my tap,
'twill make your nose red as my cap.

A general rhyme also existed at the time that the hostelry was flourishing, although it did not necessarily refer to that particular establishment:

Old Mother Redcap according to her tale,
Lived twenty and a hundred years,
By drinking very good ale.
It was her meat, it was her drink
And medicine besides,
And if she still had drunk that ale
She never would have died!

It is possible that such miraculous water existed at Harlestone and was used for brewing, but redcap was also the name for the headwear of certain elementals, so it is feasible that local folk believed the spring to be the haunt of fairies or similar beings, like the fairy pool near Brington where sprites were frequently seen gambolling among the water plants.

Stones have long held a fascination among people – with some justification. Next time you are out in the fields or walking in the street, you will probably see, if you look carefully, an isolated stone, perhaps tucked away in a corner, having no apparent use. Dotted around the county are a number of these stones, like boulders of granite or quartzite – and they are not of local origin. In some cases, these have been transported by human means from some distance away but the majority have been deposited by glacial action. They have consequently given rise to all kinds of legends, such as having been dropped or thrown by giants or the Devil. However, because of their uniqueness they have been seen as a symbol of sanctity and, as a result, they have been used throughout the ages for special purposes: for oath swearing; as assembly points for community matters such as settling disputes; for trading and bargaining purposes such as the Jo Stone at Gretton; and even marking the centre of a village. In some cases, they were considered to have certain inherent properties that could be of communal benefit in some way, either spiritually or materially.

In the extreme north of the county, in a ridge and furrow field near East Farndon, lies the Judith Stone, a large granite boulder lying in a hollow, which is believed to mark an assembly point where tribes met on important occasions during the Bronze and Iron Ages. Being on elevated ground with sweeping views, the site was obviously of strategic importance and would have been part of a communications network across the hills of the county in times of danger. The stone gets its modern name from Countess Judith, the niece of William I, who owned a great deal of land in the county.

Above: The Jo Stone at Gretton, where local agricultural trading and bargaining formerly took place.

Below: The ancient Judith Stone in a field at East Farndon, a glacial boulder used a tribal meeting point.

Sometimes the shape of a stone, whether man-made or natural, could give it a particular role in community life. Such a case was the Witch's Chair at Weldon, an L-shaped piece of rock sited some way out of the village, off the road to Upper Benefield, and used, according to tradition, for carrying out village justice. It is said that in the fourteenth century a man murdered his lover in a fit of jealousy after he found out she was attracted to another man. He was apprehended by the villagers and chained to the stone chair to starve to death. After a few days, the village officials went to check on the results, but were astounded to see him looking healthy and in good spirits. Thinking something was amiss, they resolved to find out what was going on, and hid themselves close by early the next day. They soon had their answer when a baker from Benefield arrived and promptly began giving food and drink to the prisoner. They later dealt with the baker, leaving the prisoner to fulfil his predestined sentence.

Several sites around the county have stories telling of occasions when attempts at building a church on a certain site have been unsuccessful, with all the hard work undone and the tools removed, apparently by supernatural forces like elementals or demons. It was more likely, however, to have been local pagan opposition to a Christian takeover of a particularly sacred site that had been venerated since time immemorial, causing fear, anger and superstition to come into play. This would accord with recent research which shows that, contrary to what is widely believed, few churches actually stand on former pagan sites. Church Stowe, or Stowe Nine Churches near Daventry, has such a story. For eight consecutive days, the tools, trenches and stonework from the day's work kept vanishing overnight in the valley where the church was being built and were found dumped at another site further away on top of the hill. A watch was kept on the ninth night by a specially chosen person, who could not believe his eyes when he saw a hairy creature 'of great strength', carrying out the task. The church was consequently built at a different site – where it stands today.

A variation of the legend states that fairies, annoyed that a church was being erected near their dancing place, kept dismantling the stonework but left it in piles on the ground. On the ninth night a monk kept watch, spending the time hidden and deep in prayer. This had the desired effect, for the fairies never appeared again and the work was finally completed on the chosen site. Apart from this 'nine false starts' theory for the name of Stowe Nine Churches, there is another which asserts that nine churches can be seen from the summit on a clear day but for this to be achieved one would need remarkable eyesight!

A number of stones are said to move at certain times of the day or on special days of the year. A pair of eagles on the gateposts of Drayton House at Lowick were said to be able to fly away if the clock ever struck thirteen. If you are lucky enough to be able to see through the hedges lining a field track between Weekley and Warkton, you will notice a statue on a pedestal standing in marshy ground. Known traditionally as Stone Moses, it now stands at the source of a spring which

Stowe church, built on the present site after various thwarted attempts, according to legend.

once fed water through conduit pipes to the grounds of Boughton House some distance away. A former owner, Sir Ralph Montagu, had been Ambassador to France between 1660 and 1678 and, after seeing the fountains and palace of Versailles, began to extend his home in a similar style of grandeur, landscaping his grounds to include fountains and statues, among which was Stone Moses. When a new water and drainage system was installed, the statue was moved to his present site, a move which gave rise to colourful stories. Children playing in the vicinity were warned not stay out after dark or Stone Moses would get them. And, in keeping with our theme, at midnight he slips off his pedestal and goes down to the River Ise a few metres away for a drink.

Stories have been told through the centuries of toads surviving incarceration in trees, coal seams and rock, enclosed in cavities which fit round them snugly, without food or air for several years, living on moisture generated from their skin or from a humid substance exuding from the stone: toad in the hole, perhaps? An experiment was conducted in 1825 at Oxford where six cells were made in a

Stone Moses, said to walk to the Ise for a drink of water at midnight.

The bridge at Rushton, built in 1829. Live toads were placed in the hatches as an experiment in survival.

block of limestone and six in ironstone. Toads were then sealed inside them with glass and putty and they were buried 3ft down in the ground. After a year they were opened; those in limestone had survived but those in ironstone were dead, apparently because of a crack in the glass. This may have led to such an experiment taking place at Rushton, when a new road and bridge was built replacing the old route over the Ise in 1829. Live toads were placed in small slate and cement hatches at the foundations to see if they could survive for 1,000 years. Today the hatches under the bridge are cracked and some are empty – perhaps they have since escaped!

Celestial phenomena such as eclipses and comets have always caused great wonderment or been a source of superstition. Some have been spectacular, such as the meteor seen at Middleton Cheney in 1806, the appearance of which was reported in a London newspaper as follows:

This evening precisely at six o'clock, a very bright meteor like a rocket passed over the parsonage of Middleton Cheney, Northamptonshire, in the direction south-west to north-east. It glided along horizontally not more swiftly than a bird flies, and seemed at a height of not more than 29 to 30 yards, and as it became extinct within the distance of about half a mile before it reached the hill in that direction, its height above the ground could not be mistaken. No sparks issued from it, but it was followed by a smoky train.

Other wondrous sightings that became talking points for a long time and led to all kinds of speculation included one at Gretton in the early evening of 15 September 1749, when a meteor shot across the sky, with thunder, black clouds and whirlwinds that drew up water from local streams. Columns of smoke formed over the village with 'bright arrows' darting to the ground. In September 1693, villagers in the county were startled by the strange erratic behaviour of a long bright shooting star, which, unlike normal meteors, formed a strange letter 'W'. On 27 October 1776, a large fireball was seen in the north of the county; it eventually landed in a field between Tansor and Fotheringhay, exploding with a deafening sound that could be heard for miles, its impact causing fragments to ignite and setting light to a barn. Most unnerving of all celestial sights, however, was that which appeared in May 1929 at Far Cotton:

Eyewitnesses spoke of seeing a brilliant streak of lightning go across the sky and then heard a loud explosion. Mr E. Allen of Oxford Street described seeing after the explosion, a tongue of red flame which appeared to strike him on the forehead.

Earthquakes are also no stranger to the county, a notable recent example being that felt in the north of the county in the early hours of 23 September 2002. However, one of the worst was that which occurred on 30 September 1750, rocking the area between Newton and Rothwell. The tremor lasted for between twenty and thirty seconds and caused buildings to shake and shudder considerably, none more so than the church where the vicar was taking a service. He recorded in the parish register:

I thought the Roof would crash then, or we would be swallowed up by the earth ... it was like a mighty wind, or rather the driving of many Coaches ... the Earth was sensibly perceived to heave under our feet. The church totter'd from the Foundation and the East Window shook most violently, as if all was coming down, and from the Roof, which we thought was falling on us, we heard dreadful Crackings.

A fire broke out in the town at around midday on 20 November 1675 and one can imagine the trauma it caused to the people of Northampton. A strong south-westerly wind blew the flames from the cottage of an elderly woman living in a lane near the castle. It struck the thatched buildings in its path as it spread to Market Place and Derngate, finishing almost half a mile from where it had started. In the Drapery, the fire was reported to have made 'a noise like thunder'. By the time it had abated after six hours, over 600 houses had been destroyed, although only eleven people had lost their lives. Inevitably, amazing tales arose from the event: there were stories of an apothecary's servant seen walking along Gold Street with flames on each side as he carried a barrel of gunpowder, and of three rainbows seen together in the sky after the heavy rain that followed.

Fires also had devastating consequences for other towns in the county. In 1462, Kingscliffe had to be virtually rebuilt and realigned after 'a hundred dwellings' were said to have been destroyed. In 1718, most of the old town of Thrapston – over fifty houses – was destroyed by fire; much of it was later rebuilt in brick. However, certainly the most remarkable fire was the one that occurred at Wellingborough in July 1738, when flames spread from a baker's shop in Silver Street, where oats were being dried, into the neighbourhood. The fire melted the lead of the church roof, destroyed 800 houses and left several others badly damaged, making 120 people homeless. The damage could have been worse, had it not been for the efforts of a brave sixty-year-old woman from Pebble Lane with the apt name of Hannah Sparke, who, with the aid of others, helped smother the flames with blankets soaked in beer from the large stock of barrels in her cellar! A plaque was later erected in commemoration and the heroine given 'the freedom of the town' as a token of gratitude.

In recent years, we have seen a great many floods, though in such a well-watered county these have never been unusual. In December 1720, Northampton witnessed 'the greatest flood that has ever been known in this age' when the Nene overflowed, swamped countless numbers of buildings and drowned forty sheep. One of the most dramatic floods was the Great Flood that hit Wellingborough in 1841, when the same river carried a great portion of the bridge away, entering the lower room of a house close by. The family were evacuated by the man of the house, who took his wife and some of the children to a more secure place on a sturdy section of the bridge and then returned to collect the others. On the way back, a gush of water and a large piece of ice upset the boat and drowned the man and his children. Fortunately, the woman and the children with her, all of whom were by now standing in water up to their waists, were rescued and taken to safety in a cart.

A close-knit village community would often unite and help each other through the worst of the weather. A vivid description of a severe storm in Kingscliffe in 1884 appeared in the memoirs of Adela Lock in 1957. She spent much of her childhood in the village and gave some excellent glimpses of life in the area as it was in the last quarter of the nineteenth century:

The miller waved his hands by the windmill about an approaching 'whirlwind'. Uncle ran to shut the chickens up. Hay and straw stacks were being blown over. A chimney pot fell. Someone tried to close the windows. The thatch was stripped from the cottage roofs and casements were torn off. We could only wait until the storm stopped. More pots came down, and there was the crash of broken glass. About nine o'clock, it died down, and a few ventured out with lanterns to see if anyone needed help. Men went to farms to borrow stock-cloths to put over broken roofs, but supply was not equal to demand! The brook was so swollen, its banks overflown, and the water was rushing over the road, making it impassable, and entered homes …The next morning, a survey of the damage was made, and everyone helped clear up and repair.

Nature has also provided the county with some more interesting features, among them places for hearing one's echo. At Thenford there was a tradition that if someone stood 380ft from the north front of Thenford House and spoke, not shouted, out a sentence of about fourteen syllables, the echo of the sentence could be clearly heard, repeated over and over again. By going nearer or further back, a similar effect could be achieved but the resonance was at its best from the original spot. Another renowned echo was at Rushton, close to the former Cockayne bridge over the River Ise. It was popular with children living in the locality but even an echo can be the cause of tragedy: in the eighteenth century, a little girl from nearby Barford wanted to talk to the local echo but fell in the

The 1912 flood at Geddington.

water and drowned. It is still an atmospheric, tranquil and tree-shaded place; the crumbling stonework of the ancient disused bridge is now covered in greenery and is a favourite haunt of bats.

The ivy-covered Cockayne Bridge at Rushton, long disused and a favourite haunt of bats.

six

LEGENDS AND TALES

In 1834, Thomas Haynes Bayley (1797-1839) wrote 'The Mistletoe Bough', a folk ballad which soon became a drawing-room favourite in Victorian times. It tells of some wedding festivities taking place on Christmas Eve, with the guests playing a game of hide and seek. The bride is the first to hide and finds an old oak chest in the attic. As she climbs in, the lid snaps shut and she is unable to get out, since the catch for opening it is on the outside only. For some reason, she is not found until several years later. The story certainly struck a chord around the nation and several counties adopted the tale, with the same sequence of events set in different country houses:

> In the highest – and the lowest – the loneliest spot,
> Young Lovell sought wildly – but found her not.
> And years flew by, and their grief at last
> Was told as a sorrowful tale long past...
> At length an oak chest, that had long lain hid,
> Was found in the castle – they raised the lid
> And a skeleton form lay mouldering there,
> In the bridal wreath of that lady fair!
> Oh! Sad was her fate – in sportive jest
> She hid from her lord in the old oak chest.
> It closed with a spring – and, dreadful doom,
> The bride lay clasp'd in her living tomb.

Apart from Minster Lovell in Oxfordshire, Northamptonshire has the best claim, however tenuous, to being the site of the tragedy. Some later writers in the

The earthworks of Titchmarsh Castle, one of the settings for the tragic tale of the mistletoe bride.

county, notably the Kettering poet and artist George Harrison, transferred the scene of the wedding celebrations to Titchmarsh. Despite a little poetic licence, one can see why. The facts are that in 1242, Sir John Lovell of Minster Lovell married Maud de Sidenham, whose family home was Titchmarsh Castle. Shortly after their marriage, the couple came to live at Titchmarsh, which replaced the Oxfordshire home as the main family residence. Their son and heir was born there in 1255 and the family line continued for several years. By 1363, however, the castle had long been deserted and was described as being in ruins. Rubble from the castle ruins was then used for building houses in the village and only the earthworks can be seen today. The Lovell family had lost its lands at Titchmarsh because of their association with Richard III, which was shown in a saying:

> The cat, the rat, and Lovell our dog
> Rule all England under the hog.

The important thing here is not so much the historical accuracy – the wedding reception was in Oxfordshire and the bride definitely did not die that evening! – or the suspect aftermath: why no one thought of looking there at the time, if there was a thorough search, or why such a long period elapsed before she was finally found. Although only a tongue-in-cheek invention, there is an element in the story of a distorted version of the struggle between winter and spring. Whatever the case, it is a fine tale that still stirs the imagination today.

The Dun Cow's Rib in the
church of St Peter, Stanion.

In the church of St Peter at Stanion can be found a gigantic whalebone, but when
and how it got there is unknown. Traditionally it has been known as the Dun Cow's
Rib and has an amusing legend attached to it. At one time, there was a giant cow
which was so large it could provide milk for the whole community. One day, a witch
in the village got annoyed with everyone constantly avoiding her and cast a spell on
the cow, or some say she milked it with a sieve, with the result that it could no longer
give any milk and subsequently fell over and died. The rib is supposed to have come
from the cow and is a memorial to her and the service she gave!

As with the previous story, a similar tale exists around the country, with variations. There may, however, be a grain of truth in the Dun Cow legend. It is
believed that before the Saxons came and hunted it almost to extinction, a long-
horned native breed of cow almost 6ft in height, with a white hide and red ears,
grazed throughout the land. The Saxons brought over the breeds we see today.
Seeing any survivors of such a distinctive breed would have made an impact on
our impressionable ancestors and inevitably give rise to legends.

It is said that all round Britain, there exists a strange phenomenon: layers of trea-cle-bearing rock from compressed ancient forests of trees similar to sugar cane lying deep beneath the earth, like seams of coal. It is supposedly a powerful sub-stance: in some stories, it is highly explosive; in others it is a delicacy. One legend states that the ancient Britons made use of it against the invading Roman armies, pouring it onto the surface of tracks to delay their march across the land. It is not certain how these strange tales began but it is likely they originated in the Victorian music hall. Whatever their origin, these stories seem to have been used as a ploy by certain villages to draw attention to themselves, either as a sign of exclusiveness or to mystify outsiders. Whatever the situation, the joke is at the expense of those who believe it – usually a neighbouring village!

At Crick, the treacle mines are now defunct. Overlooking the village, there is a treacle mine 'spoil heap' at Cracks Hill, from the time the Crick canal was con-structed. It is said that if you happen to accidentally wander in the vicinity, you are 'in the treacle'. Legend also has it that the M1 was deliberately diverted away from Crick because of the danger of subsidence from the mines. The deposits are no longer worked and the mines are permanently sealed up. However, all is not lost: if you are so inclined, it is possible to see the original mining equipment and a special spoon in the village hall about every four years, when one of the miners, resembling one of the Seven Dwarves, might just be present!

Cracks Hill, Crick, beneath which the highly dangerous treacle mines are said to exist.

Stories of ghostly fiddlers and drummers can be found all round Britain and Northamptonshire is no exception. These stories use a local setting and often take place in the distant past. The legends probably became more widely popular in 1837, after the appearance of a phantom drummer in a magazine story by Richard Harris Barham, as a parody of contemporary and superstitious practices. The story later appeared with other tales in *The Ingoldsby Legends*, a nineteenth-century best-seller. For his story 'The Dead Drummer', Barham took elements from a real-life crime that had taken place in 1780 on Salisbury Plain, when a sailor killed a drummer boy who was accompanying him across the lonely stretches. In the story, the ghost of the victim later reappears to haunt him and he confesses the crime to a local clergyman.

At Rushton, a ghostly fiddler was said to be heard on certain nights playing an ancient tune. When the Cockayne family purchased the Hall in 1619, a secret passage was discovered under the Warryner's Lodge. Unlike other rumoured subterranean tunnels around the county, this one did exist, although it has now been blocked up. The passage was a source of intrigue to the new owners, who offered a reward to anyone daring to enter it and follow its track to the end. The challenge was taken up by a fiddler from Desborough, who stipulated that if he did not reappear, the money was to be given to his wife. He disappeared and his wife got the money but it later transpired that the couple had craftily hatched a

Rushton Hall, from where an underground passage was said to lead to the Triangular Lodge and in which a vast treasure was said to be concealed.

scheme, the fiddler having secretly ventured into the passage earlier and found a cavity in which he could conceal himself for a long period until he was deemed to be lost and the search called off. They wisely left the district shortly after, wealthier than before.

Two different ghostly drummers are said to have been seen in the county, one at Drummer's Mound, near Barford Bridge between Kettering and Corby, and the other at Cat's Head Wood, near Brigstock. The latter is connected with a mutiny of the Black Watch, who marched from Scotland to London in 1732 for inspection by George II, only to be spurned by him on arrival. Many of them left in disgust to make their way back home, some taking a route through Northamptonshire. Captain Bell from Dingley was summoned to apprehend them in the vicinity of Fermyn Woods, where they either surrendered or were captured. It is said that, the night before, a drummer boy accompanying them had been murdered in nearby Cat's Head Wood by some of the pursuing militia and was hastily buried under a mound. For many years afterwards, a small boy could be seen dancing on the mound, playing his drum.

There are interesting legends of buried treasure round the county, some having been unearthed and other hoards still awaiting discovery. Silverstone racetrack was built on a Second World War airfield, which itself had been constructed on the site of the former Luffield Abbey, traces of which were still visible until then. A farmer by the name of Saywell once farmed the site and in 1740 he was plagued by deer from Whittlewood, one of which was strange in appearance, having the 'face of a man'. The deer kept disappearing at the same spot; Saywell dug there and found 'treasure' hidden by the monks 'in time of trouble'.

In 1576, Mary Queen of Scots was imprisoned in Derbyshire because of her implication in Catholic plots and schemes against her cousin, Elizabeth I. While she was staying there, she was robbed of a sum of money and a cask of jewellery by two men who fled southwards with the stolen goods. They were pursued, caught and taken to London where they were put on trial. There they confessed to having buried the Queen's jewellery at Geddington Chase in Rockingham Forest. A prominent land-owner, Edward Brudenell of Deene, was given the task of leading a group of men in a search for the possessions. The result of the search was not recorded, so it is not known whether the jewels were ever recovered. They may still be there today!

There were always those who claimed they could detect buried treasure, as a means of making a profit from gullible people seeking to improve their existence. According to an extract from the Lincoln episcopal visitations, such a person was apprehended at Kettering in 1527 for charging a fee to show someone where a precious hoard could be found by digging into a mound. His confession has a supernatural element and reflects the popular superstition current at the time. He stated that:

ther was iii thousand poundes of gold and sylver in a bank besides the crosse nygh hand to Kettering, and that it is in ii pottes within the ground ... A man sprite and

Geddington Chase, where treasure belonging to Mary Queen of Scots was buried by thieves and supposedly never retrieved.

woman sprite did kepe the said ii pottes.

Northamptonshire may have had its own Dick Whittington. In the church of St Mary Magdalene at Yarwell, there is an ornate marble tomb chest with a wild man wielding a club depicted on the top slab. The tomb is that of Humphrey Bellamy, a wealthy London merchant who died in 1715. As a boy he came to the village, destitute and ill, while on the way to London. He was fed and cared for by the villagers until he was well enough to travel on to the city, where he became prosperous and was made an alderman. In his last years, he came back to the village that had helped him in his youth.

Inside the church of St Michael and All Angels on an isolated hilltop above the village of Wadenhoe, there is a memorial tablet to Thomas and Caroline Welch Hunt, 'who were both cruelly shot by banditti near Poestum in Italy'. Caroline

The top slab of the Bellamy tomb inside the church of St Mary Magdalen at Yarwell.

was twenty-three and Thomas was twenty-eight. The hidden story is that, less than a year after their wedding, the couple went on a European honeymoon. In Italy, on Friday 3 December 1824, they took a detour from Rome and headed south to Salerno, to see the ruined temples at Poestum. While preparing to stay overnight at a small inn at Eboli, the innkeeper saw the affluence displayed by the couple, such as their jewellery and Thomas's ivory-backed clothes brushes. He contacted some of the local bandits and told them about his guests and their departure time. Early the next morning, the men came out of hiding from behind nearby bushes and held up the carriage with pistols, demanding some of their valuables. They were given money but, knowing what the innkeeper had told them, demanded something more extravagant. On being refused anything else, they became agitated and threatening. Thomas told them they would not dare to shoot and tried to carry on with their journey, whereupon shots rang out, apparently wounding both husband and wife. Thomas died instantly but Caroline lingered on and was able to relate the pattern of events before she too expired. Both were buried in Naples and the four bandits were caught, tried and guillotined. However, the instigator of the crime – the innkeeper – managed to avoid being connected in any way and continued to run the inn for several years after the event.

Other young lovers have, however, been more fortunate. In the summer of 1786, a seventeen-year old orphan and heiress, Miss Talbot, of Weston-on-the-Wolds was returning home from a visit to Ashley, accompanied by her male guardian. When the carriage stopped on the turnpike road near Desborough for a rest break, it was approached by two young men. The *Kettering Leader* reported what happened next:

> One of them distracted the guardian's attention, while the other, a 'Mr Burdett' of Middleton helped her out of the carriage, and both ran across the field to the hedge where a post-chaise and four awaited them. The guardian shouted to them, but to no avail. They then went on 'to the Land of Matrimony'.

The wall memorial at Wadenhoe telling of the tragic Welch Hunt honeymoon in Italy.

Riots, rebels and outlaws

Of all the characters that existed and incidents that took place, none can be more fascinating than young William, son of Sir Henry of Drayton, and his daring exploits in the Brigstock bailiwick, mainly in the 1250s. Something of a real-life Robin Hood in some of his actions, he seems to have been clever, elusive, fearless and imaginative. He must have been popular with local people, as it seems they knew him but did not reveal his identity when questioned – even at the expense of their own imprisonment. A local person was witnessed talking to William and his men during one incident and leading them to a place called Denrode. The first time William appears in the records is in 1246, when he is charged with complicity in a poaching offence after a bloody arrow was found in a neighbouring house in Brigstock. He probably continued committing offences during the next few years but the next time his name appears is in May 1251, when he was seen riding a black horse with a group of armed men and pages and a pack of greyhounds in the Sudborough and Lowick area. A shepherd and four herdsmen were eating their dinner under a hedge in a field when they saw the group pass by, with William wearing 'a tunic of green hue' and riding a horse, over which was slung the body of a deer covered in leaves and boughs. Later that year:

> John Spigurnel, the riding forester of Brigstock park, presented that as he came from the swanimote of Stanion on the Wednesday next before the keeper of Ackwellsike, they saw two evildoers to the forest with bows and arrows, who shot three arrows at them; and they went towards the thicket of Aybriotheshawe. And they say upon their oath that one of those two evildoers was Dawe, the son of Mabel of Sudborough; and that the other had a mask over his head, wherefore they suspected that he was William of Drayton, and more especially because he was accused before of an evil deed in the forest. The said William of Drayton is with no one constantly, and is sometimes in one place and sometimes in another. And therefore the aforesaid Dawe was attached, and he found twelve pledges of making answer before the justices.

William was obviously a very difficult person to pin down in movement and thought. Thereafter, there is no more mention of him in the records and he seems to vanish altogether, as suddenly as he appeared, seemingly never caught – perhaps like Robin Hood.

Robin Hood needs no introduction of course, his fame having spread far and wide over the years, whether he ever existed or not. Not mentioned in writing until 1262 but of older origin, his surname Hood was then a common surname and in such a large forest area, particularly in the north of the county, it was inevitable that a certain Robin Hood would be around, attracting outlaws and other outcasts.

Perambulators at the ancient ash tree of Fineshade, re-enacting part of a medieval forest boundary walk. From left to right: Peter Hill, Chris Wade of the Rockingham Forest Trust and Dan Keech from Common Ground *(Flora Britannica)*.

Outlaws were certainly a common feature of the countryside in the medieval period. If an offender against Forest Law failed to appear before a forest court, called an eyre, after being attached, or bailed, to do so, he would be deemed to be an outlaw. A good example, one of many in Rockingham Forest, is the following from the court records of 1255:

The sheriff says that Robert, son of Godfrey, and Geoffrey were convicted of theft and by judgment were hanged. Robert of Corby now comes and is detained in prison for trespass to the venison. And Richard does not come and he was attached by Roger of Benefield. Therefore let the said Richard be exacted and outlawed.

Intriguingly, a 'Robyn Hode' was imprisoned at Rockingham Castle in 1354, for 'trespass of vert and venison in the Forest'. At other times, there were supposed sightings of him in Corby and Brigstock. He is said to have secretly visited Brigstock some time during the reign of Henry III, who was King between 1216 and 1272. He entered the church of St Andrew but some of the villagers betrayed him and Ralph de Hanville, a royal official of the manor, sent soldiers to lay siege to the church. During the attack, he managed to escape but the priest, who was standing by the altar, was killed by an arrow. No historical evidence exists to verify that the incident did take place, but it makes a good story! The tale is

Rockingham Castle, where a 'Robyn Hode' was held in 1354 for 'trespasses against vert and venison'.

told by Charles Montagu-Douglas-Scott in his *Tales of Old Northamptonshire* and appears to be based on one of the original medieval tales, 'Robin Hood and the Monk' – written around 1450 but much older in its oral form – with the action and characters transferred to this county:

Bold Robin Hood to Brigstock came,
In the Farming-woods he lay,
And he feasted himself on his sovereign's game,
So long as he chose to stay,
For the sheriff was dead, and the verderer fled
At the sight of bold Robin away.

Bold Robin he entered the Church one morn –
'Twas Blest Saint Mary's Day –
And the people they stared at his bow and his horn,
As kneelèd him down to pray;
And there by the door knelt fully a score
Of his merry men keen and gay.

The dark-eyed priest the Mass intoned,
(A buck in his larder lay)
And up in the belfry a little wind moaned,
As a little wind moans today;
When sudden, without was a stir and a shout,
And Robin was up and away.

The arrows came rattling onto the walls
As Robin he rushed outside;
Thro' a window one flew – and the good priest falls
At the feet of the Crucified;
The women they scream and the men blaspheme
And each and all would hide.

But Robin he marshalled his own merry men
With a blast of his bugle horn,
And he fought his way to the woods
Thro' the stooks of the golden corn
And the arrows around him lay thick on the ground
Like a harvest of ills forlorn.

And lo! an armed knight was down,
Who in swift pursuit has led:

'Now carry me back to Brigstock town',
Sir Ralph de Hanville said,
'So sore am I hurt thro' my stout mail-shirt,
That I fear my days are sped'.

'And carry me into the Church', said he,
'Full soon I must confess;
The priest will be there devout in prayer
For the sum of our success,
Since I promised him well o'the red monie
If Robin we should possess'.

Straight into the Church Sir Ralph they bore;
He moaned at the least delay;
On the Altar steps in a pool of gore
The dark-eyed rector lay:
'A judgement, and right', said the wounded knight,
And he passed unshriven away.

Such was the popularity and widespread knowledge of Robin around the kingdom, that certain topographical features were honoured with his name. In the
case of Northamptonshire, two prehistoric standing stones on a slope overlooking the River Nene at Ferry Meadows, near Peterborough, were known as Robin
Hood and Little John. Both are still discernible, though they now officially lie
outside the county boundary.

Of all officials appointed to maintain Forest Law in any of the county's royal
forest areas, no role was more hazardous than that of the forester. Acting as a
kind of gamekeeper and policeman, he had to patrol the forest either on foot or
on horseback, looking out for poachers and trespassers, whom he had to pursue
and arrest. He could be recognised by his green tunic and a horn, his symbol of
office. The foresters were very unpopular with local folk, not only because they
enforced Forest Law but because they could legally demand certain fees, as well
as food and drink for themselves or their beasts, calling at a home at any time
when on duty! They were often involved in illegal money-making practices, such
as impounding villagers' beasts and forcing the owner to pay a small fee for their
return. They also aroused the wrath of villagers by removing the ball of the foot
of dogs in addition to the permitted three claws – and charging an exorbitant fee
for the unwanted task.

Inevitably, some foresters suffered injury or death in the course of their duty.
Such an example was Matthew of Thurlbear. He was patrolling the area of
Beanfield Lawn in Rockingham Forest with his brother James and other foresters,

when they were alerted to the presence of five poachers with greyhounds chasing deer. The poachers saw the foresters coming and stood their ground, shooting arrows in their direction. Two arrows struck Matthew, killing him; the poachers fled into 'the thickness of the wood' and escaped.

However, the story does not end there: three weeks later, James was invited to dine with the abbot of Pipewell Abbey. As he dismounted, he saw a greyhound with a distinctive, unusual tawny colouring, the same one that had been with the poachers who had killed his brother. The dog's owner, Simon of Kilsworthy, a guest of the abbot, was subsequently taken into custody at Northampton Castle.

The story still does not end there, for two years later it was alleged that James was frequently seen 'assembling eighteen armed men in all the bailiwicks [administrative areas of the forest], to wreak destruction to the venison of the lord king.' A case of if you can't beat them, join them!

In another incident in Rockingham Forest, a sinister 'magical' rite took place at Bullax wood near Lowick in 1255. In a gesture of ultimate contempt, the antlered head of a buck was stuck on a spindle – a version of the stang or pole used in social disapproval rituals – like a menacing two-fingered snub against authority and as a souvenir of the poachers' activities:

> On a stake in the middle of a clearing which is called Harleruling, placing in the mouth of the aforesaid head a certain spindle and made the mouth gape towards the sun, in great contempt of the lord king and of his foresters.

The forest officials, after 'raising the hue', gave chase but were further humiliated by a shower of arrows aimed at them and had to flee, unable to resist the onslaught. All the poachers were eventually caught, except two who failed to appear at a court and were declared outlaws.

In the *Gesta Herwardi (The Deeds of Hereward)*, a mid-twelfth-century book by an Ely monk known simply as Richard, a list is given of Hereward the Wate's band of outlaws, which includes at least four men from Northamptonshire: Tostig and Godwin of Rothwell, Godfricus of Corby and Villicus of Drayton, all 'among the most renowned knights in the kingdom'. After the fall of Ely in the autumn of 1071, Hereward officially disappeared 'into the remoter parts of the Northamptonshire forests to summon more men to his aid', initially passing through the forest of Bruneswald (Bromswold), a portion of which spilled over into the county from Huntingdonshire and Bedfordshire and then formed a link with the three county forests of Rockingham, Salcey and Whittlewood. The village of Lutton was formerly known as Lutton by Bromswold and Newton Bromswold, near Higham Ferrers, still retains the name.

A tradition states that at one stage Hereward and his men got lost in Rockingham Forest but thanks to the intervention of St Peter in a vision, a wolf appeared to lead them out of their predicament. And as a bonus, and a further sign of approval from the saint, when darkness drew in, burning candles appeared on all the trees to provide a trouble-free passage through the gloom. Hereward was eventually caught by William I's soldiers and placed in gaol at Bedford before being escorted to Rockingham Castle with a heavily-armed guard. However, Hereward's men lay in wait in the forest, surrounded the guard, slew them and rescued their leader.

Whether out of necessity for food, for adventure or for leisure, poaching was always a part of life – deer in the Middle Ages, rabbits and other game thereafter. There was always an element of danger or risk involved, as landowners zealously guarded what was on their property. For the men of some villages it became a specialist pursuit, some groups even being 'professional', working their way up the scale, initially with rabbits and pigeons (both of which were seen as a nuisance by some farmers and as small fry to the poachers themselves), to the more tricky method of catching hares, and then on to pheasants, partridges and other game.

Poaching gangs had set rules and conditions for their members, which in many cases had to be meticulously adhered to. Mrs Simpson of Corby described the gang in her village, and its leader in particular:

> John James was his name and he was captain of the 'Corby Gang'. When a new member was admitted to the gang, the captain would present him with an Ash plant about five feet long, known to the old inhabitants of the village as the 'Corby Stick'. It was quite straight and extended a fair piece from where it was held in the hand. If a member of the gang failed to use it when he was in danger, he was expelled from the gang.

Rivalry between gangs from different villages and towns would often lead to heated confrontations if another's territory was encroached upon. Jack Robinson of Great Oakley recalls:

> A gang would come from Kettering, and later Corby, armed with nets to catch rabbits, which could be worth sixpence or ninepence each depending on size or who was paying, a lot of money then if enough were captured. A group of the villagers would wait for the offenders at night, and the encounters would often get violent, with the use of sticks, resulting in wounds and bruises.

Until guns came into use, a basic way to catch rabbits was either by using a large net known as a 'haynest', or a 'flan', which was a small round net placed over the hole of their burrow. Other methods used for catching their quarry were more innovative, especially those for catching pheasants, one way being to soak raisins and corn in whisky overnight and then sprinkle the doped food on the ground for the birds to eat as they emerged from their night roost. This was a process which only took a few minutes, as the alcohol soon began to take effect, after which they would not be able to run or fly, making their capture an easy task. Another trick was to mix some carbide and water (to form acetylene) in a can, which was then placed among the branches of a tree or bush where the birds were roosting, the inflammable gas quickly bringing them down. Smaller numbers of poachers liked to creep up slowly to a thick hedge where they would normally be inconspicuous to a gamekeeper a few hundred yards away. If by chance they were seen, however, a heavy stone known as 'a poacher's stone' would frequently be aimed at their adversary.

A rebellious county

Beginning in the middle years of the fourteenth century, when enclosure of the land was taking place, many peasants were deprived of their livelihood because the land they had worked on for generations was suddenly converted to profitable sheep farming by the landowners, some of whom showed little consideration about the effect such an action would have on their tenants. English wool was highly prized in Europe and sheep, apart from being more profitable, did not need paying and did not have any grievances. Pasture also needed less work than arable land.

One serious regional incident occurred in 1607, when groups of alienated peasants entered the county from neighbouring Warwickshire and were joined by several local people who sympathised with their plight, many of whom were similarly affected. The main culprits were the Tresham family, who had deprived peasants of land at Haselbech, Pytchley and Rushton and nearly succeeded at Orton and Great Houghton, before turning their attention towards the area around Newton – not the village itself but land some distance away, near Little Oakley, known as The Brand. This was not Tresham land but common land for other villages, though Thomas Tresham thought otherwise and began to illegally enclose it and build a lodge, causing a popular outcry.

The Levellers (not be confused with the Civil War rebels), or Diggers as they called themselves, headed for The Brand and on 8 June 1607 began uprooting and digging up the newly planted hedges of the enclosed fields. Their leader, John Reynolds, was known as Captain Pouch because of a distinctive bag he wore on his belt, which contained a piece of green cheese as a charm and protective amulet, a common superstitious practice in Tudor and Stuart times in the face of adversity. With the charm, Reynolds believed he was empowered and claimed:

> I have authoritie from his majestie to throwe downe enclosures and that I am sent of God to satisfie all degrees whatsoever.

Tresham, alarmed at the sudden course of events, sent out an appeal for help from his fellow landowners, all of whom declined either out of sympathy for the peasants or because of a lack of interest or perhaps dislike of the family. However, he did enlist the help of two prominent county men, Sir Anthony Mildmay of Apethorpe and Edward Montagu of Boughton. The peasants with their tools and makeshift weapons were no match for the trained militia that was sent and in the ensuing mêlée at least fifty of the rioters were killed, with several more injured.

At a subsequent inquest, it was recorded that several 'townships' – including Weldon, Corby, Kettering, Benefield, Desborough and Thrapston – had been involved. The rioters were not only farm workers but also butchers, tailors, smiths, carpenters, weavers and shoemakers. In spite of only protecting their livelihood and traditional rights, all had to sign or make their mark on a document which read:

> We submit ourselves to His Majesty's Mercy, confessing our heinous offences in the late seditious insurrection and rebellion upon the pretence of depopulation and unlawful inclosure.

James I showed magnanimity and duly pardoned all except the ringleaders of the rebellion. They fared less well: having been found guilty as traitors, they were executed and their remains put on public display in county towns as a warning and deterrent to any more insurgents.

At Grafton Underwood, a dispute between two influential, single-minded men – the lord of the manor, Sir Edward Montagu, and the newly installed rector of the church, John Williams – arose over the forthcoming annual feast of St James. Both Sir Edward and his neighbour and fellow magistrate, Thomas Brooke of Great Oakley, with whom he shared strong Puritan beliefs, issued a set of stringent regulations which were to be read out by the rector to the congregation in the churchyard in advance of the preparations for the feast, as follows:

> No unlicensed beer to be sold.

> Fiddlers not invited by the villagers, or who play music different to that pre-arranged with village leaders, 'to be treated as rogues'.

> Unlawful recreations before the end of Sunday church service: offenders to be presented and punished.

> Other invited outsiders are not to linger at the end of the festivities but to depart straight away.

John Williams, however, objected very strongly. He read out in the churchyard the order obtained from the village constable and at the end, after asserting that no Puritan influence would prevail during the occasion, issued what he considered a fairer and more fitting set of rules for an occasion that should be joyful and meaningful, without restriction. These included the freedom for alewives to sell their brew without licence and for fiddlers to play what they wanted without hindrance. He decreed that the village should 'use any sportes or exercises which are not prohibited by the lawes of the land'. Sure enough, excesses did prevail including the use of cudgels by three fiddlers – one from the village, one from Oundle and another from Desborough, during which 'some had their heads broke and the blood did run down'. Despite an appeal by Sir Edward to higher authority about the rector's actions, John Williams won the day, later becoming the Dean of Salisbury, Dean of Westminster and holding the prestigious office of Lord Keeper of the Great Seal.

Wilbarston was one county village that stood no nonsense when its way of life was disrupted in any way. It was involved in at least four riotous incidents, the most inflammatory being when Parliamentary enclosure threatened their traditonal way of life. This form of enclosure involved the partitioning of plots of land with hedges. Leading local landowners had the financial resources to enclose land, after successfully petitioning Parliament for an enclosure award by paying an appropiate fee. This worked against the smaller landholder, as had been the case with medieval and Tudor enclosure, resulting in the loss of, or changes to, traditional rights of common (like grazing) in open fields – as well as the loss of livelihood and the disappearance of a communal meeting place for customary games and festivities.

In the summer of 1799, about 300 people gathered on the village hill – in olden times known as Cookstool Hill, now School Lane – and lit a large bonfire on the road to prevent a wagon, which was bringing a load of rails and posts for fencing off a small piece of land which had been allocated to them as compensation, from coming through. The local militia were called out and the Riot Act read to the crowd, after which a period of waiting ensued. Some of the more demonstrative rebels were taken into custody and, ironically, made to assist in putting up the fencing! Eventually the crowd dispersed and the work was completed. However, the matter did not end there, for another – less eventful – enclosure riot took place four years later. Nevertheless, all over the country, the familiar field patterns we see today were taking shape and were here to stay.

A similar situation had occurred at Brigstock in 1603 when Sir Robert Cecil, the Earl of Salisbury, decided to sell off parts of his newly acquired land in the deer parks that covered a vast area stretching as far as Drayton Park near Lowick and bordering Geddington, Boughton Wood and Grafton Park Wood. He sent workmen to the site to begin work on clearance and fencing off certain areas.

The villagers, understandably incensed at the loss of their traditional rights of common – and perhaps the opportunity of illegally obtaining venison as a tasty substitute for their monotonous diets – sent 'a troop of lewd women' to distract the workmen in their labours. It is not recorded what this 'lewdness' was but its occurrence was noteworthy enough to be recorded at the time. Whatever happened, the work was duly completed without violence or further interruption, after alms had been distributed to the women.

Kettering has frequently been seen as a hotbed of rebellion and independence in county history, from its role in the roots of early Nonconformism to its involvement in a variety of clandestine activities. An interesting case of the latter occurred in 1638 when royal suspicions were aroused about illegal hunting in the area, resulting in a search of every dwelling and building, large or small, within a five-mile radius of the town, for nets, crossbows and even dogs. Obviously the locals could not be trusted. More serious, however, were the Bread Riots that took place there on 11 August 1795. At 10 a.m. a cartload of flour was passing through the town centre but was blocked temporarily by an angry crowd. Three hours later, another load came through, this time accompanied by eight soldiers, causing the crowd to throw stones and drive the cart back, chasing and overturning it in the process, and to attack the soldiers. As the afternoon wore on, a larger group of soldiers were brought in to face the increasingly hostile mob. It was reported in the *Northampton Mercury*:

Mr Maunsell came, reassembled the soldiers, and blew the trumpet to arms. He then rode at the head and read the Riot Act; swords were drawn. The crowd was unmoved. The soldiers loaded their weapons and the wagon moved on, the mob shouting and pelting. Swords were drawn once again, and the soldiers turned on the mob, one of whom attempted to cut down one of the mob, and was thrown from his horse. A pistol was fired.

In the evening, the scene got uglier as the mob grew more aggressive, breaking windows around the town. Despite this, no one was wounded and few were hurt by the time the crowd had dispersed.

Some villages even squabbled among themselves – something probably not unfamiliar to today's residents! Such a case was Stoke Albany in 1796, when the church bells were inspected to see if any recasting was necessary. The results were not conclusive, however, and the village became strongly divided as to whether all or some of the bells should be recast. Members of the 'all' faction are said to have surreptitiously entered the belfry and caused the perfectly sound tenor bell to drop from its frame to the floor below, where it lay unharmed from its fall. They tried again to do damage a little later, using a sledgehammer. Vandalism is not new! In the end, the 'all' faction won and five bells were recast.

The village of Little Oakley is arguably the quietest village in the county, basking in an aura of timelessness and solitude. That was not the case in 1585, when the tranquillity of the village was shattered by the events that took place at the church of St Peter. Fifteen men from Boughton, Brigstock and Weekley, armed with swords and staves and with the aid of a blacksmith, broke into the church 'in a very ryotous manner and cawsed the churchdore to be picked open.' In the ensuing fracas, one of the congregation, Thomas Smith (a milner) was violently assaulted; they 'broke his head and rent his Dublet of his back', and another, Richard Popplewell (yeoman) was injured: 'thrown over the seats of the saide church.' They also began 'threatninge dyvers to the greate disturbance of the whole perish [sic]'.

The incident was brought to court at Rothwell, where it transpired that the reason for the attack was a dispute by a new lord of the manor, William Montagu, over a new priest, Robert Norbury, whom the Crown had appointed. His own choice was Richard Baldocke, the ringleader of the attack on the church! The problem had arisen because the previous lord of the manor had not appointed a new incumbent to replace the last one, William Carter. Nine witnesses were called to the hearing, with three commissioners presiding: Edward Watson of Rockingham, Thomas Tresham of Rushton and John Reade, Esq. – the latter adding another problem to the proceedings, having taken an active part himself in the incident! The result was that the Crown choice of priest was reinstated. He continued, peacefully, to minister until 1618. What happened to the miscreants is not recorded.

County characters

Many a colourful personality has graced the pages of the county's history and given rise to a vast body of folklore, which itself would need a book in order to do the subject justice. The whole range covers carriers, a sandman, a lamplighter, a famed long-distance walker, rogues, tradesmen, adventurers, adulterers and vagrants.

Adeline, Countess of Cardigan, was a great Society beauty who married the fifth Earl of Cardigan – of Battle of Balaclava fame – who was twenty-eight years her senior. At Deene Park, the family seat, he had a portrait painted depicting him being presented to Queen Victoria, with his wife in the background. When the Queen heard, she requested that the Countess be painted out – such had been the scandal at the couple living together before their marriage in 1858. Also in the home was the head of the Earl's favourite horse, Ronald, which can be seen gazing from the wall of one of the rooms today. The Countess was a remarkable woman in many ways. As she grew older, she attempted to maintain her beauty with thick, gaudy make-up and would ride around on horseback in such a manner. Perhaps more bizarre, however, was a made-to-measure coffin she had ordered for herself long before her death in 1915, aged ninety-one. It was kept on a trestle table in the ballroom, where visitors were usually asked to try it for size and comfort.

Scandal had also occurred in the family in the seventeenth century, when Anna Maria Brudenell, a daughter of Robert Brudenell, married Francis, Earl of Salisbury, who was twenty years older. In her early days at the court of Charles II, she proved to be the centre of attention and received flattery from admirers, and several duels were fought for her favours. After she had married, the affairs continued, eventually leading to a fatal duel that took place at Barn Elms in Towcester between a lover, the Duke of Buckingham, and her husband, who could no longer tolerate the gossip and scandal about the long-running affair. The Earl died two months later after being 'run through the right breast to the right shoulder'. The duel was recorded by both Samuel Pepys and Horace Walpole, the latter adding (incorrectly) that the Countess had held her lover's horse during the duel, dressed as a page boy! A later lover boasted about his intimacy with her, which led to her hiring a gang of ruffians to waylay him and teach him a lesson at Hammersmith. Her beauty was later captured on canvas in the guise of Minerva by the painter Lely, the painting being later bought by Sir Robert Peel.

Another interesting person connected with the county was William Hope Williams, the son of a wealthy Cornish financier who had started the banking house of Hope and Co. in Amsterdam. When his father died, he inherited a fortune and acquired Rushton Hall in 1828, becoming Sheriff of Northamptonshire. He made significant changes to the Hall, such as diverting the main road away from the property with a new bridge and extending and renovating his residence, pulling down the fine pendant ceilings inside the Hall in order to have the French style with which he was acquainted from his lengthy stays in Paris. During the building work, a stone lintel was removed and documents, bills and twenty Catholic books from the time of Thomas Tresham were discovered behind it. In December 1835, a fire – believed to be the result of an over-enthusiastic celebration – caused considerable damage to the north wing, with a long art gallery destroyed. In Paris, Williams had a large house built to a strange design with gold pillars, where he held lavish parties. He would walk around wearing diamonds all over his clothes and flashing his wealth at all and sundry. He never saw visitors before one o'clock and absolutely detested male company, preferring to have a bevy of eighteen young ladies around him, all with musical or artistic talents of some kind, who would come to the county with him on his visits. He died in his bed, apparently with his female companions in attendance.

'Planter John' was the name given to John Montagu, who had succeeded his father, Ralph, a former ambassador to France, at Boughton House. In 1708 he continued the work he had begun with his father in planting trees in the grounds of the great house, which had been modelled on Versailles. Having completed

the work, he proceeded to expand the area of woodland around his estates, subsequently acquiring the nickname 'Planter John', for the avenues of elm, lime
and beech which began to dominate the local landscape in years to come. After
his death, a somewhat implausible tradition held that his intention had been to
plant an avenue of trees all the way down to London to another home of the
family in London! The total aggregate length at the time of his death was estimated at seventy miles, with one avenue stretching for three miles! Though now
much depleted, some avenues can still be seen today, particularly in the vicinity
of Warkton.

From a more humble background came 'Old Simon' from Woodford. A cooper
by trade, his life was transformed after being spurned by his lover, and after leaving the village, ended up in London, where he fell on hard times, becoming a
vagrant. He did return and was hardly recognisable. A description of him at the
time appeared much later in Northampton Notes and Queries in 1888:

> A thick-set man wearing his hair very long and allowing his beard to grow, which
> together, gave him a venerable appearance. Upon his head was placed a hat in the
> shape of one of the earthenware pancheons in common use; other portions of his
> costume consisted of rags and shreds of books and papers, cut out much in the shape
> of a beaver's tail, around each other in a continual series, forming a kind of apron in
> front. Over his left shoulder was thrown a sort of loose cloak, much tattered.

A native of Kingscliffe, William Dakin, had a similar appearance, though the reasons are not clear as to why he chose to be so conspicuous. Also known as 'the
lunatic settled', he was frequently seen in the area, and was described in 1800, as:

> being no more than 45 years old, though the coarse dirty habit which he constantly
> wears, and the enormous length of his beard which he suffers to grow (only now
> and then does he clip it with scissors) give him a much older appearance. He later
> believed he was Jesus Christ.

One of the most astounding characters to be associated with the county was
John Baker, born in Eye, near Peterborough in 1733. He was apprenticed to a
shoemaker, but went to London in 1757, where he joined the navy for ten years,
during which time he had been involved in many battles. In 1774 he sailed to
America where he became an officer's servant, but was captured by a tribe of
native Indians who saw him as something unique. He had been born without
any gums or teeth – a situation that remained with him throughout his life. This
gave him the ability to perform facial contortions, such as pushing his nose into
his mouth, so that the bottom lip came almost up to his forehead. The Indians
fascinated by what he could do, bore a hole through his nasal cartilage as a mark
of distinction, and threaded a gold chain through it. He liked what had happened,

and thought up the idea of placing the stem of a pipe through the hole, by means of which he could pick up a small glass containing a drink with his nose and chin. Eventually released, he made his way back to England and for a while stayed in his native county, marrying twice and becoming the father of thirteen children. He fell on hard times however, and in his old age ended up in a workhouse in Covent Garden, making ends meet by performing some of his facial tricks for the crowds. He was later described by one source as 'the greatest curiosity ever seen'.

It was a long-standing custom among piemen to add a little variety to the task of selling their products by frequently tossing a coin to determine whether a customer got a penny pie for nothing, or twopence – a kind of 'double or quits' situation. At Northampton in the early 1800s, there lived a pieman named 'Fletcher' who was a well-known trader, always immaculately dressed in a scrupulously clean apron, a frock coat, knee breeches and blue worsted stockings, carrying his cloth-covered basket of wares, with pride of place given to his speciality black puddings. On one occasion at the Northampton Races, it is said that during a conversation with a stranger, he decided to be more adventurous than usual, and offered him as many puddings as he could eat for a shilling. He began to doubt his wisdom as the stranger managed to eat his way through sixteen of them. Becoming alarmed at such an extraordinary feat, he gave the man back his shilling and hastily left the scene!

seven

THINGS THAT GO BUMP IN THE NIGHT: GHOSTS, WITCHES ET AL

What is a ghost? We might say an event recording itself on the surrounding area, replayed if the circumstances and situation are suitable, like a video/DVD, to those in the right time and place. A glimpse of energy from the past re-enacted. A life cut tragically short by murder, execution, illness, accident or suicide, before its allotted time. A sense of wrong to be put right, whether by revenge or justice. Perhaps unable to leave a place much attached to in life, it can either be seen as a vague white shape shimmering and fluttering over a field or road, or clothed in a darker transparent garb. It can be felt as a chill current of air, or as a weight sinking on a bed. It can be heard as a whisper, shriek, or sob. Of all the beliefs that our ancestors had, this is one that has survived and intrigues us just as much today, and the winding, isolated country lanes and pockets of woodland of the county are ideal places for the imagination to wander – or *is* it imagination?

During the Second World War, Gordon Garth, a serviceman stationed at Spanhoe Airfield (between Harringworth and Laxton), was cycling back alone to his base after an evening in Kettering with local friends. It was a beautiful moonlit night, and he felt a sense of exhilaration as he pedalled towards Deene. It was a little after midnight as he reached the outskirts, a dip in the road inexplicably full of mist. Reaching the other side, he saw a figure on the left side of the road:

The Ship Inn at Oundle,
which is supposedly haunted.

It was wearing a very full length light grey coat with something like a hood, and as I approached, I began to sense something very unreal. The upright figure had no normal walking gait, but seemed to float along the edge of the road! I was suddenly struck with a sense of fear I had never experienced, either before or since. Although sweating heavily from my ride, I immediately felt very cold and clammy. What should I do? I thought of the long detour if I turned back – but too late – I was almost upon the figure! I swerved the bike across the road to the right, to give myself maximum clearance. The whole atmosphere seemed most unreal and although I was extremely scared, as I went past, I could not resist taking a look, which gave me a clear and long- remembered picture. The figure was probably 5'6" but looked taller with the hood, with slim to medium build, and around the neck was something like a scarf in near white; between this and the hood I could see no clear features. Male or female I know not. Then I noticed that from the bottom of the long grey coat to the hard road there appeared to be nothing!

Giving a wide berth to the apparition, he cycled on furiously until he reached his destination, waking all his comrades in the process, who told him he looked like he had seen a ghost! Similar sightings have been made over the years by local folk, further on up the road at Wakerley, near the site of the former Augustinian Priory of Fineshade.

More sensational is the sight of a ghostly monk at Barford Bridge on the A6003 Kettering to Corby road. Numerous sightings have been reported by people from all walks of life, on one occasion a car inexplicably catching fire late at night – not by vandals – but with the driver at the wheel. It is usually seen shimmering across the road in front of motorists or occasionally appearing in the back seat of the car, reflected in the driving mirror. The apparition may well have been connected with nearby Pipewell Abbey whose monks would walk across the fields to take services in the churches at Barford, Great Newton and Great Oakley, all of whom did not have a resident priest. In an unconnected incident, a Romano-British burial mound was disturbed during the building of a dual carriageway close to the bridge in the 1960s. For some unknown reason, sightings of the monk increased in frequency and still occur today.

The southern parts of the county also have their fair share of dark figures that have been seen through the ages. At Salcey a tall monk wearing a black cloak and hood glides across a cornfield on the edge of the woodland. At Milton Malsor, ghostly figures pass from a driveway, across the lane and into a walled footpath on the opposite side. After a few paces, the monks turn left and walk through the bricked-up doorway of a large house in the vicinity.

One of the most vivid of the tales is associated with Passenham where a luminous skeletal horseman, with a broken neck, has been seen on past occasions, being dragged along the road attached to the stirrups of his ghostly mount, until they reach the churchyard where both disappear.

A tradition at Cosgrove is that a prosperous family in the village forbade their daughter from associating with a humble shepherd boy. To ensure this command was met, the father managed to have the boy convicted for sheep stealing, a crime of which he was innocent. His plan backfired however, for after the boy was transported to the colonies, the distraught girl plunged into the mill race. It is said that her apparition can sometimes be seen, whenever there is a full moon.

Charles II is said to have acquired an isolated lodge in the centre of Salcey Lawn, for his mistress, Nell Gwynne. During one prolonged stay, she grew bored awaiting the king's arrival, and took another lover. Charles was not pleased and had him murdered, after which a ghost was seen rushing around the wood. Nell herself has also been seen, seated in what was formerly the orchard of the house.

One of the strangest supernatural occurences in the county occurred comparatively recently at Teeton and was well-publicised at the time in the winter of

1947/1948, when the squire, Sir Robert Fossett became ill and was taken to hospital. While he was away, his sister Margaret Leatherland was milking a cow, when she saw his face appear on the froth in the bucket. She took it outside, but the face was still there. This continued over the following days, witnessed by others who could offer no explanation. Photographs were taken, and incredulous visitors came to see for themselves, only to leave none the wiser. Scouring was tried to remove the image but was unsuccessful, and it was only about three months later when Sir Robert died, that the face finally vanished.

The county also has its fair share of 'grey ladies', ghostly horses and carriages, phantom riders and other eerie phenomena At Dallington two incidents took place the church of St Mary, the first in 1907 when a girl from Harlestone and a friend who had come up from Kent to stay with her, went for a long walk in the countryside and reached Dallington as dusk was drawing in. The local girl went into the church while her friend looked around the churchyard, but very soon rushed out after seeing the interior full of spectral kneeling people enclosed in a 'bubble-like' form. The second girl went to see for herself and followed suit. Years later, a pupil slowly coming home from school by herself came across the Grey Lady (a former Lady Spenser) occasionally encountered near the church, wearing a flowing grey cape. She excitedly told friends at school the next day, one of whom accompanied her at the end of the afternoon to see for herself. The ghost duly obliged, this time stopping to look at them, making the girls turn to run away. However they were unable to do so, a powerful force holding them back. Eventually it subsided and the girls managed to escape.

The centre of Northampton was once noted for frequent sightings of the 'Cock Lane Ghost', a saddler's apprentice who had been so cruelly mistreated by his master, that eventually he died, his body being quickly disposed of by the perpetrator of the deed. The sightings began to cause such terror amongst townsfolk that they would avoid the area after dark, and got so bad, the name of the street was changed to Wood Street, after the sawmills in the vicinity.

Ratling Irons Plantation is a spinney to the east of Thorpe Achurch. It was here during the Napoleonic Wars that French prisoners of war were chained overnight en route to Norman Cross. It is said that many of them were so badly treated and tortured by cruel escorts, that a psychic 'imprint' was left in the vicinity, with their cries, moans and the dragging of chains audible to anyone daring to enter the wood.

Legend has it that a murder was committed at Haunt Hill House in Weldon, and that rusty-coloured marks on the stone floor are bloodstains that cannot be removed. The assertion may have been inspired by the influential Walter Scott whose *Chronicles of the Canongate* (1827–8) have a tale about indelible bloodstains, likewise *'Rookwood'* by Harrison Ainsworth.

Haunt Hill House, Weldon.

It could be possible that the house was built on a piece of ground known as 'the haunted hill' – but villagers have not been able to ascertain the origin. It was built by Humphrey Frisby between 1636-1643 when he married Elizabeth Grumbold, uniting two foremost families of local stonemasons. However, there are various legends connected with the building and the bloodstains, one of which tells of strange noises often being heard often after dark, and a white figure frequently seen flitting around the house about midnight, supposedly of a nun who was once murdered there. In another legend, told by Annie Beaver, who spent her long life in the village, a white-haired, long bearded man lived in the house. One night during a deep sleep, he was awoken by the sound of a cockerel crowing eerily. Lifting his head from the pillow he saw a ghostly snow-white cock perched on the bottom of his bed looking at him. He had heard the story of the cockerel many times before, but did not believe in such superstitious things. Instead he wondered how it had got into his bedroom and jumping out of bed, made to grab the bird, arms outstretched, but it flew off soundlessly around the room, down the stairs. He gave full pursuit, then:

At last he got his hands on it and held it up in triumph thinking it would make a nice dinner the next day, wrung its neck, tied a string round its legs and hung it up on the ceiling beam. Next morning a small pool of blood had formed on floor beneath it. Getting soap, scrubbing brush and bowl of water, he started to clean it up but he was never able to remove it.

A more amusing tale about the house originates from more recent times. In the 1930s a group of boys decided to spend the night there, taking turns on shift throughout the night to see if anything happened. According to Arthur Cunnington who was present, they took a flask of cold tea, and some bread and jam, and told stories to pass the time, to prepare them for the coming ordeal:

All went well until the middle of the night when there was a sudden fluttering sound in the room, at which everyone panicked and rushed out. Talking to a gardener the next day, he took us back in. He looked around and then came out to us, shaking his head, laughing – and told us what the noise was. A starling had got stuck in the chimney!

One of the most supernatural places in the county was Boughton Green, a kilometre outside the present village. It was long considered dangerous to pass by the churchyard of the now derelict St John the Baptist on Christmas Eve. In 1875, a young and single local famer, William Parker took the risk of walking back home alone, after a convivial evening with friends at a pub in Moulton. No sooner had he neared the entrance, when he was approached by a very attractive young woman with long flowing red hair whom he found irresistable, and was soon beguiled by her charms and flirtatious behaviour, seemingly oblivious to the warnings of the legend associated with the churchyard. They kissed and arranged to meet the following month. Despite being somewhat inebriated, he noticed she made no sound as she headed towards the churchyard gate, which he thought was strange, but plodded on along the lane to his home. After a good night's sleep, he realised what had happened, telling everyone in the village to their horror. Sure enough, one month later before the tryst he died of causes unknown.

He had fallen prey to the charms of the ghost of an eighteenth-century girl who had committed suicide in the churchyard following the sudden death of her husband shortly after their wedding at the church. It is said that anyone walking by on that evening will meet either the girl or her husband, depending on their gender, fall under their spell and suffer the same fate as William Parker. The tale is probably another degenerated version of a winter/spring myth, in this particular case influenced by a Celtic tale.

This led to the appearance of a story in the *Northampton County Magazine*, which may have been handed down through the years, though the date given for the incident, 1708, is several years too early and is written in a tongue-in-cheek

The ruins of St John the Baptist church at Boughton Green, the scene of ghostly encounters on Christmas Eve.

style! The tale starts on Christmas Eve at the 'hostelrie of ye white Harte' where a group of tipplers are discussing the strange apparitions said to appear on the eve of Yuletide at Buckton (sic) churchyard. Among the assembly is Jonas White, a weaver from Kingsthorpe, who asserts he is neither afraid of mortal nor ghost. Hearing this, another of the men present, Robert Bletsoe, offers to wager his three-year old horse against White's pigs, that he would not dare set foot go to the churchyard. The bet is accepted, but unbeknown to White, another man in the group decides to play a prank on him, in which a ghost dressed in black will appear at the spot at midnight:

> After a great length of time spent in mirthe and revelrie with the imbibing of strong liquor, Jonas and his company, having fortified their weak and carnal bodies agaynst the fearfulle sightes set off, with lanthornes and thick oaken cudgels...In the meantime, the ungodlie of Moulton had ben searching neare and farre for someone to dresse as a ghoste, according to the plan set down. No person could be found willing

to undertake this unholie duty until at length it was reported that in ye Blue Bell there lay a highwayman, who had drunken excess of strong waters. Him they tooke and gave more liquor until at lengthe he had no concernment of that which was going on arounde. Then they stripped him of his clothes and and smeared his bodie with honey and afterwards covered this with sticky messe with soote, so that he looked more like a poore heathen. The drunken sotte was then conveyed to the small wood on the north side of the churchyard, there to await the hour of mid-night. At lengthe the bells of Moulton rang out midnight and Jonas, with an ashen face and trembling knees, prepared to fulfil that which he had wagered and started with a skein of thread down the path. At the same time, the men of Moulton waked the drunken highwayman and forecd him up the other end of the pathway. Bletsoe now appeared attired all in white, at the eastern end of the churchyard. The three met in the middle. Jonas White, overwroughte with terror, fell upon the grounde behind a gravestone, his face to the earthe, moaning and muttering, and beseech-ing the Lord to helpe him out of his pitiable plighte. Robert Bletsoe, on seeing the figure in blacke, thought it must be the ghost of the notorious Captain Slash and fledde, armes waving and uttering fearfulle cries, towards the place where the men of Moulton were hidden. They, supposing him to be the ghost, fledde for their lives back to their homes, where they tolde of strange and supernatural signs they hadde seen. The drunken highwaymen, who was so overcome with liquor, he had no room for feare walked up the path towards the watchers of Kingsthorpe. They, seeing a figure all in black, thought it was the very fiend himselfe, and fledde without cast-ing a looke behind. He was found next morning on the road to Moulton sleeping off the effects of the drunken orgie. Bletsoe made his way home by a devious way, and White, after waitynge til dawne before venturing to move, rose up and returned a chastened man.

In the above tale, mention is made of the notorious Captain Slash, the leader of a band of robbers which terrorised the region. George Catherall and his gang found the Boughton Fair an easy target – being one of the great fairs of the Midlands, it attracted many visitors and therefore lots of money. One night the gang crept up to where the stallholders were sleeping and released the wild beasts from their cages. While everyone was rushing around in the ensuing mayhem, the gang made off with the takings. Catherall was eventually caught and his hanging took place at Northampton racecourse in July 1826. However, a superstition lin-gered long afterwards that the site of the Fair was haunted by Captain Slash.

Haunted hostelries

Oundle supposedly has two haunted hostelries. The seventeenth-century Ship
Inn in West Street has had its fair share of ghostly sightings. A new landlord saw
one of his predecessors, who had hanged himself from a bedroom window, brush
past him on one occasion, and it was said that guests found it difficult to sleep in
a certain room. The nearby Talbot Inn has a well-known association with Mary
Queen of Scots who was beheaded at nearby Fotheringhay Castle. A staircase said
to be from the former castle is supposed to be the scene of her appearance, and
between February and April, appears at the foot of a bed, to look at the occupant.
One guest heard a woman sobbing in the next room, and on investigation found
it to be unlocked and unoccupied. In 1965, a woman was roused from her slum-
bers with the feeling of being held down, unable to call out, move, or turn on the
light. On another occasion, a group of visitors was discussing the queen, when
one of them said jokingly, 'Where's Mary?' at which a picture crashed to the

The Talbot Inn, Oundle, scene
of many experiences involving
the ghost of Mary Queen of
Scots.

floor. Fires have also inexplicably broken out, and there have been cases where unseen forces have prevented occupants of one room from leaving, when they try to open the door.

In the autumn of 1998 experts spent the night in the Thornhill Arms at Rushton, after new owners, Garry and Sue Haynes, their children, staff and customers had all seen woman in an old-fashioned cloak floating past in area between the toilet and doorway. They reported:

> Our pet mongrel began acting strangely and would not cross the first floor landing, despite any titbit it was offered or after a great deal of coaxing. You could feel cold spots in the entrance, a key to the cellar turned by itself in the lock, a light bulb disappeared from its socket, and heavy doors slammed shut.

One wonders if the cause was from the building's use during the Civil War, when it was used as a kind of mortuary for storing soldiers' bodies before burial. Interestingly, a few body-length slates have survived in the cellar and can be seen today.

The Thornhill Arms at Rushton.

The Bell at Finedon is one of several hostelries claiming to be the oldest in England, but actually dates as a public house from 1872, replacing a much older one of that name which was sited some distance away. It has its ghosts, one of which is supposed to creep into the passage at midnight for a quick drink, presumably spirits of some kind!

The most haunted hostelry in the county has to be the former Black Lion in St Giles Street, Northampton (not to be confused with an older hostelry of that name near the rail station) now the Wig and Pen, which has experienced unexplained phenomena of all descriptions. The switching on and off of lights was a frequent occurrence, and continued even after the wiring system was checked. The cellar area was particularly prone to the sound of footsteps, a heavy barrel was seen being moved from the ramp to the cellar gangway – without a sound, and animals would keep away from the area. Chill air, and a feeling of discomfort and apprehension were normal sensations. On at least one occasion, a strange vapour appeared and lingered in one corner for three minutes, then vanished as quickly as it had come. Among apparitions reported over the years are those of a heavily-built man with a black dog, and a woman in a riding habit. One couple looking after the pub heard an infant crying, and thinking it was their own,

The notorious Black Lion pub, now called the Wig and Pen, in Northampton.

got out of bed to attend to it, but found it fast asleep. What is astonishing is the true-life history of the building. On Christmas Eve 1892, the occupier, Andrew McRae, murdered his mistress, Annie Pritchard, and then boiled her head and some of her bones in a copper which he normally used for preparing the bacon that he sold. Their baby also vanished and was never found. Needless to say, he was caught, tried and duly hanged.

Perhaps the most remarkable incident in recent times is that which occurred on a hot summer day during the 1960s, when two boys from Northampton were cycling around the countryside, calling at Woodford on the way. Entering the empty church of St Mary, one of them took photographs of the interior and its furnishings and later had them developed as slides, which were later shown during a family get-together that Christmas. They were amazed to see a transparent white figure of what appeared to be a knight kneeling at the altar. After much media coverage, expert opinion was sought by sceptics to see if the image was a superimposed forgery, but on examination it was proved to be a genuine image.

The altar in the church of St Mary, Woodford, which was the scene of a ghostly apparition.

Elementals

Our ancestors' belief in elementals shows itself in the names of ancient sites dotted around the countryside. At Nether Heyford is 'Thurspit', one of six hollows or pits believed to have been made in the county by giants or demons (Old English 'thyrs'). Harrow Hill in Brington parish was believed to be a particular supernatural, and hence sacred, site as its name implies (from Old English *hears*, meaning heathen shrine). Places with the prefix 'worm' were in many cases snake-infested, and can be accounted for; others however, like 'Wormpath' in the parish of Towcester, could well mean frequented by a 'dragon', the Old English 'wyrm' having multiple meanings. There are two hollows known as 'pokepyt' believed to be the haunt of goblins, a spring called Puckwell in the parish of Aynho, the settlement of Puxley, and Puckwell Hill Field at Glapthorn, all of which get their name from the Old English 'puca' for a goblin.

Such was the belief in elementals that until the late nineteenth century, the circular fungal marks sometimes seen in fields and known as 'fairy rings' were believed to be caused by their tiny feet when dancing in the moonlight. Brington

A magnificent fairy ring in a forest glade at Westhay Wood, near Kingscliffe.

parish was believed to be the most likely place to encounter the elementals, who also loved to bathe on summer evenings and play among the sedges and reeds of isolated pools and ponds, one celebrated occasion being in 1840 when several people are reported to have witnessed the secretive beings. It was said that their favourite ring resisted attempts at ploughing it out, and that if you ran round it nine times on the first night of the new moon, you would hear a fairy festival taking place in their underground world below.

Fairies could be found in different shapes and sizes, and they also varied in the way they interacted with humans. Many were friendly, and would do favours for a household, provided they were not seen, and were left water to bathe in. Hence many county women would sweep the hearth clean, and leave a bowl of water, before going to bed. However the elementals were not always so amenable. They were said to sneak into a dairy, and suck at cows and sheep, or go into the buttery and take away anything edible, leaving some kind of substitute in its place.

A young man returning home from a feast in a neighbouring village was walking through a wood when he was confronted by fairies playing football in a clearing. He asked to join in and they invited him to do so, but as soon as he managed to

A view of the pond in the parish of Little Brington, supposedly once a favourite haunt of fairies.

kick the ball, it burst, the force of the explosion knocking him senseless. When he awoke the scene was deserted. In a variation of the story however, on awakening he found himself surrounded by golden coins which had filled the ball.

Children of course have always been fascinated by fairies, elves and goblins, especially in story form. The county, with its spinneys, leafy glades, meadows, ponds and streams, would have been peopled with such creatures and fired the imagination. One girl in particular was sufficiently well-educated and talented enough to write delightful and masterful lengthy verses about all kinds of subjects, but it is her poetry about fairies in particular which are impressive. She spent her early years in Pytchley and Gretton, where her father, Abner W. Brown, was vicar. Those early years playing in the beautiful countryside were the inspiration for the wonderful poetry she wrote between the ages of twelve and twenty-four, when she was tragically struck down by an epidemic sweeping the area. Shortly afterwards, in 1869, her father collected a huge volume of 255 poems, mainly by his daughter, and published them under the title, *Lyrical Pieces*, as a tribute to her. The following is part of one of her fairy poems, 'The Fairies' May-Day Gathering' and shows what a talent was lost, not just to her family, but to the county:

A seventeenth-century woodcut of fairies dancing.

Artemis, Titania,
Radiant fairy queen,
Flashes, through the twilight air,
Glistening in green.

Hark! she calls her fairy nymphs.
In wild elfin rhymes;
Listen to her lily bell
And her harebell chimes.

Come ye fairies, haste, ye fairies;
Hither away to the greenwood dale,
Come, where the emerald moss is blooming;
Joyously dance o'er the blossoms pale.

Come, where brackens are tall and verdant,
Shining with necklace of pearly dew;
Come, where asphodel beds are fragrant,
Come, where clover is young and new.

Haste! for glowworms are trimming their lamps;
Haste! ere cowslips are withered and dead;
Mushrooms are peeping to be your thrones;
See! blue vervain is rearing its head.

John Clare also included fairies in some of his verse. One such charming example is a short poem entitled, *Fairy Elves, Those Minute Things*:

Fairy Elves, those minute things,
That sleep and dream in flowers,
That come on Summer's golden wings,
To dance in moonlight bowers.
That on a mushroom table sups,
By glowworm's trembling light,
And drink their dews from acorn cups,
The summer's pleasant night.

The 'redman' – similar in appearance to a small elf but preferring a solitary existence, inhabiting wells and hollows, and usually seen wearing a red cap – was less common in Northamptonshire folklore. One of the more interesting tales however, tells of three brothers who lived at Rockingham, each of whom was visited in turn by a hairy redman begging for food. The two eldest drove him away, but the youngest and cleverest, knowing of a redman's secrets and habits, managed to trap and imprison him until he revealed the whereabouts of crocks of gold stored somewhere in a nearby underground chamber. He subsequently became rich, and left the county to live in a fine house at Barn Hill, Stamford, where he married the prettiest girl in Rutland.

The 'boggart', a mischievous and cunning elemental, was much more common in the county folklore. One tale commonly found around parts of Europe, has a Northamptonshire version with an agricultural setting for the confrontation between a man and a boggart. A version in the folk dialect of Lindsey in Lincolnshire in the 1880s (said to be identical to that of our county) begins:

> Ther isn't noä boggards here-aboots 'at I knaw on, but when I liv'd i' No'thamptonsheer, I heerd tell o' won at reckon'd at best farm i' loordship belonged to him, if ivrywon hed the'r aun, an' he let foäks know it an' all.

The story goes that a farmer was busy working on his land when a boggart approached him, telling him in a surly tone to stop. The farmer ignored him, pretending not to have seen or heard him, and carried on working as the boggart tried again and again to get his attention. Eventually the farmer got tired of the coaxing and wheedling, and told the boggart he must go through the legal process if he wanted to 'get houd a' land'. At this the boggart changed tack, and told him there was no need for lawyers to be involved and offered to share the land equally with him when harvest time came round. To avoid any further confrontation the farmer agreed, whereupon the boggart told him that neither of them must go back on their word. The farmer assented, asking him whether he wanted what was above the ground or below it. Studying the surface carefully, he accepted what would grow beneath it and told the farmer he would return at harvest time. The canny farmer sowed the field with wheat, thereby reaping the husks, and leaving the stubble and chaff for the boggart.

Feeling cheated, the boggart asked for a reversal of roles for the next harvest, with the upper part going to him, but again the farmer tricked him by sowing turnips, so the boggart only got the leaves. Not wishing to be outdone a third time he challenged the farmer to a mowing match, with the whole field as the prize. However, once again the farmer was one step ahead and the day before the match he took a cartload of iron bars and put them in the half of the field that the boggart was going to plough. When his scythe continually kept striking the bars, he thought he was being obstructed by dock leaves. Looking ruefully at his blunted blade he asked for a break in order to wring out his shirt and have 'a bit o' bacca'. The farmer, nearly finished, asked him why he wanted to rest when he had hardly mown a stretch, and that he himself was going to carry on regardless, non-stop until midday. Unable to counter this, the boggart flung down his scythe in disgust, telling him he could keep his mucky old land, and (in the words of the dialect version of the tale), he 'goa's an' niver cums back noär moor'.

Will o' the wisp

Nowadays we know that these phenomena are caused by methane from decaying vegetable matter, and that being lighter than air tend to float, dance around and abruptly change direction. The north of the county was particularly noted for sightings, and many accounts were handed down by villagers and travellers about mysterious lights trying to lure them to their deaths. In his diary, Clare notes that he had frequently seen them as had the 'alewife' of the Exeter Arms, who told him she had often seen as many as fifteen 'in and out in a company as if dancing reels and dances' on Eastwell Green. There had been a great upstir in his village about the regular appearance of a ghost in a neighbour's field, wrapped in a large white winding sheet. It was that of an old woman who had recently drowned in a well. Clare and his friends decided to go out each night to see this apparition for themselves, but saw or heard nothing. What they did see however one evening was a bright light which began to get larger and then 'glided onwards as if a man was riding on horseback at full speed with a lanthorn light.' Presently, it was joined by another from the south-east, both of them 'dancing a sort of reel', before chasing each other playfully and disappearing.

In the following extract from his diary (which is housed in Northampton Library as MS15) he perfectly encapsulates the sense of fear of the supernatural felt by county folk, as he recalls another occasion, this time in his younger days, when he encountered a will o'the wisp while returning from courting a girl over at Ashton, some miles away. He was feeling terrified on the long walk back home, alone and in darkness, when he saw something that seemed to be waiting for him on the path. He climbed a stile to see if it was human or supernatural:

It came on steadily as if on the pathway and when it got near me within a pole's reach, perhaps as I thought, it made a sudden stop as if to listen to me. I then believ'd it was someone, but it blaz'd out like a whisp of straw and made a crackling noise like straw burning, which soon convinced me of its visit. The luminous halo that spread from it was of a mysterious terrific hue and the enlarg'd size and whiteness of my own hands frit me. The rushes appear'd to have grown up as large and tall as whalebone whips and the bushes seem'd to be climbing the sky. Everything was extorted out of its own figure and magnified. The darkness all round seemed to form a circular black wall and I fancied that if I took a step forward, I should fall into a bottomless gulph which seem'd yawning all round me, so I held fast by the stile post till it dart'd away, when I took to my heels and got home as fast as I could.

A nineteenth-century engraving of a will o'the wisp.

The Wild Hunt

Among the most evocative images of the county's folklore are those of the Wild Hunt. The original source of all these traditions are probably folk memories of the Anglo-Saxon god Woden and his Scandinavian counterpart Odin, leading a hunt through the skies with a band of dead warriors, looking for warrior heroes who had fallen in battle and, with the help of the Valkyries, transporting them to Valhalla where a glorious future life awaited them.

As Christianity became established, the pagan war leader was transformed into the Devil, riding through forests or the sky, looking for lost souls. The hunting party was now a gruesome band of undesirables consisting of the unbaptised, criminals and demons, riding red-eyed steeds and accompanied by fierce black dogs that also had red eyes. Tales also sprang up that the hunter was once human and loved hunting so much that on his death he spurned the chance to go to heaven in order to carry on his favourite pastime. Another legend was that he was condemned to hunt for eternity as a punishment for hunting on the Sabbath. Whatever the case, seeing or hearing the hunt was, like the appearance of an eclipse or comet, a bad omen, portending disaster or death.

In England, the earliest written accounts of the Wild Hunt take place around the northern edge of Rockingham Forest, in the vicinity of Stamford and Peterborough. The Anglo-Saxon chronicles for 1127 state that:

> as soon as he arrived, it was heard and seen by many men, many hunters hunting. The hunters were black and great and loathly, their hounds all black and wide-eyed and loathly, and they ride on black horses and black he-goats. This was seen in the very deer-park in the town of Peterborough and in the woods from Peterborough to Stamford.

This happened continuously from February through to Easter. The 'he' mentioned in the first line is a French cleric, Henry, abbot of Poitou, who was the cause of the Wild Hunt appearing. He had earlier obtained 'through his great wiles' the archbishopric of Besançon and had since lost both bishoprics, deciding thereafter to try his luck in England. Through Henry I, he obtained the abbacy of Peterborough which was 'basely given away between Christmas and Candlemas', according to the monks and local folk who were obviously not happy at the new appointment, hence the ill omen.

Tales of the hunt also occur elsewhere in the county. Sternberg mentions that the wild huntsman is not confined to any particular district and (allowing for a little exaggeration perhaps) is common to almost every parish, and may be seen:

> ...on a calm summer's night when the pale glimmer of the young moon scarcely penetrates the dark foliage of the trees ... slowly riding along the green-sward border of some old green lane or lonely road.

The forests of Rockingham and Whittlewood became the setting for a Wild Hunt in county literature. A member of a visiting royal hunting party sees the beautiful daughter of a forester and falls in love with her. She leads him on, playing with his feelings, making promises one minute, spurning him the next, until she finally jilts him, causing him to decapitate himself. Seeking revenge in death – for which she shows no remorse – he reappears at the spot where they first met, riding a black horse. Seeing him, she flees into the woods and is pursued by the headless spectre and his hounds, and is torn apart. This scene is re-enacted for eternity and the tradition of fatality applies to anyone witnessing the scene, for they will also come to a nasty end. In *Historical Legends of Northamptonshire* (1880), Alfred T. Story describes the huntsmen:

...in their quaint dresses of Lincoln green dashing across the glades on fiery steeds cheering their hell hounds with unearthy glee.

Later, Charles Montagu-Douglas-Scott set the legend in ballad form as 'The Wild Huntsman of Whittlebury', the first verse of which begins:

> Ho, ho! for the Whittlebury's huntsman true
> The huntsman who hunts by the keen moonlight!
> Hurrah! for his hounds that a maid pursue!
> She crosses a moonlit ride in view,
> Tallyho! and a scream that startles the night,
> Forever, and aye when the moon is bright.

Supernatural animals

A spectral hound known variously as Black Shuck, Padfoot, Shag and Shagfoal was a lingering superstition in the region. Depending on the area in which it was seen, it could appear in different forms: as a shaggy black dog with fiery red eyes (the inspiration for *The Hound of the Baskervilles* on Dartmoor); as a great 'bear-like' creature (around the Helpston area of John Clare); as part-dog and part-horse (at Thorney) or as a creature the size of a calf. To touch it, even to see it or speak its name, was considered an ill omen. It usually haunted lonely places such as country lanes, bridges, fields and sometimes appeared close to a village. The black dog in the Cottingham area, however, was quite amicable. Its favourite haunt was the road between Cottingham and Rockingham, where it was said to appear by the side of any wayfarer travelling alone, gladly providing company, protection and guidance. However, if an attempt was made to touch or stroke the animal, it would instantly vanish.

Sightings of another animal have been a talking point in more recent times. Every year, there are reports in the media of sightings of a large black cat seen around the county, particularly in the central and northern parts. Whether such a beast exists or not is a moot point but there are many who testify to having seen such a creature or its tracks. County newspapers like the *Evening Telegraph* have offered rewards to anyone producing concrete proof on film or other documentary evidence. In 2003 alone, there were five sightings: near Aldwincle, in Corby village, in Cranford and two around Gretton. A woman from Desborough claimed in 2001:

> I totally believe it exists. Before when I had seen reports about it, I had my doubts and thought it was a big domestic cat. But when I saw it for myself for the first time, I realised it was real ... It was halfway across a field, crouched down as if it was either eating or drinking from a puddle.

Described variously as being the size of a lion, having yellow eyes and a black coat, a distinctive head and long tail, no evidence has yet been forthcoming but the situation could change at any time. Like crop circles – which actually date back in recorded form to the seventeenth century – they are becoming part of modern folklore, the first recorded sighting in Britain being in 1860.

Witches

At church, it was customary to bless holy water once a year for use at baptisms, for the sick and on special occasions. It was widely believed that witches were liable to use the baptismal water from the font for their charms and spells. Therefore, to safeguard against this, fonts were often fitted with a stapled lock to prevent the contents from being stolen. Ten staples survive in the county at Barton Seagrave, Cottingham, Cranford St Andrew, Duddington, Flore, Little Billing, Nassington, Pitsford, Roade and Thurning.

So-called witches were indeed a social problem. It is human nature to follow a set pattern in life within a community for the sake of harmony. If anything disturbs that pattern and something goes wrong or interferes with the status quo, the cause is found and removed. A sudden illness, an unexpected death or damage to property, crops or livestock had to be attributed to something or someone. In past times, when communities were smaller and everyone knew each other, those causes were not hard to find. On a personal level, there may have been a recent quarrel or disagreement between two people or more, perhaps over the refusal of a request, followed by a curse or threat. There may have been a long-term problem affecting the community, usually caused by social misfits like the poor, the old, the infirm or the mentally unstable, or by outsiders like vagrants, all of whom created a social burden. Anyone living alone could be seen as suspicious and would be the focus of superstition, rumour and a lack of trust. There was commonly an unpopular individual such as a gossip, a spiteful person or one of 'loose living'. Finally, anyone performing some kind of social service such as a wise woman or midwife could find themself vulnerable in a tense situation, if something went wrong. Once the cause of the misfortune was found, gossip or rumour would cause widespread fear and anger in the community, eventually reaching the ears of someone of higher social standing or influence, who consequently would take the case to court, which in turn would lead to an indictment and trial as a witch.

A manuscript containing an unusual woodcut and entitled 'A brief extract of the Arraignment of nine Witches at Northampton: July 21, 1612' can be found in the British Museum. Apart from describing the largest witch trial ever held in the county, the manuscript is unique in many ways for it describes behind the scenes pre-trial brutality and forced confessions using the swimming test, scratching, beating and bodily examination (looking for the witch's teat). It also gives an insight into the

A staple font in the church of St Mary, Duddington. These fonts were intended to prevent witches from stealing holy water.

religious teaching of the time as put into the minds of ordinary folk. For example, one of the accused, Agnes Wilson, was asked how many gods she acknowledged, to which she replied two – God and the Devil – an innocent statement by an uneducated churchgoer, who was only stating what everyone was told, but damning evidence in court.

The first of the nine trials concerned Joan Vaughan, who was described as 'a chicken of her dam's hatching', a reference to her mother, Agnes Brown, who had an evil reputation. Vaughan was gossiping with a group of neighbours when Mistress Belcher, a local member of the gentry, passed by. Vaughan made a pointed comment or gesture that caused the lady to take offence and strike her, to which Vaughan retorted, 'You'll be sorry you did that!' Mistress Belcher replied that she neither feared her nor her mother and dared her to do her worst.

Shortly after she arrived home, Belcher was seized with a agonising pain and was confined to her bed, her face contorted, crying out 'Away with Joan Vaughan!' News reached her brother, Master Avery, who went to her aid but was unable to alleviate her pain. He suspected witchcraft and saw Vaughan as the perpetrator. The court clerk then tells how the brother ran towards the house of Vaughan and her mother, to take them to his sister for her to draw their blood – a way of breaking a witch's spell – but:

...as he came nearer the house, he was suddenly stopped and could not enter, whether it was an astonishment through his fear or that the spirits had power to stay him I cannot judge, but he reported at his coming back, that he was forcibly stayed and could not for his life go any further forward – and they report in the community that he is a gentlemen of stout courage.

Making his way back to his home, he was confronted by two 'hellhounds' which tormented him, causing the same symptoms as his sister. Avery could take no more and managed to get Vaughan and her mother apprehended and consequently put in jail by Sir William Saunders of Cottesbrook, where they were held down and scratched by the brother and sister, whereupon their symptoms vanished. More sinister was what happened next:

Not long after Master Avery and his sister having been both in Northampton and having drawn blood of the witches – riding both homewards in one coach, there appeared to their view a man and a woman riding both upon a black horse. Master Avery having spied them afar off, and noting many strange gestures from them, suddenly spake to them that were by and (as it were prophetically) cried out in these words 'that either they or their horses should presently miscarry.' And immediately the horses fell down dead.

At the trial it was stated that a fortnight before they were arraigned, Brown and two other 'birds of a feather' were seen riding a pig to see 'Mother Rhodes', an old witch who lived in Ravensthorpe. However, before reaching their destination, the old witch died, but in her last breath told bystanders that three friends were on their way to see her, but she would meet them within a month of her death. After being found guilty, Vaughan and Brown still declared their innocence, and cursed and blasphemed up until the point they were hanged at Abington Gallows.

Another of the arraigned witches was Helen Jenkenson of Thrapston, who had long been regarded as an evil person and was much suspected of crime before her eventual apprehension for 'bewitching of cattle and other mischiefs which before time she had done around Thrapston'. She had also supposedly bewitched a child to death. Her chief accuser, Mistress Moulsho, was a woman of influence and standing, a member of a family mainly associated with nearby Twywell:

Mistress Moulsho had a buck [tub] of clothes to be washed out. The next morning the maid, when she came to hang them forth to dry, spied the clothes, but especially Mistress Moulsho's smock, to be all bespotted with the pictures of toads, snakes and other ugly creatures. Which making her aghast, she went presently and told her mistress who, looking on them smiled, saying nothing else but this, 'Here are fine hobgoblins indeed!'

A woodcut from 1612, showing three Northamptonshire witches 'all abyding in the towne of Gilsborough and riding to a place called Runenstrop all upon a sowes back.'

She then went purposefully to the house of Helen Jenkenson, and 'with an angry countenance' told her of this matter, threatening her that if her linen were not cleared from those foul spots immediately, she would scratch out both her eyes. Not staying for an answer, she went home and found her linen as white as it was at first. She later tricked Jenkenson into coming to a convenient place where she could be searched, to see if anyone could find any insensible mark on her body (it was believed that the Devil kissed his chosen ones on part of the body, which subsequently could feel no pain). Mistress Moulsho was one of the searchers and supposedly 'found at the last that which they sought for, to their great amazement'.

The people of Raunds all considered Arthur Bill and his parents to be witches but it was Arthur, 'a wretched poor man both in state and mind', who was arraigned at Northampton for bewitching Martha Aspine to death and malevolently affecting several cattle in the area. While he was awaiting trial, he began to imagine that his father was going to testify against him and so sent a message to his mother to bring him along to the cell. As soon as they arrived, mother and son:

> both joined together and bewitched a round ball into the throat of the father where it continued a great while, his father not being able to speak a word. Howbeit, the ball was afterwards had out, and his father proved the principal witness against him.

Obviously family ties were not strong enough here! And matters worsened when the mother cut her throat after several days of conscience-searching and making loud imprecations, cursing and wailing, which was heard all round the neighbourhood.

Several years later, in 1674, Anne Foster, who was active in the area around Eastcote, Astcote and Pattishall, was also arraigned at Northampton, for taking revenge on a wealthy farmer who had refused to sell her some meat. She was alleged to have caused his house and barns to catch fire, bewitched his cattle and left thirty sheep 'with Leggs broken in picces and their Bones all shatter'd in their Skins'. Like the witches at the 1612 trials, she was found guilty and hanged.

During the eighteenth century, a series of pamphlets were circulated round the county giving an account of an astonishing event which was said to have occurred during March 1706, in which two women were accused of being active as witches around the villages of Cotterstock, Glapthorn, Benefield and Southwick. Elinor Shaw (originally from Oundle) and Mary Philips, both of Cotterstock, were said to have done much evil in the area. Twenty-three witnesses were said to have given testimony against them, accusing them of crimes ranging from bewitching a woman and two children to death and harming eight men and thirteen other children, to 'destroying forty pigs, a hundred sheep, eighteen horses, and thirty cows'.

According to the first and most widely circulated of the pamphlets, the two women had an argument at Southwick with a Mistress Wise, whereupon Elinor later made an effigy of her and stuck pins into the image before roasting it:

> That same night the woman became violently ill and died. One witness said he was driving his sheep to pasture, when he heard a clamour coming from the dwelling of Mistress Wise. Going to the source of the noise, he saw Shaw threaten Mistress Wise with harm, and grievous mischief. There was mention of a bowl that Wise had not given back to Shaw. On hearing this, Philips laughed mockingly and with her clenched hand made a menacing sign at the woman of the house, saying as they left, 'Leave her be, I will bounce her well enough!'

At Glapthorn, it was alleged that the two women were walking by a dwelling outside which a group of children were playing. The women spoke to the children and, as they left, touched one of them on the head. The child later sickened, was unable to eat and, during the night, died. Both women were later found guilty, sentenced to death and placed in prison at Northampton St Giles. Ten days later, on 17 March, they were partly hanged on the gallows and then when nearly dead, were promptly burned until they were no more.

All this is somewhat surprising because belief in witchcraft had declined by the end of the seventeenth century due to more advanced rational and scientific thought, changing attitudes and a relatively peaceful period in history after the turmoils of the Reformation and Civil War. The trial of the Cotterstock witches is astonishing because it ended in execution, years after the last officially recorded execution for witchcraft took place in Exeter in 1685. But did it ever happen? The pamphlets were circulated a long time after the supposed trial and contained varying and contradictory details. These have been accepted as fact but they are a gross deception – for the trial never happened! Let us look at the real facts.

The trial was never publicly reported in any form at any time, neither does any legal record exist. No mention was made of it by the three eminent contemporary judges, Chief Justices Parker, King and Burn, who helped a writer, F. Hutchinson, compile *A Historical Essay on Witchcraft* (published 1718), which listed all the witch trials that ever taken place in England. At the time it is supposed to have taken place, the trial was never reported in a broadsheet (there being no newspaper in the county until May 1720) and no references appear in overseer and churchwarden reports at Northampton St Giles for 1706 (or the year before or after) either to the execution or the preparations for the event. There are two other giveaways that this was a forgery: the women were burned, which never happened in England, in whole or part, and the event took place in 1706, twenty-one years after the last ever official witch execution took place. Even the names of the women cannot be traced: a look through the parish registers for the places concerned draws a blank. The fact is that they were based on an earlier and spurious pamphlet from 1700, which was itself loosely based on the famous witchcraft trial at Chelmsford in 1566.

In 1648, an incredible spectacle is said to have occurred over a period of three days at Welton, when a ten-year-old girl who was believed to have been bewitched coughed up three gallons of water, 'to the great admiration' of those who witnessed the scene. Later, her older sister ran around the village exclaiming that her sister was now vomiting stone and coals. The news spread like wildfire and folk testified to having seen as many as 500 pieces coughed up, some weighing as much as a quarter of a pound (about 125g) and so large that they had difficulty finding their way out of her mouth.

Wilby and the surrounding area seems to have been a favourite haunt of witches, who had the power to transform themselves animals, usually a cat, fox or hare.

In one tale, a woodcutter lived on the edge of the village. His wife was a wise woman providing cures and remedies but, as so easily could happen to such women, her skills rebounded on her when something went wrong. Such was the case when the hens in the village were suddenly unable to lay eggs, the cows could not calf, milk went sour for no apparent reason and nobody could bake any bread successfully. Rumours began to spread and intensified after a child playing in the woods felt her face being scratched and, running home terrified, fell faint on the floor. The next morning, as the child's condition deteriorated, the wise woman's cat was seen in a tree outside the bedroom, watching the open window with great interest. Shortly afterwards, the woodman's lunch began to disappear while he was working close to where the food basket lay. After the same thing occurred the next day, he decided to resolve the matter and keep a close watch. It was the cat. The next day, as it was opening the basket, he took his axe and chopped off its paw. With a loud wail, it ran off limping in the direction of the cottage. When he got back home, he found his wife lying in a pool of blood, her hand missing.

A similar incident occurred at Syresham: a man and his son were walking through the woods when the boy begged his father for a branch to play with. He obliged and began to break one off a gnarled old oak tree but immediately dropped it in astonishment as blood gushed out of the trunk. Shortly afterwards, a woman long suspected of being a witch was seen around the village with her arm bandaged up. She was consequently 'swum' and found guilty of being a witch.

Cogenhoe had a renowned wise woman, Old Betty. On one occasion a soldier committed suicide by drowning in the Nene. An extensive search was made for the body but was fruitless, until Old Betty recommended putting a piece of quicksilver in the centre of a loaf, saying the bread would float on the water and remain on the spot where the body lay. This was attempted and sure enough they found the corpse entangled in weeds. Locals said that Old Betty was always doing strange things and children feared her, saying she was a witch.

The children of Guilsborough were told that Pell's Pool on the road to Cold Ashby was the home of a nasty witch and that if they misbehaved she would come out of the water to catch them. Also in the same area there was a family, known as 'the witch family', who kept to themselves, spurning the company of other villagers. People were very wary when passing by their home.

eight

SUPERSTITION AND BELIEF

Today we live in an age where superstition plays a relatively minor role in people's lives, although a few vestiges of the past remain, such as horoscopes. However, superstition would have dominated the lives of our ancestors in thought and action: there were certain taboos and observations that had to be made at various times for peace of mind. When darkness fell, there was no street lighting and if there were any lights within the home, they would be primitive tallow candles with reeds. Few people would venture into the darkness outside, except to the nearby alehouse, for the only inhabitants of the night would be spirits, witches or the lawless. Early to bed and early to rise would have been the norm.

Cutting trees, sowing corn and other agricultural tasks were carried out in harmony with certain phases of the moon or at specific times of the day, or even using a charm, if a successful outcome was to be achieved. The process of converting milk and cream into butter, 'making it come' (coagulate and solidify), usually followed a time-honoured county tradition, involving a ritual chant as if coaxing, soothing and talking to the contents. There were two general forms:

> Churn butter churn!
> In a cow's horn
> I never see'd such butter
> Sin' I was born

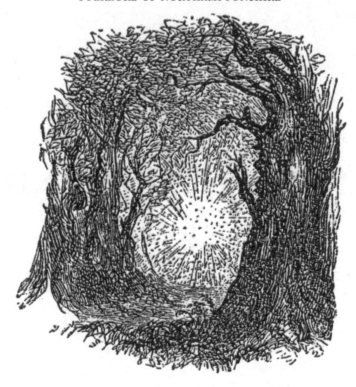

A nineteenth-century engraving of a forest, a place to grip the imagination.

Peter's standing at the gate
Waiting for a buttr'd cake

Churn, butter, churn!
Come butter come!
A little good butter
Is better than none!

Similarly, other domestic tasks and weddings never took place at certain times or days of the year which were considered unlucky. Certain plants and objects were considered to be favourable and protective; others were claimed to be evil and were to be avoided and never brought into the home. What seems incredible to the modern mind is that people still carried on believing and carrying out set rituals, whether they came true or not.

Certain days of the year were believed to give powerful indications of what the weather would be like for the coming period. Whatever the weather was like on a Friday, Sunday would be the same, and the sun would always shine at some point on a Saturday, regardless of what kind of weather prevailed. If it rained on Easter Sunday, there would be 'plenty of grass but little good hay'. The weather on Valentine's Day would determine whether March would be a good windy month for the laundry: 'In Valentine, March lays her line'. At Martlemas (Martinmas), which occurred on 11 November, it was customary for farmers to check the direction from which the wind was blowing, as this was said to determine the weather conditions for the next two or three months. Other weather conditions that day would have a similar bearing on the future and there would be an appropiate saying, for example:

> If there is ice that will bear a duck for Martlemas, there will be none that will bear a goose all winter.

Another day for predicting the duration of a season was Candlemas on 1 February:

> If Candlemas Day be fair and bright, Winter takes another flight
> If Candlemas Day be cloud and rain, Winter is gone and will not
> come again.

Some years ago, a resident of Brigstock, Mrs E. Britton, collected spoken and written sayings from people in the area. These included many words of wisdom regarding the weather:

> Onion skins very thin, mild winter coming in;
> Onion skins thick and tough, winter weather cold and rough.

> In February if thou hearest thunder, thou shalt see a summer wonder.

> As many fogs in March, as many frosts in May.

> A dripping June keeps all in tune.

It was also thought that the behaviour or movements of certain animals, birds and plants was an indication of what kind of weather was on the way. If cats were seen eating grass, it was a sign that rain was coming. Sheep bleating in the evening or grazing in the middle of a field meant that a storm would be imminent. Rooks building their nests higher than usual in the trees was a sign of good weather; if lower, it was otherwise: 'Rooks high, it will be dry; rooks low, winter will show.'

The pimpernel was seen as nature's barometer, as it has a habit of closing its petals if rain is threatening. It was affectionately known in the county under two names, either 'John-that-goes-to-bed-at-noon' or 'the shepherd's weather glass'. The knotweed (knapweed) was similarly valued for its predictive qualities, its seed vessels showing the state of weather by expanding when dry and closing when wet. The lesser celandine has similar habits, its petals shutting when rain is in the offing. To our ancestors, the petals also gave some indication of the time, as they closed by five o' clock in the afternoon and did not open again until around nine o' clock the next morning, even if the weather was fine, warm and dry.

John Askham, the Wellingborough writer and poet, looking back nostalgically to his days at dame school between 1829 and 1832, described in great detail the superstitious nature of his teacher, an elderly woman in old-fashioned clothes, whose chief occupation was eternally knitting stockings:

> ...she was the epitome of old errors, a repository of recipes, a cyclopedia of superstition. She was a believer in signs and tokens. She had tokens for life, and tokens for death; the latter were generally raps on the headboard of the bed, or hollow cinders out of the fire; these she could adapt either to life or death; if she inclined to death, it was a coffin, if to life, a cradle. A running over of a candle would be moulded by her superstitious fancy into the resemblance of a winding sheet: if a bright spark flew out of the candle, it was a sign of having a letter: the throbbing of her corns prognosticated a change in the weather: if her back was a sign of snow: the aurora borealis denoted war; she could see swords in the clouds quite plain.

Around the county, each day of the week had its merits or disadvantages. Monday and Thursday were said to be the best days for a wedding – but during Lent, especially Ash Wednesday, it was considered to be a bad omen. Finding a horseshoe was a good omen, but not a knife. In general, iron was a good metal to come across, but not silver. If out nutting, opening a nut with a double kernel was favourable, provided both kernels were not eaten – one had to be one thrown over the shoulder. The first egg of a pullet would bring luck if given to a loved one. An old shoe was thrown at anyone about to undertake a new venture, to ensure their success. Crows were particularly auspicious and if two were seen together, especially flying over your head, it was a sign of good fortune, though if a single crow landed in front of you, it did not augur well.

The fortunes of a child's life could also be influenced in certain ways. When a baby was taken to visit friends for the first time, it was customary for them to give it an egg which, if preserved, would bring good fortune. One wonders how our ancestors managed to do this! Perhaps the strangest belief, however, was that a thin membrane known as a caul or kell which sometimes covered the face of an infant at birth could betoken good fortune if preserved throughout the child's adult life. If carried, it could even could prevent drowning. However, should it be lost, it was believed to signal misfortune. Such was its scarcity and esteem that advertisements were placed in the *Northampton Mercury*, offering large sums of money to anyone having such a highly valued commodity.

Superstition was also attached to the use of money. It was customary for a shopkeeper to give a coin or two back to anyone buying goods, regardless of how much they had spent, not as change but as token of good luck. This was known variously around the county as either 'lock penny' or 'luck money'. When hawkers had their first sale of the day, the money they received, 'handsell', was spat on in the hope of good luck for the rest of the day's trading.

Many people today would flinch at carrying a calf's tongue or a piece of fish wrapped in rushes in their pocket, yet it was believed that anyone doing so would be protected against assault, leaving them unscathed after such an encounter. It was also said to provide a ready supply of money!

It was customary to dress up in new clothes on Easter Sunday and if someone did not wear a new item of clothing, that person would not prosper for the rest of the year. In a house, care was also taken to avoid breaking a mirror or letting a child look in one before it was a year old, or misfortune would follow. Other bad omens were dropping a small piece of furniture on the floor for no apparent reason and hearing your name being called when there was nobody in the vicinity. Folk also avoided entering the front door of a house and going straight out through the back, in the belief that such an action would lead to them never returning.

Houses were protected from lightning and other harm by 'raising the branch', which was the custom of hanging a branch from the roof or chimney, and drinks were passed round whenever a new roof was built or replaced on a home. Another apotropaic device was to wall up an animal to watch over a new building, the body of the animal eventually becoming mummified and its spirit housebound. Later, thatchers would add the form of an animal or bird to a roof, not just for decoration but for a similar purpose.

Some occurrences were unpreventable, such as the hooting of an owl, which was always considered a bad omen. At Cogenhoe, a shoemaker and his wife were well known for their colourful ghost stories and their knowledge of 'ow owls talk'. They would tell visitors about how an owl once flew round a nearby farmhouse, shortly after which the farmer's wife fell downstairs to her death, and how another owl foretold the death of one of their own relatives.

However, there could be humour in a situation involving an owl. Such was the case with a man from Little Oakley, who was staggering back home alone across the fields after a heavy drinking session in Geddington. Passing somewhat noisily through a spinney, he heard what he thought was a loud voice uttering a long-drawn-out 'Who?' He gave his name, only to hear the sound repeated twice more. Muttering expletives, he went on his way out of the spinney, not realising what he had disturbed!

Plants have attracted a whole body of folklore for themselves. The elder tree was treated with special reverence. Known as 'eldern' in the north of the county and 'edders' elsewhere, its branches were used – like those of rowan – as a protection

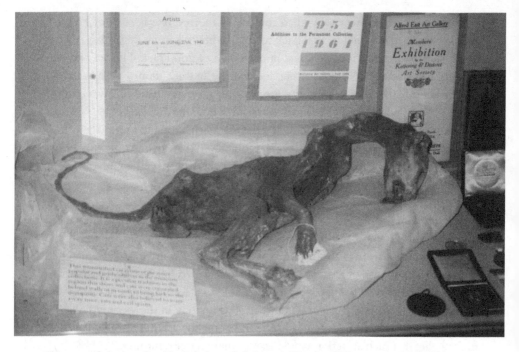

This mummified cat was found beneath the roof of a house in Kettering. Walling up animals in buildings was once a common way of protecting homes from misfortune, such as lightning damage or harmful human influences.

Animals made out of thatch were not just for decoration but, unknowingly for many folk, were a modern form of house protection.

against witches. This accounts for why so many were planted by the side of houses and tracks in the county at one time. The long stems of elder and hazel called 'etherings' or 'ether-winders' were also intertwined between stakes in hedge-laying to bond or strengthen new fences. The blooms of lilac and hawthorn, or 'may', was never taken inside houses, in the belief that it would invoke a future death. A legend surrounding may as a plant of fatality describes its association with the Black Death, when it sprang up everywhere and spread in the untended fields of the depleted population. Its blossom has a sickly scent which is nauseating to many. Intriguingly, in the 1970s, a group of scientists analysed a chemical component found within the plant that is similar to that found in decaying corpses.

Daneweed (field eryngo) was formerly found in the area around Watling Street, from which it took its other county name of Watling Street thistle. Though widespread in much of Europe, where it is considered to be troublesome once it establishes its deep roots and begins to spread, it does not really flourish in the British climate and is consequently scarce in this country. Long ago, a tradition came into being after it was found 'in the hills near Daventry at Danes Camp' and it was said that if it was cut on certain days, it would bleed 'in memory of them defending their conquered territory against the Saxon army'.

The excretion from the wild rose, known locally as 'briar ball' or 'save lick', was rubbed by boys on the cuffs of their coats as a charm to prevent them getting flogged. Another plant, however, did not have the helpful effects it was intended to have: at the school in Nassington in July 1895, the medical officer of health, C.N. Elliott, was called in from Oundle to investigate absences. In his report he wrote:

> I visited the village on account of a number of children being absent from school owing to a rash on their faces, hands and arms, supposed to be due to some infectious disease. After the examination, I came to the conclusion, firstly that the children were not suffering from any infectious disease, and that there was no reason why they should not attend school; and secondly, that the rash was caused by the children rubbing their hands and arms with the juice of the plant called 'Petty Spurge'. I had no doubt this was done to escape school. In all, there were about 25 cases. The rash resembled 'herpes', but some children had blisters as large as half-a-crown.

It seems that a boy had discovered the effect that the sap of the plant had on the skin and, seeing it as a good way of getting out of school, had passed on his discovery to others. No doubt the truancy ended in a good hiding for all concerned and was never attempted again!

One can imagine what our county ancestors would have made of other natural marvels of strange appearance. For instance, there were two kinds of a brain fungus, a jelly-like substance with a moist and rubbery appearance when fresh, that soon goes rock hard on drying, and is found on the roots of old trees, rotten wood or on the ground. It was believed to fall from the clouds and, when fresh and moist, it was said to be possible to spot it from some distance away. The yellow form was known as 'fairy butter' and the black form as 'witch's butter'; both were also known collectively as 'scum' or 'scoom'.

A similar substance, but an algae rather than a fungus, was a white translucent form of nostoc, which was believed to come from space, the residuum of a meteor. It was said to be found close to the spot where a shooting star had landed and was consequently known as 'star jelly', 'star shot', 'star fall'n' or 'ground jelly'. However, John Morton, in his survey of the county's natural history in 1712, believed that it came from the 'coddy moddy' or seagull dropping the half-digested remains of its food to the ground while in flight. There was also an ancient belief that if frogs came out onto wet ground that soon became frosty, they would turn into a jelly-like substance, like their spawn.

It was only natural that our ancestors would find objects on the ground which had an odd appearance and for which there was no obvious explanation. They therefore ascribed an origin to them and gave them a valid name. Neolithic and Bronze Age flint arrowheads were believed to be of elemental origin and to cause illness if removed, and were known as 'elf bolts'. Many finds were fossils from the vast Jurassic sea that once covered the county. Gryphaea or 'devil's toenails' are especially common, some being of immense size. Northamptonshire folk would call them 'grandmother's toenails', 'Poll parrot's bills', 'bird's bills', 'crow stones' or 'crow pot stones'. The dark

Some of the fossils which abound in the county and which once gave rise to much speculation about their origin.

brown pointed sheaths (alveoli) of belemnites, an ancestor of the squid, were believed to land during thunderstorms and were thus known as 'thunderbolts'. Less common were 'hearts' (pholodomya), huge heavy heart-shaped fossils from ironstone or limestone deposits. The coiled serpent or spiral shape of ammonites led them to be called 'snakestones' (also a common name outside the county) and shark teeth were called 'sparrow beaks'. If iron pyrites were found in the northern parts of the county, they would be called 'kernels'. In the 1950s, a villager of Yarwell recalled:

> When the river [Nene] was dredged and deepened many years ago, a great many long-buried creatures came to light: great ammonites nearly a foot across, fossilised fishes and bones of great lizards.

Man-made objects from earlier times could also cause interest, especially coins. 'Danes money' was a name applied not to the currency of the Danes but to any ancient coins found in the soil. However, in the area around Chipping Warden, any old Roman coins that were unearthed were known (for reasons that are unclear) as 'Warden folk costerpence'. In 1849, a ring was found amid the earthworks of Pipewell Abbey, inscribed '+ AGLA + ADROS + UDROS + TEBAL + GVT + G', which was a charm invoking God's help against epilepsy and toothache.

Predicting the future

Knowing what was going to happen in the future was of vital concern to everyone, regardless of age, gender or occupation, therefore certain rituals were carried out, often solemnly, at auspicious times of the year. On New Year's Day, it was common around the county for the head of the family to open the family Bible with his eyes closed and the text of the first page he touched with his finger would indicate the events of the coming year.

Of all types of divination for the future, however, none gripped the imagination of girls and young single women more than that of knowing if and when they would marry, who it would be and if it would last. There were regularly placed days throughout the year when they could perform a simple ritual, either alone or with friends:

St Agnes' Eve (21 January). If the following ritual was carried out successfully, a girl would dream of her husband-to-be. After a day of fasting, except perhaps for some parsley tea and a little bread, sheets and pillowcases were to be changed and a clean shift or smock worn. Before retiring to bed, the girl had to chant: 'St Agnes, I do pray to thee, I, a maid who would married be, so thou my husband show to me.'

St Mark's Eve (24 April) and also at Halloween. An individual girl would eat an egg yolk and fill the shell with salt, with the result that a future lover would visit before the morning. Groups of girls would also get together to make a Dumb Cake, so-named after the ritual accompanying it. The cake was basically a thin pastry consisting of flour, egg, salt and water and was marked with the initials of each girl's name, using a pin or bodkin, and put on a gridiron over the fire to cook. At midnight, the cake was broken into three pieces and, leaving the door open and putting any pets outside the house, each girl would walk backwards silently, eating a portion of the cake, the rest being put under her pillow. Those who were to marry would shortly hear a knock at the door or a rustling in the house while lying in bed, or would dream of their future love. Those destined to remain single would dream of freshly dug graves or rings not fitting a finger.

Another ritual carried out by a group of girls was to watch the doorway of the church entrance during the day until the evening, when one of them would lay a branch or a flower in the porch. The girl who had laid the branch would return at midnight, with as many of the group who were willing, to take it from the porch to the church gate. Shortly after doing this, a vision would appear in the form of a marriage procession with her likeness hanging on the arm of her would-be groom, the number of bridesmaids and men being the number of months to wait until her wedding. If she was not to be married, however, the vision would be that of a funeral cortège, with a coffin draped in a white sheet, borne by shoulderless bearers.

Midsummer Eve (St John's Eve). A shift was washed and left to dry on the back of a chair. At midnight, the image of the would-be lover would appear to turn the shift. Alternatively, the girl might pick a rose and take it home, walking backwards without speaking to anyone on the way. The rose was then put on paper until Christmas Day, when the girl would wear it at church, where it was believed her future husband would take it from her.

St Martin's Eve (10 November) and St Thomas's Eve (20 December). A girl would peel a red onion which was then wrapped in a handkerchief and put under her pillow. Wearing a clean smock, she would then go to bed and, if successful, dream of her lover. The ritual would be accompanied by a chant, one of which was used in the county from the seventeenth century onwards: 'St Thomas pray do me right, and bring my love to me this night, that I may look him in the face, and in my arms may him embrace'.

On Tanders, 'dreaming bannocks' were made, each piece of dough consisting of eggs, flour, butter and salt with a little spice, to which was added a magic ingredient – a tiny pinch of soot. These were placed on a gridiron and toasted, then eaten in silence before retiring to bed. Like most other divination rituals, it was said that you would then dream of your destiny.

nine

EVERYDAY LIFE

Anecessary part of life for all villages, where money was in short supply, was to make ends meet by going round the lanes, fields and woods in groups and gathering items for use at home. Gathering spare fleece was known as 'a-wooling' and collecting firewood was 'a-sticking'. However, an integral part of the agricultural year and a big annual event for all the villages in the county was gleaning, gathering in the fields for loose corn left behind after harvesting. In the north of the county this was known as 'leasing'. When collecting barley grains, handfuls were scooped up and poured into aprons. With wheat, more care was taken, as explained by Charles Kimbell of Boughton:

> the ears were placed one by one tidily in the hand until the gleaner held as much as could be grouped, then the struggling stalks were twisted round and round beneath the ears and the stalk ends tucked in to hold firmly together.

Often a second gleaning – a 'pickling' or 'prowling' – would be carried out for any grain missed first time around. This was done by the women and children and could provide valuable extra, and free, food for families and chickens. A bell known as the Gleaning Bell was rung as a signal for the gleaning to start. In some villages, such as Gretton, Slipton and Aldwincle St Peter, this would be at 7 a.m. at others, like Twywell and Duddington, it was normal practice to ring two bells, one at 8 a.m. for the start and another at 6 p.m. for the cessation of work.

John Askham wrote a vivid description of his experiences of gleaning in the area around Wellingborough in the mid-1800s. He describes a 'motley party', dressed in old clothes – rags and tatters – and with a bag tied round the waist

THE BOUGHTON ESTATE

WOOD GATHERING TICKET.

This Ticket entitles... *Mrs. L. Wymant (Geddington)*

to enter Boughton Park and the Avenues on the Estate for the purpose of gathering sticks on any Wednesday or Saturday between the hours of 8 a.m. and 4 p.m., *except during the months of May, June, and July, when no gathering will be permitted.*

This permission does not apply to the Plantations and the Wilderness in the Park nor to the Woods on the Estate.

Any person transferring this ticket to another, or breaking the Rules, will forfeit this permission.

CYPRIAN R. KNOLLYS.

Estate Office, Boughton House.
August 15th 1916

A permit to go 'a-sticking' in Geddington parish.

to put 'short ears' in, arriving after a 'long' journey to begin back-breaking, leg-scratching work in fields that stretched for great distances:

> When the signal 'all-on' was given, the gleaners spread themselves over the field; and it was not an uncommon thing for a mother and a child or two to gather such a burthen before night that they could hardly stagger home with it.

It was not uncommon for groups from neighbouring parishes in the county to fight over disputed gleaning territory, usually on boundaries. These disputes were a serious matter: more than pride was at stake and the prize of more grain for the victorious was worth the trouble. These fights could get quite vicious, with scratching, kicking, hair-pulling and tearing clothes being a common feature. One particularly noteworthy incident took place in the north of the county in 1869, when a grudge arose between Nassington and Yarwell.

The incident revolved around the extra-parochial areas of Old and New Sulehay, which lie close to the boundaries of both villages. For centuries, Old Sulehay was considered to belong to the parish of Yarwell and New Sulehay to

Crop gatherers in the fields around Collyweston.

Nassington but that year an inspector from the former Local Government Board was sent to meet the overseers of each parish and, after deliberating on the matter, awarded both areas to Nassington. This obviously did not go down well with the folk of Yarwell, as the residents of Old Sulehay attended their church, the men worked on a Yarwell farm and the women gleaned in the fields there. Officially the protests stopped but Yarwell had other plans and when harvest time came and the first field was ready for gleaning, the women got there first and began gleaning long before the Gleaning Bell was sounded. When the women of Nassington arrived, the gleaning was almost finished. They ordered the Yarwell women to leave and a scuffle broke out as the leader of of the Nassington group got an unexpected response, finding herself being pushed across the boundary ditch. This was followed by a loud shout: 'Get back to Nassington where you belong!'

From the sixteenth century, the county began to develop as a cordwaining, or shoemaking, centre. In Northampton, it became the largest single occupation and this was intensified when the town secured military contracts in the following century, using the welted sole process and handstitching. Further military demands necessitated expansion, which also meant a lucrative income for those with the financial means to establish a workshop, such as Thomas Gotch who set up in Kettering in 1776 and soon began to prosper and draw further local competition. By 1835, it was a full-blown industry, especially after the introduction of sewing machines and the process of rivetting shoes, which was developed later that century, which also saw a boom in sales, albeit at the expense of village craftsmen around the county.

The shoe trade had specialist names for some of its workers and processes. The highest paid craftsmen were the skilled 'clickers' who 'skived' (cut) all the leather and shaped it in the required fashion. Most people, however, used machinery for their particular role in the factory. There was an amusing side to the work, as explained by Norman Mason who, like most other people in the Kettering area, worked in the trade for many years:

> We used to say that when we walked to the bus after work we could tell which factory people worked in by the way they walked ... A lot of the people worked in factories where there was piecework and that meant they got paid by the number of pairs of shoes they handled and worked on so they worked at a much faster rate and it showed in the way they walked.

Women of all ages learned how to make lace to support themselves or to supplement family income. They often sang special worksongs, the movement of the bobbins being timed by the modulation of the tune.

Charles E. Kimbell of Boughton described one such person at work in the village during the 1880s:

> fixing in a round hard cushion which the worker held on her lap, was an intricate grouping of pins, each one attached by white cotton to a bone bobbin. The bobbins varying in shapes and colours lay flat on the cushion and were manipulated by the deft fingers of the worker who seemed to ply the bobbins mechanically, swirling them over at such a rapid speed that anyone unititiated into the mysteries of lace making would watch the process with wonder and marvel at the delicate pattern of the white lace issuing at the base of the pins.

The earliest references to woodturning in the county appear in the sixteenth century, when just one woodturner was recorded in the Rockingham Forest area. This was mainly due to the restrictions of Forest Law regarding the use of timber. After the decline of the law in the late 1600s, however, the craft really began to develop, flourishing mainly in Kingscliffe, where abundant supplies of cheap or free wood were available. It reached its heyday in Victorian times, when at least ten different craftsmen could be seen working in groups outside their houses. The finished product, for which the village became renowned, was known as 'treen' and visitors came from far and wide to see and buy the high-quality goods. A description of the woodturners at work during the early 1880s has come down to us from a Yarwell villager, Lucy Adela Lock, who thoughtfully wrote down a description of life in Rockingham Forest and her visits to Kingscliffe as a little girl in *Memories of a Villager*:

> I would watch them work in their shops. They would sit in front of their lathes, which they worked with their feet. One man sat on a wooden block and chopped logs of wood into 'billets' of the right length for a wooden tap, tool handles, etc. The next man shaped it roughly with a tool and passed it to another who used finer tools, which made it more like the article it was intended to be. The last man bored holes and used chisels which made it more smooth and shapely. The finishing was done by hand. I have seen a woman using a small poker which she burnt patterns on things e.g. egg cups, candlesticks, etc. Then they would be rubbed with sandpaper, and polished or varnished: Oak, cherry wood, box-wood (for taps), apple wood (for tool handles), willow (for spoons, bread boards), etc. It was fascinating to watch shavings curling away from the lathes. The people fetched them to light fires and put under mats, or on damp floors.

A fissile form of limestone exists in the north of the county around Deene, Wakerley and Collyweston. It was celebrated from Roman times onwards as the ideal material for roofing, being of a hardwearing and durable nature. These thin layers, known as 'logs', were formerly made into Collyweston slates, which enjoyed a high reputation for many centuries. They were somewhat heavy and required great skill in order to manoeuvre and fix them into position. The slaters of Collyweston certainly possessed this skill and their services were in great demand. Only a dedicated few now carry on the tradition, which began to decline when the coming of the railway brought cheap slate from Wales.

The hard, finely grained rock which lies at the base of the limestone beds was extracted from the quarry during the winter months and the logs laid out on the ground to be exposed to night frosts. They were watered to keep them wet, which allowed the frost to penetrate deeply. When they were ready, they were split with special chisels which were inserted into the cracks by the slaters. Yellow-white or with a bluish tinge, the finished product or 'colleys' were sought-after everywhere. Different names were given to the colleys according to their size, given here in inches:

6	Even Mope
6.5	Large Mope
7	Even Mumford
7.5	Large Mumford
8-8.5	Job

A group of Collyweston slaters pose with their tools in the early twentieth century, behind a screen erected to protect them from the wind.

9–9.5	Short-un
10–10.5	Long-un
11–11.5	Shortback
12–12.5	Middleback
13–13.5	Longback
14	Batchelor
15	Wibbett
16	A Twelve
17	A Fourteen
18	A Sixteen
19	An Eighteen
20–21	In Bow
22	Short Ten
23	Middle Ten
24	Long Ten

A lot of iron ore-deposits lay near the surface in parts of the county and these were initially worked by hand, using the precarious plank and barrow method, where ironstone was placed in wheelbarrows, carted along narrow lengths of

A Collyweston slater, Robert James
Spaull, at work with his specialist tools in
Collyweston churchyard in the late 1960s.

wood which spanned deep chasms below and loaded directly into railway wag-
ons, or transported by horse and cart to the nearest railway station. Falls from the
planks were a common occurrence, with injury or death a distinct possibility,
a risk which was part of the job until as late as 1930. A vivid account of those
years was given by Annie Wignall, the daughter of a local doctor, in 1974. She
described the life of the workers:

> ...a workman trundling his barrow across a springy plank would sometimes lose his
> balance and crash to the rocky strata some 30 feet below. A messenger would then
> dash by bicycle to fetch a doctor – if there happened to be such a machine at hand.
> But not every ironstone worker owned a bicycle. They mostly walked to work ... By
> modern standards it was a tough life, but to quote one of the workers: 'Ah, we'd have
> fun, those times. If a man fancied a walking or running match, he could have it. If he
> cared for a good game of cricket or football, he could have it. And if anyone wanted
> a thick ear, he could have that too, for the asking!'

Equally as dangerous was the task of processing the iron into steel. At the Corby
steelworks, accidents were inevitable with the chance of burns, concussion and
even death always present. In the 1960s, Colin Eliot recalled the days when his
father undertook dangerous missions as a maintenance fitter, always having to be
on call to release the explosion doors which had jammed at the top of furnaces:

The 'plank and barrow' system used for transporting newly quarried ironstone at Corby in the 1890s.

When I was a small boy I remember him being severely burned; I screamed in terror at the sight of the burns hanging like grapes ... I realised why my mother dreaded the sound of the 'knocker up' either knocking on the window, or throwing stones to wake up my father in the middle of the night.

A similar number of accidents occurred during the construction of viaducts when the railway came to the county. These accidents were mainly fatal, as the number of inscriptions on tombstones testify. However, some were lucky enough to escape with their lives, albeit at some cost, as with the case of a Geddington railway worker named Talbot who was working on the viaduct spanning the valley at Harpers Brook, between Great and Little Oakley. Surviving his fall, he ended up with an injured leg that henceforth led to villagers calling him Bent Axle Talbot, a name that he graciously accepted for the rest of his days.

Watermills and windmills could also be dangerous places. In September 1597, it was reported that William Miller, 'the son of Will Miller' was buried after a fatal accident:

he fell into the water and the stream carried him under the new corne mill wheele, which quashed him all to pieces.

A particularly grisly incident occurred at Bulwick in November 1863: a miller, Jeffrey Sarrington, was going about his daily work at the watermill when he caught his sleeve on a cog wheel and was pulled into the machinery. A report of the incident described the ensuing events:

He shouted to his apprentice to stop the mill and bring a knife, with which he attempted to sever his mutilated arm, but being blunt, it needed whetting. He gave the knife to the boy and ordered him to sharpen it, but a suitable means was impossible to find. Whereupon, the miller asked for a metal candlestick that stood nearby, to take off the rough edges. He then naggled away at his arm and kept at it, but became exhausted after a while and asked the boy to finish the task. Eventually, he disengaged the stump leaving the mutilated part between the wheels, then he bound the stump in a handkerchief, went home and took to bed. It was near midnight when a messenger was sent to the surgeon at Kings Cliffe to come and attend to the miller. On examination it was found necessary to remove more inches from the arm.

The post mill at Great Oakley, scene of a tragedy in 1865. The sixteen-year-old son of the miller, James Pain, collapsed and died whilst helping his father at work.

Even work that seemed innocuous could be fraught with danger for our ancestors. To keep newly-sown seed or growing crops in the fields free from stones and hungry birds, boys were often employed to patrol an area, usually with a rattle, stick or gun. What may seem a relatively harmless task could end in tragedy, such as the fatal shooting recorded in the journal of an Aldwincle farmer, William Coales:

> the above poor boy, John Allen Coales, met with a sad accident this Day, July the fourth 1863. He was scaring Crows away from some Potatoes at the 2nd Gates, and was Laying or Hanging the Gun on the Bushes of an Ash.

The well-being of livestock was always of paramount concern, although those entrusted with that care might seem unusual to us today. Living at Syresham during the 1870s was a small man nicknamed Doctor, who had a prominent nose and who was always seen carrying a shoulder stick slung over his back with an old tin can attached to the end. He was a self-appointed vet, who boasted that he could cure all kinds of animal, or anything else for that matter. He asserted that 'what he did not know wasn't worth knowing'. His wife used to help him when she was not gathering horse manure around the streets and lanes for her garden, travelling great distances to get a sufficient quantity. Legend has it that on one occasion Doctor was called upon to examine a cow and a horse at a nearby farm and the farmer ordered a ploughboy to assist him. The task took a few days, during which time the young man took a great interest in what the 'vet' was doing and asked him why he was giving the same stuff to both the animals, to which he replied:

> Me lad you don't know – you're born to it. You got a lot to larne. Shake it up and down for the horse – backwards and forwards for the coo!

Housework in olden times was much more strenuous and wearisome than it is today, with a variety of daily or weekly chores that had to be done and were vigorously adhered to at all times, without the aid of technology and labour-saving devices. Chores that would have been familiar around the county for many up until the Second World War were recorded by Mary Hercock, the daughter of a Blatherwycke gamekeeper, in 1980:

> Every day the oil lamps had to be filled and the wicks checked and trimmed. The sticks had to be chopped, wood to be sawn and the coal bucket filled. In the bad weather we collected the coal left at the bottom of the field on a sledge. The fireplace in the kitchen, containing an oven and small boiler for hot water, had to be blackleaded, and we also had an oil stove with two burners and an oven. Outside the house was a copper to heat water for baths and the weekly wash, the water obtained from a pump in the garden. Candles had to be ready for upstairs light.

Of course, some household tasks did not always run smoothly, for potentially devastating accidents were always waiting to happen, a case in point being one which occurred at the Queen's Head, Yarwell in the 1920s. Lance Lock recalled the incident in his memoirs:

> Frances Simmons, worked there as a girl with Mrs Stafford. They did the washing one day when the copper wouldn't go. Mrs. Stafford decided to put some gun powder on the fire and probably put too much on – 'one hell of a bang,' said Frances, 'which blew the copper door and blew soot all over the wash house and the clean washed clothes'.

Fairs and markets

Of course life was not all work and hardship. Going to a fair or market was a great social affair, an occasion for making new acquaintances, meeting old friends, bargaining and buying and in some cases hiring labour, and enjoying oneself. Holding such an event would have been prestigious and lucrative for any town or village. Some were granted by charter from the King and others were set up by the lord of the manor, who could make a lot of profit from levies and tolls on trade during the event. Fairs were usually held annually, to coincide with a saint's day or an event in the agricultural year, and lasted three days. In most cases, fairs were dedicated to the saints of the local church. Markets, on the other hand, were held weekly and were mainly for the sale of food items, attracting both buyers and traders from a wide area both in the county and from outside. A lord of the manor was responsible for keeping law and order, settling disputes, preventing bloodshed and keeping drunken individuals in check.

Boughton Fair was one of the most important and widely attended fairs in the Midlands. It was proclaimed annually, somewhat unusually, by a representative of the lord of the manor long before the event itself, to allow for the bidding of stalls and booths. Traders would come from all over the region, selling cakes from Banbury, rakes from Weldon, Corby and Geddington, and 'treen' (woodware) from Kingscliffe. Held on the triangular green outside the village between 23 and 25 June, the first day was devoted to the sale of items of woodwork and metalware, the second day to horse racing, wrestling, games and sports and the third day to the mass sale of cattle, sheep and, above all, horses. In the late afternoon, after the main event, there were sideshows with curiosities, theatre acts and displays of animals – some exotic – accompanied by widespread drunken revelry which went on well into the evening with constant outbreaks of fighting – and petty theft.

Robert Lucas (1747-1812), vicar of Hardingstone and later Pattishall, wrote a poem about the fair, beginning with a detailed description of various folk getting ready for the event and then conjuring up the atmosphere of the fair itself:

See! Pots capacious, lesser pots entome,
And hogsheads barrels gorge, for want of room!
From their broad base, part in each other hid,
The lessening tubs shoot up in a pyramid,
Pitchforks and axes and the deepening spade,
Beneath the pressing load are harmless laid,
While way out behind where pliant poles prevail
The merry waggons seem to wag his tail.

Theatre

The eighteenth century saw the theatre becoming a very popular form of entertainment in the county, performances often being given in a venue such as a hotel or inn. Northampton was the obvious choice, being the main town. However, some of the larger villages were able to experience the theatre without having to go into a town, as travelling theatres came to them, setting up a stage on a green or some kind of booth. Such was the case in Brixworth, Earls Barton and Kingscliffe.

AT the THEATRE at Brixworth, in Northamptonſhire,
by Mr. JACKSON's Company of Comedians, on
Monday, January 23, will be preſented
LOVE in a VILLAGE.
In which will be introduced a STATUTE for the HIRING of
SERVANTS.
To conclude with a DANCE by the Characters.
To which will be added,
MISS in her TEENS.
On Wedneſday, January 25, will be preſented,
King RICHARD the Third.
To which will be added,
DAMON and PHILLIDA.
And on Friday, January 27, will be preſented,
The WAY to KEEP HIM.
To which will be added,
HOB in the WELL: Or, The
COUNTRY-WAKE.

An eighteenth-century handbill advertising a touring theatre performance at Brixworth.

Food and drink

People today would give a great thumbs down to much of the food eaten by our ancestors, who did not have the money or range of products we have nowadays. 'Chitlings' – animal intestines – were very popular and were linked together in knots, the thicker parts being known as Tom Hedge, and boiled. Other innards used to make dishes were the lungs or 'lights' and one dish known variously as 'light pie', 'pluck pie', 'sweet pie' or 'pluck pasty' was widely eaten. It was a form of pasty, containing finely chopped lights, apples, currants, sugar and spice. Ugs pudding (black pudding) was another favourite. 'Race' – the heart, liver and lights of calves – was a special treat, and 'crow', which was calf or cow liver fried in pig fat, was a particular favourite in farming families. Boiled egg and rook pie was a popular dish with the men, the feathers obviously being removed first!

Other dishes would be more appealing to the tastes of today. Squab pie was a widely eaten dish in the villages around the county, the filling consisting of apples, onions and fat bacon; a variation known as 'tantarrow' used meat instead of bacon. 'Ock 'n' Dough' was a very popular meat and potato dish, with interesting variations: the potatoes are cut in half and pressed into the pastry round the dish, surrounding the meat like a giant island surrounded by potatoes. The county had a variation of toad-in-the-hole or pudding pie: instead of using sausages in the recipe, small pieces of bacon or even steak were substituted and the dish was not baked but boiled.

For centuries, the pig has provided a vast range of products, especially tasty, affordable meat in different forms, and many a county home once had their own animal. After the pig had been dispatched by a local slaughterman or butcher, the blood was drained and the carcass cleaned up. Flo Colyer of Weldon gave a detailed account of the custom in 1976:

> The entrails were removed and emptied into a large pancheon of water. The bladder was blown up for the boys to use as a football – and a good one it made too. Nobody relished cleaning the intestines, but there were no plastic sausage skins in those days, so the smaller intestines were required for the purpose, and everyone was partial to the chitterlings from the large intestine.

It was then customary to salt the flitches for ham and bacon and to make sausages, pies and black puddings. The leaf (belly fat) and flare (loin fat) were removed and boiled down to make lard, any remaining scraps being made into 'flitters' which, with a little pepper and salt sprinkled on, made an excellent teatime meal. It was also a tradition in some areas to make gifts of some part of the animal, farmers often making and sending a pork pie as a gift to another farmer, or perhaps a needy person. In most cases, however, family and friends were the recipients, as Flo Colyer explained:

It was customary when our pig was killed to send portions of 'fry' (liver and fat) to relatives and friends and neighbours. The most fortunate received a piece of pork or perhaps some sausages as well. They returned the compliment when their pig was killed in the season.

Popular food could sometimes have unusual ingredients added, albeit by accident, as in one case at Nassington, where lads working for the local butcher George Mould, or Uncle George as he was affectionately known, accidentally put sand in the sausage meat instead of pepper! Mr Mould also had another tasty surprise, when the village band that he led ended up at his home after a performance to enjoy a well-earned cup of tea. It is said that his son, not wanting their company for some reason, laced their tea with lots of sugar and Epsom salts, to get rid of them. One hopes that their music had not been the cause.

Certain dishes had amusing names: 'mommy' or 'pommy' was any food cooked to a pulp, such as crushed apples, and 'sleepy' was the pulp of pears. 'Parliament' was a thin rectangular piece of gingerbread and 'queen cake' was a heart-shaped pastry influenced by playing cards. A great favourite was yeast dumplings known as 'popabouts'. Milton Malsor was renowned for its '100 to 1 pudding', which was so-named because it contained at least hundred and one pieces of potato but only one piece of meat. Even more hilarious was a very popular form of plum pudding eaten in the eighteenth and nineteenth centuries, known variously as 'whispering pudding', 'hooting pudding' or 'screamer' because there were so few currants in the pastry, they had make those sounds in order to communicate with each other!

For special occasions, however, there were special dishes. Tander cakes made of yeast, flour, salt, sugar, warm water, egg, crystalised lemon peel, lard, currants and caster sugar were eaten sliced and buttered on St Andrew's Day, washed down with tea. Cattern cakes or 'wiggs' were made from dough, lard, sugar and caraway seeds and were consumed on St Catherine's Day. At the Long Buckby Feast (Buckby Plum Pudding Feast), which was originally held in August but now takes place in September, a kind of rich bread pudding is still specially baked for ten hours the day before and eaten cold the next day. For Rothwell Charter Fair, it is customary to eat boiled ham, salad and Rowell Fair tarts, the latter using an age-old recipe, with variations to suit family tastes, but consisting basically of cream cheese (originally using milk and rennet for curds), mixed fruit, breadcrumbs, butter, caster sugar, eggs, lemon rind, nutmeg – and 'a little something from the bottle', such as sherry.

At Earls Barton, where growing leeks was once a source of pride, leek pie is still made. The vegetables were originally taken to the village green and fed through a chaffer and water trough to be washed. The pastry was made and cuts of beef and

A selection of freshly baked Earls Barton leek pies.

pork added, then the pie was taken to the baker for cooking. The epithet Barton Leek was formerly given to anyone hailing from the village. Whether it was said in jest or jealousy is not known but presumably the villagers felt flattered that their unique dish had attracted such attention!

Our modern concern with diet and health would have been ignored or treated with disdain in the eighteenth century by those members of society with the money – and inclination – to indulge in a new passion in the form of eating contests or 'gorging matches'. One such occasion was recorded in the detailed diary of the Oundle carpenter John Clifton on 7 August 1782. One wonders if the servants mentioned usually dined on such fare, in which case any vacancy for their position would have been much sought-after:

Today Mr Edens gave another specimen of his Noble abilitys in the Bolting way in Dr Walctt's kitchen, he being invited in to Dine with the Servants. First he devoured a fine plate of Ham and fowls. Second, a Charming Mess of Nice Beans and Bacon as any common man could cram down for Dinner. Third, a Precious Plate of Haunch of Venison. Fourth, Another exact the same quantity. Fifth, Another exact the same again. Sixth, A fine Hunk of Bread and Cheese and as much Ale as made six Horns with what he drank at his Dinner. Bless his poor Stomach! He said himself that each Plate of Venison weighed full three quarters of a pound, besides a full flow of very rich Sauce.

Not so appetising, perhaps, was the Sunday dinner awaiting a certain landlord of West Haddon in the nineteenth century. A poem describing the supposedly true incident was written by William Page in 1928. It tells the story of a travelling navvy going into the Crown public house for beer, bread and cheese. Setting his basket down, the landlord notices a freshly caught hare. Licking his lips, he goes away, kills his cat and when the navvy's attention is elsewhere, substitutes the dead animal for the hare. After his meal, the navvy sets off on his journey but after some distance notices the basket is lighter than before. Discovering he has been duped, he returns to the hostelry on the Sunday morning and finds the landlord has gone to church. He asks the serving girl for some small beer and, as she goes off to the cellar, he takes out a leg of mutton from a steaming cooking pot nearby, replaces it with the cat and cheerfully makes his way out, justice done. He is far away by the time the hungry landlord returns and asks for some of the broth but is about to have two surprises:

> Now when it was tasted, he said in great wrath,
> 'Oh wench, what the plague have you put in the broth?
> All around it is swimming a great lot of hair,
> You may eat it yourself – I'll not, I declare!'

> 'Come, bring up the mutton, and mind you make haste,
> The turnips and capers, the butter to taste',
> So Betty with all needful things did prepare
> To take up the mutton, not doubting 'twas there.

> But alas, it had gone, and nowhere could be found,
> Though they searched for the navvy, the roads all around.

Before the advent of piped water, Elsie Harrison of Little Oakley, who was over 100 years old when I interviewed her, recalled seeing freshwater eels in the well at the rear of her garden on frequent occasions. Even as late as the 1970s, you might see transparent freshwater shrimps in a glass of tap water in the north of the county. This would give rise to the humorous comment that it was full of protein! Water, or 'frog wine' as it used to be called in some parts of the county, was formerly drawn from wells using pumps which sometimes had fanciful names such as the One-handed Lady.

Ale was once drunk by young and old, in varying degrees of strength, and there was also 'buttered ale', where beer was boiled with sugar, butter and spice, and cobbler's punch or hot pot, in which warm ale was thickened, sweetened, and mixed with spirits – gin being a particular favourite. Home-made wines were also popular, as was 'cool tankard', which was a mixture of wine, borage, water, lemon and sugar.

A less inviting drink, used in some cases as a food, was 'kettlins', also known as ketley broth and teakettle broth, in which hot water was added to bread and salt, sometimes with pepper, milk or butter added. It was a common and integral part of life in poorer homes, where money was short and families were large.

When tea became cheaper, and hence more widely drunk, in the mid-nineteenth century, it gave rise to some pet names, one of which was 'Willy call your father'. If the tea was over-diluted with water, making it weak, the man of the house might say, 'You've put the miller's eye out'. Bottles of cold tea became a popular refreshing alternative to beer for some workers, especially those who needed to take extra care in their tasks, such as the workers in the nascent iron and steel industry in the north of the county. Tea is a diuretic, of course, and the more one drank, the more a visit to relieve oneself would be necessary, which gave rise to the expression: 'I shall pee over nine hedges and the tenth.'

On St Martin's Eve (November 10), it was customary, according to John Clare, to gather around the hearth and place large apples on the fire to cook, after which they were added to a pitcher of 'creamy' ale with nutmeg. The drink was known as lamb's wool, after the fleecy appearance of the froth. There were more elaborate, pre-prepared versions, such as this one which was used in parts of the county in 1886:

> One gallon of light ale or stout
> Half a cup of sigar
> An eighth of a teaspoonful of nutmeg
> A quarter of a teaspoonful of cinammon
> Half a teaspoonful of ginger
> Twelve small apples
> Two cups of heavy whipping cream
> A quarter of a teaspoonful of salt
> Two tablespoons of brown sugar

Take the apples and either broil, boil or bake them until bursting. Heat three quarters of the ale until warm, add the remaining quarter together with the other ingredients, bring to the boil, then simmer until frothy. Pour into a bowl, and whip the cream until it peaks. Add this to the mixture. Serve when ready.

Medicine and cures

Folk medicine had an important role in everyday life for the majority of people, who could not afford a physician. Even if one was available, common folk tended to put more trust in the specialist knowledge and skills of someone in the community: a wise woman, who had probably learnt her craft from what had been passed down through generations of her family. She was the community doctor and midwife, offering expert advice and treatment for free or at little cost. She would know which plants or other sources to use for alleviating pain or for healing and curing, based on an observation, understanding and bond with the world of nature. Living in an age of superstition, she would frequently use incantations or charms, giving more apparent credibility and power to the task in hand.

John Askham, in one of his sketches of life in Wellingborough in the 1800s, describes the skills of Jenny Clay, a wise woman renowned in the district for her knowledge and dexterity:

> Her case of surgical instruments consisted of a pair of scissors and a worsted needle, and with these simple instruments and an everlasting supply of green salve, the preparation of which was a secret known, we fear, only to herself, she effected cures in all kinds of eruptive disorders which baffled the skills of surgeons who had walked the hospitals and rejoiced in their diplomas. Nothing came amiss to her, from a whitlow to a cancer. She had cured whole cargoes of scald heads ... [her green salve] would draw or heal, irritate or mollify, as the case required; it suited all, young or old, in whatever form it was applied. Everybody went to her surgery who was able to get there.

In addition to her wonderful salve, she used other remedies such as applying treacle possets, tallowing the nose, and 'pinning a stocking around the throat', all of which had been in common use since at least the eighteenth century.

Another noted wise woman who lived at Syresham in the late 1800s would cure whooping cough by opening a nut and substituting the kernel with a spider, binding up the shell tightly in muslin and telling anyone afflicted to hang it round their neck for six weeks. She was in fact following a commonly held belief that the spider would ingest the cough and the patient would thus be cured. She also made poultices from crushed snails for applying to a carbuncle or boil but in this she was not always so successful, for it was said that her method only worsened the agony on one occasion – and a doctor had to be called in as a last resort.

One of the last wise women in the county was Kerenhappuch Briggs of Wadenhoe, who was always to be seen around her garden and the village lanes, fields and woods gathering quantities of selected wild plants to make brews, salves and potions for neighbours in need. Her skills were locally recognised and her services much in demand, even to the extent of occasionally helping to nurse ailing members of the manorial family at Lilford Hall.

A rare image of Northamptonshire wise
woman Kerenhappuch Briggs.

Another well-respected herbalist and midwife was the quaintly named
Reservoir Woods of Gretton, who came from an old Romany family. She was
regarded as 'a wonderful woman with her herbal drinks, lotions and ointments'
and on her death in 1911, a gravestone was erected by public subscription, in
recognition of her services to the community and as a token of the affection in
which she had been held.

Even without a wise woman, in the days when there were not many doctors around, folk had their own remedies for ailments. A way of countering
cramp was to form a cross with one's shoes and stockings before going to bed.
Elderberry wine in hot water was a favourite tonic if you felt under the weather,
and a good decongestant for colds was a boiled onion made into a thick gruel
with salt and pepper to be eaten before going to bed with a shawl or towel over
the head.

For earache, there were two commonly used remedies: a baked onion or a flan-
nel bag full of hot bran tied on with a handkerchief. For toothache, a favourite
was to make a brown paper strip plaster soaked in vinegar, which was then thickly
coated with more paper to be tied round the face at bedtime. Bread poultices

were another remedy. However, in some villages, like Polebrook, a curious if horrifying method was to take henbane seeds with a nip of whisky!

For clearing the blood, shoots of wild hops and young nettles were boiled and used as a vegetable. For nosebleed, knotweed (polygonium) was applied. For spots, a drink made from nettles was very effective, especially if the leaves or shoots were cut early in the day before the essential oils were evaporated by the sun. In fact, the nettle was and still is a very useful plant: it was traditionally used as a tonic, as it is rich in vitamin C, as well as for milk curdling and as a salad plant, being good for the digestion. It was also well known everywhere as a stinging nettle and it was common practice to rub a dock leaf on an affected part when stung, adding saliva and chanting, 'Nettle in, dock out, dock rub, nettle out'. Strangely, the juice of a nettle is also an antidote for its own sting.

Another plant, rarely heard of today but often featuring in the county's mummers' plays as a wonder cure, was elecampane, a wild sunflower-like plant with aromatic roots and leaves which were widely used in herbal medicine and were effective in treating respiratory disorders. The plant was also made into a candied sweetmeat.

Some remedies, however, seem decidedly strange – and off-putting – to modern sensibilities. For instance, around the county, the hair from the tail of a black cat was rubbed on a stye; currant plasters or heated soap and sugar were applied to draw out poison; and for chilblains, the remedy was to soak the feet in a chamberpot of urine. In 1973, Annie Beaver of Weldon recalled some of her grandmother's remedies:

> If you had whooping cough, a fried mouse was supposed to be good, but my father did not seem to agree. For burns, ringworm etc. an ointment made from house leeks pounded with pure lard was considered a good remedy. The powder of dried puff-balls was used on cut hands. Failing that a good thick cobweb was used.

Sometimes, just to be sure, folk combined traditional methods with modern medicine. A combination of modern and traditional methods was recommended for the treatment of wounds in Kettering and Wellingborough in the early twentieth century. Once again, puffballs seemed to work magic and yet another kind of green ointment applied:

> Wash, and prepare a plaster of green ointment from chemist. Lay the dust of a puff-ball about the thickness of a sixpence or shilling. Rub the dust into the ointment, and put the plaster over the sore for nine days. Then take off and wash. Apply proper salves to complete the cure.

Gypsies visiting the county were seen to have a predilection for a certain animal that many ordinary folk would have found distasteful, yet it certainly had its uses. In 1846, a former gravedigger of Castor reported:

...they were fond of hedgehog both for food and medicine. The roasted flesh was always described as delicious. The fat was regarded as a valuable specific for rheumatism.

Perhaps we might also add frivolity and merriment, with the use of disdain and contempt, as a way of dealing with disease. The following little ditty comes from the Oundle carpenter and workhouse overseer John Clifton, who recorded it in his diary during a particularly virulent outbreak of the contagious, disfiguring disease smallpox. The diary makes fascinating reading and vividly portrays eighteenth-century life in the area:

> Poll Muckason Joins us tonight, she'll Tip us a Jorum of Diddle
> Small Pox is our Delight, and we'll foot it away to the Fiddle!
> Fol lol de rol, lor rol lol lol!
> And the Small Pox we have got,
> Not one shall appear on our Faces,
> Forty Five Sir, we thinks a Good lot,
> And they shall all come out in our A – – – s! Fol lol lol!

Spring water was widely used for healing or curing, as well as for drinking and for ritual purposes such as baptism. The main kind of water used was chalybeate – impregnated with iron salts – which gave it a reddish colour and ferric taste. This was used internally as a tonic and restorative, which was said to be particularly good for anaemia, and applied externally to treat ailments such as rheumatism and afflictions of the eyes. Though it was used whenever it was needed, there were certain occasions – such as on a saint's day, at sunrise or at noon – when it was considered to be extra powerful. For instance, 1 May was the day to visit the Kingthorn spring at Green's Norton.

Powerful healing water could be obtained from many wells all round the county. In Robinson's Grounds, among the hills and hollows of Elkington, the water was said to be 'very effective especially for the eyes'. St Loys Well at Weedon Lois was stated to be 'the best in the west of the county' and it was said that 'even the blind and leprous went there and were infallibly cured'. Guilsborough had a petrifying spring near the Grange which was 'good for several diseases' and Nether Heyford had several medicinal springs including Holy Well. It was also possible that the water could prolong life, as at Maidford, where one woman, Elizabeth Smith, lived until she was 122 years old!

At Broughton, hidden among the trees of Under Hill Woods and close to Pytchley Brook, is another famed spring for curing eye complaints. Children knew if their eyes were sore and were bathed there, they would be better. It had always been used but was rediscovered in the eighteenth century by a woman staying at the rectory. For many years, she had suffered from sore eyes but had been unable to alleviate the problem until she applied the spring's water and obtained a complete cure. In gratitude, she had a monument erected – a protective stone archway covering the spring. A similar arch-covered spring can be seen in a spinney at Boughton near Northampton.

When spas started to become fashionable again in the seventeenth century, the county proved a magnet for health seekers. Wellingborough was especially popular after a visit by Charles I and there were thirty-five wells recorded there in 1830, including Hemmingwell, Whytewell, Hartwell, Red Well and Hollywell. The water was also used for mineral waters and in a very popular stout made by one of the town's brewers, Dulley & Woolston.

At Kings Sutton, two springs were particularly efficacious, attracting visitors from far and wide. One of these, St Rumbold's Well, was advertised in 1668 as being beneficial for disorders of the internal organs, nerves, muscles and even the brain. Another noted spa was in the parish of Kingscliffe; it had been widely used since around 1670 after being 'publickly recommended' by a physician, Dr Thomas Browne, who lived in the village. In his unpublished 1829 history of the village and its environs, Revd Henry Key Bonney, rector of the parish and later an archdeacon, described the quality and content of the water:

> It both smells and tastes of iron. It will deposit a white sediment with oil of tartar, and with galls it precipitates a purple sediment, but turns of an opake red with logwood, and of a deep green with syrups of violets … it has been used with great success in disorders from obstructions, and in eruptions of the skin; it has also cured several lame persons.

Today the spring can still be found, covered with foliage despite being cleared and relined in the 1980s and with its walls inscribed with nineteenth-century graffiti, lying in isolation in a field some distance from the village. The water was used both externally and internally and children would sometimes be asked to run across the fields with kettles and fetch home some of its water for making tea. One girl growing up in Victorian times described it as pinkish in colour and salty in taste!

It was not just spring water that was believed to be effective. If you visited Marston St Lawrence on Holy Thursday during the nineteenth century and it was raining, you would see the villagers performing an annual ritual of going around the streets and fields 'in all directions' to collect drops of rain as it fell. This day was seen as particularly auspicious and it was commonly believed that water collected at that time could cure all kinds of eye complaints.

Children at play

Children had a vast array of games to play, chasing, hiding, using a ball, rope, top or anything else they could get their hands on. Church towers and spires seem to have had a special attraction for boys in the county. On at least two occasions, the spire of the church of St Peter at Oundle was climbed by schoolboys, using the crockets which are spaced several feet apart. It is recorded that the reward for those who successfully completed such a daring, unsanctioned feat was a caning from the headmaster. At Geddington, children delighted in taking aim at the church steeple with their catapults; at one time, the tail of the weathercock on the tower was missing for many years as a result of one overenthusiastic barrage. At Boughton, a favourite pastime was to throw stones over the church tower without striking the building.

Children enjoyed making use of what nature provided around them. They created 'fairy gardens' in local fields by arranging stones in a set pattern and placing wild flowers and leaves inside the walls. Certain plants had attractions and qualities that could be used for amusement. 'Keks', also known as 'sags' or 'segs', were the hollow stalks of cow parsley, a non-poisonous member of the hemlock family, which children used as pea-shooters or to make musical pipes by

Children relaxing and playing at Collyweston, *c.* 1906.

cutting the stems below one joint and partially slitting them to the next joint. In the medieval period, the dried stems were packed with waste tow or flax from spinning and then soaked in tallow or wax. When lit, these would give a light, albeit very smoky, if folk had cause to venture out into the dark, unlit streets. These torches, known as 'keckies' gave their name to the plant. In the south of the county, children rubbed together stalks of figwort, a cleansing plant once much used for skin complaints, to produce a squeaky sound like a fiddle, chanting: 'Fiddle de fiddle de fy fum, all the way to Sysham'. Another plant used in the county was Shepherd's Purse, locally known as 'pickpocket', which children picked, chanting: 'Pick pocket, penny nail, put the rogue in the gaol.'

A game peculiar to Boughton in the nineteenth century was played by a group of boys who would choose a victim and blindfold him, after which they would make knots at the ends of their handkerchiefs. They would then surround the victim, singing a dirge-like song, after which they prodded, or 'popped', their fingers into the 'cap', or mask, worn by him, the favourite area being around the eyes. He was then asked to guess the identity of the companion who had popped him. If he failed to guess correctly, they would beat him with the knotted handkerchiefs until he got it right.

Not so much a game but certainly a profitable venture for older children, and a means of supplementing their pocket money, was to seek out certain animals considered by farmers or cottagers to be pests. They could be dead or alive. One villager recalls:

> ...the most popular way [to make money] was the selling of rats' tails for a penny each, the tail of course was proof that the rodent had departed this life. And even more profitable was the sale of moleskins, for which, if they were in good condition and dried, we were paid the fantastic sum of 9d ... needless to say, moles were in very short supply.

ten

MUSIC, SONG AND DANCE

For his twenty-first birthday, John Clare purchased a bound book of blank pages at the cost of a week's wages (eight shillings) from a bookseller at Market Deeping. He used this to copy down his best and earliest poems, the collection being entitled *A Rustic's Pastime (In Leisure Hours)* and dated 'Helpston 1814'. The manuscript is now housed in Northampton Library as MS1. These early efforts already show a sensitive mind and a good command of language, and reflect a great love of the nature flourishing in the Northamptonshire country-side. Several of the pieces are simply entitled 'Song' or 'Ballad', this form of verse reflecting Clare's interest in music and folksong.

Being an avid collector of folk songs and ballads, he wrote several down in 1818 in an 'oblong book' under the title *A Collection of Songs, Airs and Dances for the Violin* (Northampton MS12). This included some of his own compositions such as 'Cherry Cheek'd Patty' and 'Maid of Shy Light', as well as well-known pieces such as 'The Cuckoo', 'Oh Dear What Can The Matter Be?', 'The Disconsolate Sailor' and another 'Ballad' with the opening lines:

> A faithful shepherd courted me
> He stole away my liberty
> When my poor heart was strange to me
> He came and sailed and stole it then.

When my apron would hang low,
Me he sought through frost and snow,
When it puckered up with shame,
And I sought him, he never came.

This theme of spurned love and illegitimate children is a common one in many folksongs of the era, and the image of the apron recurs in similar folksongs that travelled far and wide, such as 'Careless Love', 'Make Me A Pallet On The Floor' and 'A Brisk Young Soldier Courted Me'.

Clare was also very fond of the fiddle and learned to play the instrument from the gypsies who came every year to the Castor Feast, a week-long celebration during which the hostelries were open all the time and continual fighting, dancing and fiddle playing took place. In a manuscript held at Peterborough Museum, Clare describes how he got to know them at their camps, particularly the 'Boswell crew', a popular tribe well known in the district and famous for their fiddlers and fortune tellers.

Fair Green in Rothwell was an open space in the nineteenth century, although it is now built over, where dancing traditionally took place every Saturday night to the accompaniment of a fiddler, one of whom, a Mr Field, was considered to be so good it was said he could go on playing if he only had one string left. The dancers would give him a penny or two and he would go home to his wife, tell her to hold open her apron, and pour all the coins into it.

Wadenhoe hosted some of the finest fiddler players in the north of the county. In the early years of the twentieth century, one of them, Jim Smith, was said to have walked along the street during one wet Christmas Eve, playing with damp strings. As he went along, things started to happen, as described by one villager:

Cling! – one went. It was th' E. He carried on. We got half-way round; Ping! – the second one went. He finished up with the G-string. But he could still get the tune.

Another fiddler, named Curtis, would regularly walk from Pilton to Wadenhoe and play dance tunes, after which he made straight for the village pub. At closing time, he would return to the dance and be expected to play some more:

He'd walk in the room, put his foot round the leg of the chair and kick it halfway across the room, and then he'd sit down on the floor. And, boy, couldn't he play! He'd play there the polka and he wouldn't half make 'em do it. And there were some of the old gals that were getting on for sixty!

At Syresham in the nineteenth century, dances were held on the village green and even in the skittle alleys, such as the Bell Inn. Once again, music was provided

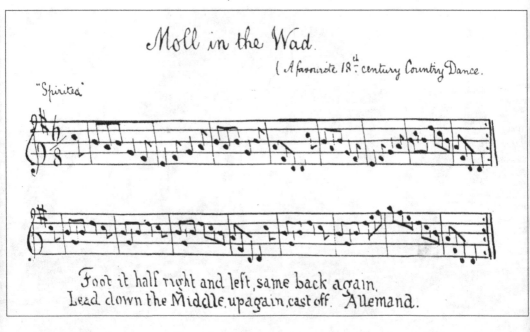

Part of the tune for the dance called Moll in the Wad.

by a fiddler, with the addition of a concertina player. Unusually perhaps, it was customary for anyone dancing to pay the musicians before a session, each player going round with a hat to collect a coin, a penny being the normal rate.

A popular dance in the county, Moll in the Wad, was recorded by schoolmaster and writer Charles Wise of Warkton in around 1905. It was an eighteenth-century courtship dance that was often performed in one form at family parties but, like many others, had virtually disappeared by the end of the nineteenth century. It was of a lively nature, made even more so by exaggerated steps and added lyrics which were improvised, sometimes bawdily, by the younger men participating. The additions would have fitted in well with the theme and title, Moll being a generic girl's name and Wad, a variation of 'wold', being an open space away from habitation, presumably for privacy, like Lovers Lane.

The Northampton Morris Men performing one of their Cotswold-style dances, 2002.

Morris dancing

Nothing today perhaps gives more of a taste of old England than morris dancing in the spring and summer. Though its origins are obscure, it is not based on an ancient fertility ritual but is probably of Arab origin, being part of a military training exercise with swords and dance-like movements to the beat of a drum. It was probably seen by knights in the Holy Land during the Crusades and consequently found its way back to Europe, where it gradually evolved into a dance at royal courts. Its modern form, known as Cotswold, has at least six morris men dressed in white, wearing ribbons and bells and waving handkerchiefs while performing intricate steps to the playing of a concertina or other instrument. The dance is part-pantomime and the role of its participants – who are based on traditional characters such as the Fool, Maid Marian or the Queen of May and a hobby horse – is usually, but not always, to mime traditional stories. Groups had, and still have, their own distinctive emblem or badge, usually depicting a real or mythological creature, such as a raven, eagle, dragon or, in the case of Northampton, a

The image of 'The Oss',
which is incorporated into the
design of the club badge of the
Northampton Morris Men.

unicorn. The Northampton group now have a horse-like creature, introduced in 1979 by one of their members, Ian Philips.

A early glimpse of a morris dancing group was given by Sternberg in 1851, when he described one of the characters as 'a clown or tomfool' with a feather in his cap, wearing an old quilt, covered with rabbit skins and holding a stick with an inflated bladder attached to the end by a cord.

The oldest surviving group in the county is at Brackley. Its roots lie in the seventeenth century, when semi-professional troupes usually performed under the patronage of local gentry. In 1603, another group, whose provenance is not recorded, performed at Althorp for James VI of Scotland, who was on his way to London to become King of England.

At the time of writing, there are eight groups based around the county: Moulton; Braybrooke; the Aynho Apricots, a female group; the Northampton Morris Men, founded in 1955; the Royal Oak, formed at Eydon in 1985; the

Rose and Castle, a group that was formed at Blisworth in 1977 and uses a form of clog dance that originated in the north-west of England; the Witchmen, who perform a style called Border Morris and are based at Kettering, or 'the Dark Side' as they prefer to call it; and Queen's Oak Morris, a female group formed at Potterspury in 1984 who also perform Border Morris dancing. This style of morris dancing, which comes from the English counties bordering Wales, is believed to be pagan in origin and is more boisterous and flamboyant, with an emphasis on the spirit of the dance rather than intricacy. The dance favours the use of sticks instead of hankies and its participants wear dark clothes and, more often than not, perform with blackened faces, in traditional guising fashion.

The Witchmen, a Northamptonshire-based group of Border morris dancers,
performing their unique form of the dance in dark garb and make-up at Ashton.

An old rhyme

A popular ditty that was once sung and played around parts of the county gives a colourful and humorous glimpse into the way in which our ancestors relaxed. It describes the vocal abilities of a group of participants at a village event:

> Old Gamble bawls, his daughter squawks
> Old Bodkin beats the time;
> They make a noise and fright the boys
> And spoil the doctor's rhyme.
>
> And Cooper Joe, he sings so low,
> We hate to hear him crow, oh, oh!
> Yet Baker Natt, he sings so flat,
> And flatter still sings Matt.

Folk music

Most of the folk songs sung in the county were variations of tunes sung in other parts of the country. One renowned folk song, which was derived from a seventeenth-century Scottish ballad known as 'Hame came our gude man at e'en', is about a drunken husband returning home and finding another man in his bedroom. Asking his wife several questions about the man, he is told it that it is something else – not what he thinks it is. The ballad later appeared elsewhere under various other titles such as 'Our Goodman', 'Four Nights Drunk', 'Drunkard's Special' and 'Seven Drunken Nights', the latter becoming a hit in the 1960s. The versions had different tunes and variations in the lyrics. The ballad even travelled across the Atlantic to the shores of America with new settlers, in a version known as 'Cat Man Blues', beginning with the lines:

> I came home last night, asked my wife 'what was that?' She said, 'Don't be suspicious, 'tis nothing but a cat'.

The Northamptonshire version is known as 'Youks, Bob!'. It is shown here in dialect form; 'cwots' are matted fleeces of wool. The song begins:

> I went into my che-amber to zee what i cud zee
> An' there I saw cwots hangin' up one, two and three.
> I went in to my lovon wife, to know how they cam there
> Wi'out the lafe o' me.
> 'Ya old fool, ya blood fool, why kaint ye very well zee?'

They are three blankets ya mudder sent to me.'
Youks, Bob, an' that's fun, blankets wi' buttons on,
The loke I nivver zee.

The Northamptonshire Poacher

Although other Midlands counties lay claim to this once popular, ancient ballad, inserting their name in the relevant place in the first and last verses of the lyrics, Northamptonshire has avidly asserted its ownership in the past and the song can still be heard occasionally around folk clubs around the county, in the version printed below:

When I was bound apprentice in famed Northamptonshire
Full well I served my master, for more than seven year
Till I took up with poaching, as you will quickly hear.
Oh, 'tis my delight on a shiny night, in the season of the year.

As me and my comrades were setting of a snare,
'Twas then we seed the gamekeeper – for him we did not care,
For we can wrestle and fight, my boys, and jump o'er anywhere!
Oh, 'tis my delight on a shiny night, in the season of the year.

As me and my comrades were setting four or five,
And taking on him up again, we caught the hare alive;
We caught the hare alive, my boys, and through the woods did steer.
Oh, 'tis my delight on a shiny night, in the season of the year.

I threw him on my shoulder, and then we trudgèd home,
We took him to a neighbour's house and sold him for a crown;
We sold him for a crown my boys, but I did not tell you where,
Oh, 'tis my delight on a shiny night, in the season of the year.

Bad luck to every magistrate that lives in Northamptonshire,
Success to every poacher that wants to sell a hare,
Bad luck to every gamekeeper that will not sell his deer.
Oh, 'tis my delight on a shiny night, in the season of the year.

The Sudborough Poachers

Poaching was a favourite theme in county folk songs. One particularly gory incident that occurred in the county in 1837 was recorded in a ballad that became
something of a best-seller at the time and was remembered well into the twentieth
century. It happened in Slade Field at Deenethorpe and is a notable example of
what could happen to poachers if caught in the act. A group of twenty-five men
from Sudborough and Brigstock had met up in a local hostelry and headed along
the green lanes with rabbit netting and sticks. However, a keeper on the Cardigan
estate at Deenethorpe had received intelligence of the intended incursion and
posted fourteen assistants at Burnt Coppice to lie in wait. The gang, with their
'bag' of 180 rabbits, were set upon and, after the ensuing mêlée, they fled, leaving
yards of netting behind as well as three of their members, who were taken away
for interrogation. The next morning, a gruesome discovery was made when a
fourth poacher was found disembowelled near the scene of the affray. Strangely, in
the ensuing post-mortem, the victim was pronounced to have died from exertion
and it was stated that no mark had been found on his body! The three prisoners
were tried at Northampton and found guilty but on account of good character
references, and having large families, were given a year's hard labour. One version
of the ballad gives the names of other gang members. This version was given to
the author by a descendant of one of those involved in the affray on that tragic
night long ago and is more in keeping with the village's original account:

In 1837 it plainly doth appear,
A bloody scene was felt most keen, until death did draw near.
Poor Samuel Mayes of Sudborough town, a lad of well-known fame,
Who took delight both day and night, to hunt the lofty game.
Mourn all you gallant Poacher men, poor Mayes is dead and gone
While our hero brave lies in his grave, as ever the sun shone on.
With nets so strong we marched along, unto brave Deenethorpe town,
With nut-brown ale that never will fail, with many a health drunk round.
Brave lunar light did shine that night, as we to the woods repaired,
True as the sun the dogs did run, to chase the timorous hare.
Then to the Poachers, the keepers they did start,
And in that strife took poor Mayes' life, they stabbed him to the heart.
For help he cried but was denied, there was no one that by him stood,
And there he lay till break of day, dogs licking his dear blood.
Farewell, dear heart, for I must part, from my wife and children dear,
Pity my doom – it was too soon, that ever I came here.
Farewell, those dear brave lads, whate'er revenge they held,
That cruel man with murderous hand, which cause me for to yield.

The ploughing match at Weldon in 1904

Ploughing matches, in which teams of ploughmen tried to outdo each other in a race to see who could be the first to complete a furrow or more, were very popular in the county until the First World War, after which time they disappeared as mechanisation transformed farming methods and ideas. The following verse was written by W. Dudley after one such event and several copies were made and handed down by descendants of the participants. It has also been set to music:

> 'Twas at a wedding party, two friends together met
> And thereupon decided, to have a little bet.
>
> The wager was on this wise, at a recent ploughing match;
> One team just finished in the time, the other were 'no catch'.
>
> William Northen argued that four hours, was not enough to plough
> A half acre in match style and that four and a half they should allow.
>
> John Singlehurst replied that he had a ploughman that could do
> An acre and a half of land in eight hours and horses two.
>
> 'Five pounds you can't!' Billy Northen said,
> 'Five pounds I can!' said John,
> 'Here, Clark, just take these two five pounds, and now the bet is on'.
>
> The bet was made, the day was fixed, the ground was measured out,
> John Clark was made the referee, to see it carried out.
>
> The day was fixed for Saturday, October twenty nine,
> At seven o' clock the whistle blew, the day was bright and fine.
>
> Clem Burbridge with the reins in hand, kept forging well ahead,
> At ten o' clock a respite had, and had his horses fed.
>
> Then Dr. Stokes came on the field with camera in hand,
> The team, the boss and referee, to snapshot on the land.
>
> Among the goodly crowd we saw Ted Chapman, Binder, Branson,
> Nor could we fail to miss him out, and that was old John Preston.
>
> He wins, he wins with time in hand, at half past one was done,
> And no-one now can honestly say, the match was not well won.

Charles Henry Montagu-Douglas-Scott.

The Witch of Weldon

Among the many ballads written by Charles Henry Montagu-Douglas-Scott of Warkton, grandson of the fifth Duke of Buccleuch and an enthusiastic collector and writer of county tales and legends, were two about local witches. Neither of the stories can be verified as fact but like so much of local history, who knows what may have been lost in the mists of time or never recorded in written form – after all, absence of evidence is not evidence of absence! One of the tales takes place in Stanion and is about an attractive young lady whose gaze at any young man would cause him to 'fall into dire calamity' of some kind. When matters come to a head, the villagers accost her and lead her blindfolded down to Harpers Brook, where she is ducked in the water several times, causing her to expire, whereupon the spells on the bewitched men are undone.

The Weldon ballad tells of two witches, one young, the other old, both having mixed fortunes within the community:

There lived a young Witch in old Weldon town – Heyday and be merry!
Her eyes they were black and her skin it was brown, As smooth and as brown as a berry!
Light was her tread and her lips were as red, As ripe and as red as a cherry!
With a folderol doll and a rumbelow, And a folderol dee, doo-day!

Over all the young shepherds she cast her spell – Heyday, and be merry!
Not a woman in Weldon that wishèd her well – As bonny and brown as a berry!
At the women she hissed, but the laddies she kissed – And luscious her lips as a cherry!
With a folderol doll and a rumbelow, And a foldero dee, doo-day!

There dwelt an old Witch in old Weldon town – Heigh-ho and aweary!
Her eyes they were black and her skin it was brown, All wrinkled and dirty and dreary!
Heavy her tread, not a tooth in her head, And her haunts and her habits were eerie!
With a folderol doll and a rumbelow, And a foldero dee, doo-day!

The shepherds laughed out when she passed them by, Heigh-ho and a weary!
Not a woman in Weldon but fearèd her eye, So black and so wicked and eerie!
She cursed as she went, all crippled and bent, All withered and tattered and dreary!
With a folderol doll and a rumbelow, And a foldero dee, doo-day!

The May songs of Northamptonshire

At one time, it was customary to take a May garland around the parish to call at
the more prosperous houses, such as a farm or manor house, where the leader of
the group would receive a dish of cream from the dairymaid. There is a reference
to this custom in the old May procession songs. Puritanism made its effect felt in
the words of the standard May song, especially in the northern area of the county.
Instead of reflecting the joy of the season, the lyrics were laden with admonition
against sin, and an emphasis on humility and repentance, some villages more so
than others. The versions sung at Nassington, Geddington, Oundle, Polebrook
and Northampton were long and full of reprimand:

> Here comes us, for May is up,
> Repent before you die,
> There's no repentance to be had,
> When in the grave you lie.
>
> To die in sin is a fearful thing,
> To go where sinners mourn,
> It would have been better for our souls
> If we had never been born.
>
> Now we've been travelling all the night
> And best part of the day,
> And now we're returning back again
> And have brought you a bunch of May.

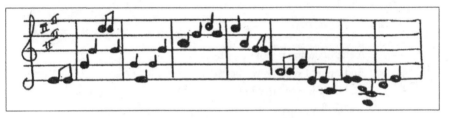

The tunes to two May songs. The tune above, top is sung around much of the county; the one below is a version from Brigstock.

A bunch of May, which looks so gay,
Before your door to stand,
'Tis but a sprout, but well spread-out
The work of our Lord's hand.

Repent, repent ye wicked men
And now we do begin,
To lead our lives in righteousness,
For fear we die in sin.

Take a Bible in your hands
And read a chapter through,
And when the Day of Judgement comes,
God will remember you.

Arise, arise you dairy maid,
Out of your drowsy dream
And step into your dairy quick
And fetch a cup of cream.

The tune to the Gretton and Pytchley May song.

> A cup of cream, it looks so white
> And a jug of your brown beer,
> And if we live to tarry in the place,
> We'll call another year.
>
> We've begun our song, we're almost done –
> No longer can we stay.
> God bless you all, both great and small –
> We wish you a joyful May.

Further south in the county, the religious content appears to have virtually disappeared. The version at Bozeat gives a good idea of what was sung:

> A branch of may, my dear, I say
> Before your door to stand,
> It is but a sprout, but well spread out,
> By the work of our Lord's hand.
>
> Arise arise your pretty maiden eyes
> Out of your drowsy dream,
> And step across your pretty dairy room
> And fetch a bowl of cream.
>
> Beside a cup of your fine cream
> A glass of water clear,
> And if I live to tarry round the town
> I'll call on you next year.

I have a purse which hangs on my arm
It's lined with a silken thread,
And all I want is a silver piece
To line it well instead.

So now I've sung my pretty maiden song
I can no longer stay,
So goodbye to you, God bless you all
This merry, merry month of May.

Of course there were other May songs. In *The Story of Blisworth*, written by Mona Clinch in 1939, Mona recalled the time when decorated pushcarts and May dolls were carried round the village. Apart from the standard May song, she remembered the lyrics to two others. The first song is:

This is May, fresh and gay
All is sweet and bright today
Come away, do not stay
Come abroad with us today.

The May Day parade outside Warmington School, *c.* 1916.

The second is the enchantingly hypnotic:

> Here we come a–Maying, through the meadows straying,
> Maying, maying, you and I.
> When the daisies grow, and drive away the snow,
> When the blackbirds sing for the dear warm spring,
> Then we come a-maying through the meadow,
> Straying, maying, maying you and I.

A fragment survives of a Woodford May song which was recorded by John Cole, a folklorist who died in 1848. He had a great interest in the customs and festivals of the village, publishing a great wealth of material. Though no tune was written down, the words have been set to music by Robin Hillman of the county folk group Ock 'n' Dough:

> Blackbirds and thrushes sing early in the morning,
> All go weeping with my garland, for the lad that I love.
>
> Here's cowslips and roses, and sweet smelling posies,
> All go weeping with my garland, for a lad that I love.
>
> These lilies and roses, and sweet blooming posies
> All go weeping with my garland, for a lad that I love.
>
> These bobbins and spangles, hang over these flowers,
> All go weeping with my garland, for the lad that I love.

The folk music scene today

Continuing a fine tradition in the county, there has been a tendency for modern folk groups based in the area to write songs about past events, which were notorious at the time but have long since been forgotten, and facets of everyday county life from a bygone era.

Sandy Denny, former singer in the renowned British folk-rock band Fairport Convention, lived for a while in a cottage in the south-west of the county at Byfield, where members of the band frequently stayed and became familiar with the county and its traditions. For many years now, the band have held an annual public get-together at Cropredy just over the county boundary near Banbury. Over the years, they have got to know the locality and some of its history. One such story was later turned into a song, 'Close To The Wind' by writer Stuart Marsden, which they duly recorded. It deals with the notorious Culworth Gang, a band of ten to fifteen local men who committed at least forty-seven robberies in the south-west of the county between 1777 and 1787. All were eventually caught after two of the gang were arrested at Towcester. They were all hanged, except for one member who was reprieved and transported to Australia.

The words of the song are the thoughts of one of the men as he lies 'in a darkened dungeon' awaiting his execution, musing about the gang's deeds which have finally come to an end. Some of the gang wrote 'letters of repentance' to their wives and families which still exist, including one by John Smith to his wife, Elizabeth, begging his children not to follow in his footsteps and to live a right-eous life. In a postscript to the letter he added:

> I desire my Son John to marry Elizabeth Beard and beg of him to be good to her and the Child, and take warning by me that they may live in Comfort. I desire you will take care of these lines and cause them to be read to all my Children every Sabbath Day.

Unfortunately, John ignored his father's request and and became a highwayman, finally being caught and executed, his mother bringing home the body in a don-key cart to Culworth.

In 1995, workshops were held around the county by Empty Pocket, a three-piece folk singing group consisting of Paul Rogers, who plays guitar, mandola and man-dolin; Yasmin Bradley, playing guitar and keyboard; and Mike Milne, playing guitar and bodhran. Their mission was to tease out tales and other information about Northamptonshire village life, both past and present. The visits proved fruitful and inspiring and led to the writing and recording of thirteen songs, all of which had catchy lyrics and tunes, with themes ranging from Mary Queen of Scots to the Ashton World Conker Championships. One of the songs was 'Boiled Egg and Rook Pie', considered by one reviewer to be a potential county anthem, comparable to 'On Ilkla Moor Baht 'At'. The pie was once very popular around the county, espe-cially with menfolk, and consisted of pastry containing the aforesaid ingredients, minus the feathers, of course! The humorous lyrics by Paul Rogers sing its praises, with a rousing chorus introducing the song and repeated after each verse:

> *(Chorus)*
> Boiled egg and rook pie is the village delight,
> You can eat it by day and dream of it by night.
> Of all English dishes there's none ranks so high
> As a slice of old Ashley's boiled egg and rook pie.
>
> It's a bad day for rooks on the 14th of June,
> 'Cos they hunt them with guns from the morning till noon.

And the ones that are prized and will boil up the best
Are the fledglings that perch on the edge of the nest.

Now Mrs Aldwinkle, she's up with the lark,
And does fifty press-ups while it's still dark.
And what is it keeps her so young and so spry
It's a generous slice of boiled egg and rook pie.

They had five alehouses, but now there's just one,
And you might well enquire where the others have gone,
The good folk of Ashley they drank them all dry,
After feasting all day on boiled egg and rook pie.

On the 14th of June, all you rooks must take care,
Of men with long guns and big nets, you beware,
And deep in the bowels of the nest you must lie,
Or else you'll end up 'neath the crust of a pie.

Ashley was also the source for another song, 'The Grand 5-Seater Loo'. Outside toilets were, of course, the norm for the majority of homes in some parts until modern times, and many of the older generation can remember a venture outside on a cold or rainy night to relieve themselves. There were variations from the single-seater toilet to the occasional double, or even triple, versions. Yasmin Bradley was inspired to write a song about one with five seats. Once again, there is an introductory chorus, which is repeated after each verse:

(Chorus)
There was Elsie, Bob and Vesta, George and Aunt Esther,
You never could be lonely when there was a loo to share,
You could pass the time of day there, catch up with gossip too,
In Ashley's great invention: the Grand 5-seater Loo.

Now Ashley might be small but the plumbing was unique,
Some called it an oddity and others said a freak.
But there was no denying in terms of sanitation,
Ashley in Northants was the forefront of nation.

For Elsie had wed Bob; they would never be apart,
For togetherness is the key in matters of the heart.
And especially late at night when the call of nature came,
With Bob from her side, it was never quite the same.

Now Bob was a romantic; he loved his Elsie dear,
He didn't like to think of her without his presence near,
On one St Valentine's, he got wood and a hammer too,
And he built his darling Elsie, an extension to the loo.

It wasn't many years before the children came along,
They seemed to like the company and didn't mind the pong.
For money was so short and house was so chilly,
You could spend a cosier evening on a 5-hole WC!

Family came to visit, friends came round to see,
Intelligence even came to Hitler's Germany.
But disaster was to strike as the bombs began to hum;
And the Grand 5-Seater Loo was blown to kingdom come.

The shoe industry which had flourished in the central area of Northamptonshire, helping to transform it from a predominantly agricultural county, declined sharply in the last quarter of the twentieth century, as a result of cheap foreign imports, causing unemployment and empty buildings. In 1993, Paul Rogers wrote a song vividly describing the situation, the lyrics of which would certainly strike a chord with those local people who were affected at the time. The opening verse and repeated chorus are the same:

What have they done with the workers in leather
The clickers, the lasters, the women and men
Who made boots and shoes for the poor and the gentry
In factories down by the banks of the Nene.

The tannery's closed and the signboard is fading,
They're using it now as a goods vehicle park,
But the smell of the leather still clings in the corners
And conjures up ghosts of the past in the dark.

The factory bands would all play on the feast day,
In uniforms braided with red, gold and blue,
And the children would dance to the drums and the trumpets,
Till the proud marching column had passed out of view.

There were boots for the soldiers and shoes for the townsfolk
And slippers that many a princess could wear,
Now they've all disappeared in the interests of progress,
Till very few know and even less care.

Another group on the county folk circuit are the four-piece Ock 'n' Dough, who take their name from the dish that was once so popular in Northamptonshire. They have built up a large repertoire of songs and gained a large following along the way over the years, performing lively tunes and ballads. Like Empty Pocket, they have also collected folk tales and stories of famous county events and in addition worked on a John Clare project, setting his poems to music.

One piece written by the group is based on the coming of the railway to Northamptonshire, the first appearance of which was in 1838, in the south-west of the county en route to Rugby via Blisworth. A line through the east of the county from Bisworth to Peterborough was subsequently opened in 1845, though not without controversy as can be seen in the following poem, 'The Northampton to Peterborough Railway (The Kettle of Hot Water)' written in 1843, two years before the opening. Such an innovation was seen by some as a threat to the traditional way of life in the county and arguably they were right, as an irrevocable transformation did take place. A tune has been composed by Janis Zakis, the accordionist, reflecting the movement of the train shown in the irregular metre of the lyrics:

> Of all the great wonders that ever was known,
> Some wonderful things have occurred in this town.
> The great Peterborough railway will beat them all hollow,
> And whosoever thought of it such a wonderful fellow.
> Why, 'tis said when it's finished, which will be in two years,
> If they can find fools to buy all the shares,
> That Northampton will become the first place in the nation,
> You won't know the old place by the great alteration.
> No drunken stage coachmen out breaking people's necks,
> Overturn'd into ditches, sprawl'd out on your backs.
> No blustering guard that through some mistake,
> Fires off his blunderbuss if a mouse should but squeak.
>
> *(Chorus)*
> Loaded with passengers, in and out, oh what a wonderful sight.
> A long string of carriages, on the rails, moved by a tea kettle spout.
>
> Oh no my good friends, when this railroad is finished,
> All coachmen and cattle will forever be banished,
> You will ride up to London in three hours and a quarter,
> With nothing to drive you, but a kettle of hot water.
> And any old woman that's got enough sense,
> By raking and scraping to save a few pence,
> If at service in London, she has got a 'darter',
> She may soon ride to see her by this kettle of hot water.

'Ev yer breakfast in Peterborough on tea, toast and butter,
And need not put yourself into a splutter,
You can travel to London and dine there at noon,
And take tea in Peterborough the same afternoon.

What a chance for the Cockneys, who are fond of fresh fish,
They will have all kinds alive on a dish,
Fen geese and fat turkeys and all such like good cheer,
There's be more go in one day than now goes in a year.
As to the nags that devour more corn in a year,
Than would support three parts of the neighbouring poor,
They'll all be taken to the knacker's yard,
And converted if possible into pork lard.
As to innkeepers and Ostlers, and all such riffraff,
This railway will disperse them before it like chaff,
They must all list for soldiers or take on for marines,
And curse the inventors of railway and steam.

All great coach proprietors that have rolled in their wealth
Are to ride upon the donkeys for the good of their health,
And to keep up their spirits are to strike up a theme,
Of the blessings of railroads and the virtues of steam.
So these are a few of the great alterations,
That this great Peterborough Railroad will make in the nation,
But if the shareholders be not careful and mind what they're after,
They might all get blown up by this boiler of hot water.
No drunken stage coachmen, etc. (as verse one)

Another interesting piece for students of county folklore has also been set to music by the group. Known as 'Irthlingborough Waterloo', it is based on a remark made by the Duke of Wellington, who on a visit to Woodford House to see a friend, General Arbuthnot, commented that the landscape between Woodford and Irthlingborough resembled that on which the Battle of Waterloo had been fought in 1815. Today, on the Finedon-Thrapston road, a fine round building built by the General after the visit can be seen. Known as Waterloo House, it was intended as a residential tower with an open gallery at the top for viewing purposes and has a stone tablet facing the fields, inscribed 'Panorama. Waterloo Victory, June 18, AD 1815'. Many years later, in 1913, Wellington's remark led to the appearance of a film crew on the site, in which the battle was re-enacted for the silent cinema. It was a memorable occasion by all accounts, due to the enthusiasm of the participants and the cuts and bruises sustained – just like those experienced by today's history re-enactment groups in order to achieve a degree of realism:

Waterloo House.

(Chorus)

Boneparte, oh Boneparte, come fight again, oh Boneparte.
The good men of this country free, will take you on for a small fee.
A hush fell over the battle scene,
As five hundred men with lances keen,
Readied for the cavalry charge,
With horses strewn from the knacker's yard.
The cameras roll, the extras yell,
As the unemployed from Northampton fell.
The screams of dying rent the air,
Not a life did the hussars spare.
And Boney rode his horse with pride,
The producer running at his side,
With a stick to prod the unwilling beast,
More used to pulling drays in streets.
For three long days the battle raged,
And in between with hard won wage,
The extras drank the pubs all dry,
Bringing a tear to a brewer's eye.
Soon came the end to all the fun,
And all the folk who'd battle done.
Retired with broken heads and bones,
Seven shillings and sixpence eased their groans.

In Comes I!

An integral part of the Christmas season, and sometimes beyond, was the mummers' play. The name is believed to come from the Greek 'mommo', meaning a mask, and in ancient and medieval times mummers were singers, dancers and musicians wearing animal costumes, such as the head of a stag or horse, for courtly entertainment. The later form, which appeared embryonically during the seventeenth century, was a play which took its basic derivatives and cast from the incredibly popular tale 'The Seven Champions of Christendom', which had been published in1596, together with other ingredients which came from a civic play produced in London during 1550s and other Tudor pageants. By 1730, the standard form of the play was well and truly in place.

Its theme was based on the ancient battle between good and evil or, on a deeper level, winter fighting spring, though it is extremely doubtful whether the players knew this, for their main purpose was to have a bit of seasonal fun and to make some money to share out among themselves. Apart from the two fighting opponents, the other characters would include someone to introduce the play, one or two doctors, perhaps the hero's mother, and one or two entertaining personalities to wind up the performance and collect money. Unlike a Hollywood movie, the hero gets killed in combat but is miraculously revived by a boastful doctor who has travelled far and wide. The names of the characters changed over the years, according to what was fashionable or by local interpretation. The hero could be St George, King George, Robin Hood or some kind of military figure. His opponent might go under the name of Turkish Knight, Saracen Knight, Napoleon or be a dragon. Sometimes the hero's (unnamed) mother might be present, and the healer could be Father Christmas, or a doctor who might be named after a local person or after something rhyming with 'blood' such as Rudd or Mudd. The name Mudd is of interest since Dr Mudd was a real person who was notorious after the American Civil War for giving medical aid to the fleeing assassins of Abraham Lincoln, which consequently gave rise to the expression 'your name is mud'. The strange characters who conclude the performance might be a Fool, Beezlebub or Big Head – 'big in head, small in wit'. At one time, Aynho had a motley collection of characters in its version of the play: an old Mother Christmas with a broom, King George, the Duke of Cumberland, Dr Gullet, Dr Phurcy, Beezlebub, Short Shirt Jinny, and Old Big Yead Jack with his bag on his back. Whatever their names, the characters would colour their faces and wear strange clothing which might be covered with ribbons and strips of parchment, partly to avoid recognition and partly to reflect the nature of their role.

Interesting versions took place in the south of the county. At Syresham, a pre-First World War play included a molly, the Duke of Cumberland, King George and two doctors, one of whom was unnamed and the other called Jack Finney with a bottle of miraculous elecampane. In this play, however, when George is revived and rises, he starts fighting again! The two adversaries have to be parted by Molly, after which Beezlebub comes on the scene with his dripping pan, followed by Big Head to perform and conclude the play as a musician. An affectionate tribute to the old tradition in the village was performed in the 1990s with a host of interesting characters beginning with a molly with long grey hair who introduced the cast, followed by St George and the Turkish knight as military adversaries, one of whom brandished a pig bladder filled with peas as a weapon. There were also two doctors, one of whom was seen to be a 'useless braggard', and Beezlebub 'ridden as a black nag'.

Perhaps the most unusual form of the play performed in the south of the county – or anywhere else for that matter – was that at Thenford, where more abstract names were given to the two opponents, and Beezlebub was promoted to introducing the play. There were eight players, including the doctor's horse and a treasurer. The faces of the characters were daubed in black (using burnt cork), white chalk and yellow ochre. Beezlebub wore coloured patches and a paper cap and carried a broom. The two adversaries were Activity, who wore a fox- or hareskin cap and tippet (a fur covering over the shoulders), while Age wore a smock with rags and a cap with a sprig of holly attached. The doctor wore a jacket, a sheepskin shirt with a bell at the back and a cap also with a sprig of holly. Jem Jacks, his assistant, wore rags stuffed with straw and held the box of magic pills, and the Fool carried a whipcord on a stick, with a bean-filled inflated bladder at one end:

> *Beezlebub*: In comes old Beezlebub, on his shoulders he carries a club,
> In his hand a dripping pan – don't you think he's a funny old man?
> Sweep, sweep! Make room for me
> And all my jolly company!
>
> Enter *Activity*: Activity, Activity, if any man interrupts me,
> I'll cut him down as small as a fly,
> And send him to the cook to make a mince pie!
>
> Enter *Age*: I am the man that dare to bid you stand
> Although you say you'll cut me down as small as a fly
> Although you say you'll cut me down for a mince pie
> Guard your body and guard your blow
> And see who shall on the ground be so.
> A battle! A battle! Between you and I
> And see who on the ground shall lie.
>
> (Age *knocks* Activity *down and calls the Doctor*)
>
> *Age*: Five pounds I will give for the three farthing doctor!

Two scenes from the Moulton mummers' play, performed annually on Boxing Day. *Above:* St George and the Turkish Knight are in combat; *below,* ina reversal of roles, it is the Turkish Knight who appears to be slain! Here the mysterious doctor revives him.

Enter *Doctor*. I am the doctor!

Age: Where do you come from?

Doctor. From France, from Spain, to fetch the dead to life again!

Age: What can you cure?

Doctor. I can bring an old woman to me that's been seven years dead
And seven years buried, in her dark earthly bed
If she takes one of my pills, it will fetch her to life again!
Itch, stitch, palsy and gout –
Pains within and pains without!

At this point the doctor gives a pill and waves his hands and Activity rises up, restored to life once again, to the cheers of the crowd. Then the Fool rattles his bladder at each of the characters and knocks each one down. They all get into a wild scrummage on the floor and mayhem ensues, to the cheering, shouting and laughter from the crowd, while the treasurer goes round shaking the money box for contributions.

Another version of the play, this time from Boughton, has come down to us and is reproduced below. In order to perform the play, the mummers followed the normal pattern of going from house to house but instead of knocking at the door, they tapped on the window of the largest room. To refuse them admittance was considered a crime and would lead to misfortune befalling to the occupants.

Herald: Make room, make room! Every garland all.
On Christmas Eve we're bound to call,
And if there is no offence,
When we're done, we'll all march hence.

Little Whit: In comes I who's never bin yet
With my big head and little wit –
My head is big, my wit is small,
I come tonight to please you all!

Beezlebub: In comes I Beezlebub – on my shoulder I carry a club.
In my hand a frying pan, don't you think I'm a handsome man?

Soldier. As I was passing by the school,
I heard you call my brother a fool.
Stand back, stand back, you dirty dog,
Or by my sword you'll die,

I'll string your giblets round your neck,
And make the buttons fly!
(*They fight*)

Doctor: In comes I, the noble doctor from Spain,
To raise the dead to life again.

Soldier: What can you cure?

Doctor: I can cure ixy, pixy, palsey and gout.
I'll cure this man, there is no doubt.
Here's a pill for you, young man.
If this does not work between now and eight o' clock tomorrow,
You will be a dead man, but in a trance,
I pray young man, now get up and dance!'

(*He does so to lots of cheers and applause*)

On one occasion at Northampton in the nineteenth century, six mummers in white garments seized the maid when she answered the door and, in a show of pretence, muttered threats to her. This had been arranged earlier when she had been bribed to play along with the scheme. She consequently took them into the dining room while the surprised family were eating supper, whereupon the mummers began to act out the play. One of the performers could not help laughing and gave away his identity – he was a member of the family from next door, who were all taking part!

Verse

The Lynches are a wooded area, originally ridges of ancient ploughland, over-looking the Nene, stretching down a slope from Thorpe Achurch towards Lilford Hall. From the eighteenth century, they became celebrated as a renowned venue for game shooting, attracting participants from far and wide. The following verse, 'Ballad of the Lynches', written in 1879 anonymously by G.W., gives a flavour of one such event, describing it like a military operation and mentioning names of people and places connected with the county, though many today might object to words like 'hero' when describing the actions of those involved! There is said to be a tune to accompany the words, but attempts to trace this have so far failed:

The Christmastide had passed away; the New Year had begun:
'The Lynches must be shot today', cries Lilford's eldest son.
The Lord of Lilford he had gone a-sailing on the main,

And flies the Royal Squadron Flag adown the coast of Spain.
His lady fair and sons at home – two gallant youths, I wot;
And they have sworn a mighty oath, 'The Lynches must be shot'.
Now summon forth the beaters, that they the woods may beat,
And promise them a guerdon of bread, and ale, and meat.
No matter though the woods be thick, the beater knows no fear:
I trow they would do anything for glory and for beer.
Forth troop they at the summons from all the country's side;
From Achurch and from Pilton they march with honest pride,
From Wigsthorpe's distant hamlet (where Nevitts all were born),
Prepared to face the thickest brakes, and brave the sharpest thorn.
'Come, look alive, you beaters!' it is the warning cry
Of Jones, the great head keeper, from whom the poachers fly;
A very small acquaintance with Northamptonshire he owns,
Who does not know the voice and form of Mr Samuel Jones.
Tight are the breeches of the youth who loves the fox to chase,
And tight the garments worn by those who royal circles grace;
But tighter far than such as these, by many a painful inch,
The breeches worn by Jones the day on which they shoot the Lynch.
A group of friends stand round him; but none such garments own:
Donald (who comes from where such things are very near unknown) –
Harvey from Farming Woods, is there, a friendly face to show;
Stout Dixey comes from Titchmarsh, Perkins from Wadenhoe;
George Hollyce, who surveys the nets; and, radiant as a star,
The purple nose of Nevitt scents luncheon from afar.
And now the beaters stand in line as if 'twere for a race,
And Mr Jones looks down to see as if each is in his place.

From Oundle and from Thrapston, the traveller, half afraid,
With wonder hears the thunder of the distant cannonade;
And the crafty poacher sighs to think that he and his good mate
May pay a visit to the Lynch, but just a night too late.
Now fierce the combat rages, and valiant deeds are done,
And each turn destroys the foe with glorious feats of gun.
'Twere hard to single out a name to trace on history's page,
Amid that band of heroes of every size and age;
Still must we speak of Burroughes, a man of Norfolk fame,
Who 'fetched em down', as Jones observed, with more than mortal ain;
Tom proved himself a worthy son of him now far away;
And Mr John the spot was on through all that famous day;
Still the red hat of Lyveden was foremost in the fight;
And Hunt, of Wadenhoe, 'pulled them down' when almost out of sight.

And long as we may hope to live, still will the tale go round,
Of how we shot the Lynches when the snow was on the ground.

The celebrated county verse 'Pancakes and Fritters' is a variation of 'Oranges and Lemons'. The fruit first arrived in London during the Stuart period and the name 'Oranges and Lemons' was first recorded in 1665 as 'a square for eight dance'. Elements of this were used to accompany the rhyme, which did not appear until 1744, and in early versions it had additional lines including 'Old shoes and slippers, say the bells of St Peter's' (shoes were traditionally thrown at newly married couples). The St Peter's line was retained for the first version appearing in the county but 'pancakes and fritters' replaced the initial words. This version was short and applied only to the town of Northampton, mentioning four parish churches and St John's Hospital:

'Roast beef and marsh mallows'
Say the bells of All Hallows,
'Pancakes and fritters' say the bells of St Peter's
'Roast beef and brides' say the bells of St Giles'
'Pokers and tongs' say the bells of St John's
'Shovel, tongs and poker' say the bells of St Pulchres'. [Holy Sepulchre]

Later, a longer version appeared, which mentioned other places around the county:

'Pancakes and fritters,'
Says the bells of St Peter's.
'Where must we fry 'em?'
Says the bells of Cold Higham.
'In yonder land furrow',
Say the bells of Wellingborough.
'You owe me a shilling,'
Says the bells of Great Billing.
'When will you pay me?'
Says the bells of Middleton Cheney.
'White bread and sop,'
Says the bells at Kingsthorp.
'Trundle a lantern',
Says the bells of Northampton.

It is often erroneously said that these rhymes were recited on Pancake Day but there is no recorded evidence for this. There certainly was a custom in the county of putting a corn dolly in a furrow on Plough Monday to bless and encourage the coming year's growth, for which there may be hidden evidence in line six of the rhyme, a pancake or something else made of corn being used as a substitute.

Richard Braithwait (1588-1673) was a writer of verse, whose *Tales of Drunken Barnaby* were posthumously published in 1716, nearly 100 years after they were written, under the pen name Coryambaeus. The tales describe the escapades of an inebriated traveller making his way from London to Westmorland via Wisbech. En route, he enters Northamptonshire, where he drinks his way through the county, stopping at Daventry, Weedon, Towcester and finally on the northern boundary at plague-stricken Wansford, where he falls asleep on a haystack which gets swept up in a flood and carries him along the Nene. Some way along the river, he awakes. Some bystanders ask him where he is from and in his befuddled condition he mentions his homeland, England. The event is celebrated in the name and on the sign of a riverside hostelry at Wansford bridge, the Haycock Hotel. The verses were reprinted in *Northamptonshire Notes and Queries* in 1899:

> Thence to Daintree with my Jewell, Famous for a Noble Duell,
> Where I drunk and took my Common, In a Taphouse with my Woman;
> While I had it, there I paid it; Till long chalking broke my credit.

> At Daintree earely might you find me, But not th' Wench I Left behind me,
> Neare the Schoole-house where I boused, Her I sought but she was spoused,
> Which I having heard that night-a, 'Farewell (quoth I) Proselyta'.

> Thence to Wedon, there I tarried, In a Waggon to be carried;
> Carriers there are to be found-a, Who will drink til th' world run round-a:
> 'Pay good fellows, I'le pay nought heere, I have left more than I brought heere.'

> Thence to Tosseter on a Tuesday, Where an artfull Batchler chus'd I
> To consort with; we ne're budged, But to Bacchus revels trudged;
> All the Night-long sat we at it, Till we both grew heavy pated.

> (*He then proceeds to Wansford*)

> On a Hay-cock sleeping soundly, Th' river rose and tooke me roundly
> Downe the current; people cryed, Sleeping downe the streame I hyed;
> 'Where away', quoth they, 'from Greenland?'
> No; from Wansforth-brigs in England!

Dialect and Glossary

In Britain we commonly refer to a north/south divide to show differences in lifestyle and wealth. Yet the term could well be applied in a historical sense to Northamptonshire, a county whose dialect and customs were shaped by circumstance depending on which part you lived, whether south, centre or north. The reason that the county is unique is its part-Saxon and part-Danish Viking heritage. The Treaty of Wedmore in AD 793 resulted in Northamptonshire being left with much of its area under the Danelaw, the boundary set at Watling Street, which is now the A5.

The arrival of the Danes and other Norsemen was a good thing for the development of English. They did get on well with the Anglo-Saxon inhabitants (despite the bias of early writers), intermarrying with them, and merging into society, with a combination of both languages forming the names of some of the county's settlements. Their language was identical in many ways but simpler and this helped modify the more heavily inflected Old English, simplifying it and adding several monosyllabic words to the vocabulary. In addition, Northamptonshire, like other counties under the Danelaw, had a range of local, more specific, words. In Danish grammar, the singular and plural forms for 'to be' are the same: 'er', for am, is and are. This influence can be seen in old dialect of the county, in 'I are', 'he are', 'it are' and so on.

The county was divided into two areas of dialect – the Anglo-Saxon area and the area under the Danelaw – with a third appearing around the centre where the two areas met, which synthesised into a standard, perhaps purer, form. In all parts of the county, it was the vowels that had the greatest diversity of sound variation. The old Midlands vowel inflections were apparent: for example, 'sheep' would sound like 'ship', 'dog' like 'dig' and 'voice' like 'vice'. Other peculiarities were 'ees' used for 'yes', 'sen' for 'self' – as in 'hissen' and 'hersen' – 'istray' for 'yesterday' and 'nunch' for 'lunch'. The old Anglo-Saxon (and modern German) plural ending '-en' was often used instead of '-s', as in 'housen'. In common grammar, the verb 'to be' would take the following forms: 'bin' instead of 'are', 'bistn't' for 'aren't', 'be' for 'am', 'beant' or 'baan't' for 'am not' and 'wur' for was. 'Wo't' meant 'won't' and 'caint' was 'can't'. 'Must' was 'mun' and 'mustn't' was 'maunt'.

When Anne Baker and Thomas Sternberg brought out their respective pioneering books on the county's dialect and words in the mid-nineteenth century, they were both limited to what research had been made in the fields of etymology and philology at that time. Since then, great advances have been made. Both Baker and Sternberg were, however, somewhat guilty of not isolating county words from regional words and hence there was a mixture of both in their glossaries. This does not matter too much, since a lot of word exchange had been going on through the ages and still does, as more 'outsiders' come into the county bringing new words and pronunciation, which become part of everyday speech and vocabulary. A good example can be found in the Corby area today, where there is much Scottish inflection and a common expression is 'yous' – as in 'see yous later' – whether addressing one person or several. A substantial immigrant population from many Eastern European countries was initially based in the same town and has since spread elsewhere, quickly becoming integrated and adding new forms of dialect and customs to the county's heritage.

Much of the old dialect of the county had already disappeared by 1850, a casualty of time, custom and demographic change. What survives today is also in danger of vanishing, yet you can still frequently hear expressions like 'me duck', meaning 'my dear', in the street, in a shop or at the market.

Most glossaries tend to be in the form of a dictionary, listing words alphabetically. However, with such a rich heritage of vocabulary and dialect in the county, an effort has been made in this section to group words and phrases thematically to simplify and facilitate the task for the reader.

Creatures and insects

arriwig, battle twig	earwig
asker	newt, lizard
bandy	stickleback
bee skip	beehive
bree, cleg	gadfly
bum	buzz
chilp	chirp
cock, cogger	banded snail
conker	small caterpillar
dodman	snail
emmer	ant
forkin Robin	earwig (north)
goggle shell	large snail shell
Harry-long-legs	daddy-long-legs
hornet	large dragonfly
hug-hog	hedgehog
Jenny Spinner	daddy-long-legs
joey	rabbit
kit	young ferret or hare
lady cow, clock-a-clay	ladybird
long-legged tailor	daddy-long-legs
midgeon	gnat
miller	moth
mouldiwarp	mole
mouldy band	ant hill
Old Sally or Sarah	hare (young or old)
paddock, poddock	frog or toad
pismire	ant
pollard, poll-head	tadpole
polly wriggle, pot ladle	tadpole
powhead	tadpole
puddock (ON)	buzzard, kite
pug	fox or squirrel
puss	hare
ram-cat, gib-cat	mole
tiddy hog	millipede
titty puss	kitten
urchin	hedgehog
woodseer	froghopper

Birds

bluecap	blue tit
butter bum(p)	bittern
cawdy-mawdy	seagull
clodhopper	wheatear
cobweb	spotted flycatcher
eekle	woodpecker
fern owl	nightjar
firetail	redstart
hoolet	owl
knave	blackbird
neb (ON)	beak,bill
Old Frank	heron
Philip	sparrow
piana	magpie
pink	chaffinch
redcap, proud tailor	goldfinch
Royston crow	hooded crow
sheep rack	starling
stag	male turkey
starnel	starling
writing/scribbling lark	yellowhammer

Flowers, plants, trees

akkern	acorn
bloodwall, bloody warrior boodle	wall flower corn marigold
bunny rabbit	antirrhinum
bunts	puffballs
butter and eggs	daffodil
Candlemas bell	snowdrop
cat haws	hawthorn berries
Daneweed	field eryngo
deal apples	fir cones
featherfew	feverfew
frog seats	toadstools
hell weed	bindweed, honeysuckle, red clover
Kiss me at the garden gate	pansy
palm	sallow
pisshead	dandelion
Queen Anne's Needlework	geranium
slon, slun	sloe
sweethearts, beggar weed	goose grass
lice weed,	"
scratch weed	"
bur weed	"
water blob	marsh marigold
witchen	rowan
yellows	dyer's greenweed

Actions

ax	ask
ball off	finish quickly
baste	beat severely
batten	work hard
battle	trudge around the home in wet or muddy shoes
bear a bob	help out
bear the bell	excel at
becall	abuse
beggar	overwork the land (exhaust the soil)
belice	beat with a strap
bewottle	confuse
bezzle	guzzle down
bibber	shiver with cold
blaat	spread gossip
blink	evade (a question)
bob	move suddenly
boffle	thwart
butter the paws	coax, wheedle
chopse	talk loudly and vulgarly
chumble	nibble
clam, clem	starve
clang	eat voraciously
clip	climb
crack	boast
cree	soak clothes in lye
croffle	walk with difficulty
dare (north)	frighten
dather, dither	shake with fear/cold
delve (north)	dig
disannul	abolish
dixen, dizen	dress showily
drib, dribble	milk a cow dry
drop out	quarrel
flit (ON)	move, remove
friddle	waste or pass time
fridge	rub
gammock	go house to house in a festive mood
glize	stare
grin	sew/stitch poorly
gern, gurn	(1) yawn, grin (2) look or speak maliciously
get a planting	get a beating
gline	look sideways
goddle	furtively deceive
gollop	eat greedily
grin	to sew poorly – the stitches so wide apart they look like teeth
gulsh	drink voraciously
hag	tire out
hedge hog	reveal, divulge
hike	move hastily
hill (up)	cover, clothe
hockle	shuffle along
jilt	throw, fling
job	poke, jab
keek (ON)	peep
klip (ON)	climb (e.g. a tree)
lape	walk through mud
learn	teach
limb	pull about roughly
match	manage
maunder	matter
moil	tire, toil
moon	stare
nanny	go at full speed
nap (ON)	catch hold of
offer	hold something in place
play with a bear	give a disadvantage to
play gooseberry	get one's own back
prig	steal
pull back	sit back
pun about	be slow and fussy
quarter	drive a cart carefully avoiding ruts
quilt	beat, hit
quirk	turn quickly
rake	wander around
roil	disturb (water)
rub up	kid or fool someone
rym	move, remove
science	walk self-consciously
scrigg	squeeze
slive	slip past
smore	smoulder
sound for	long for
sprottle	sprawl
take on	fret, grieve

tell	(1) recognise
	(2) count (ON)
	(3) speak effectively
tind, tin	light, kindle
toot	peep, espy
tramp	go on foot
trig	trot, run
whang	throw or strike violently
be wonted	get used to
yawp	talk noisily

Descriptions

addled	rotten, decayed
adeal, adell	like, resembling
arseways	stubborn
article	useless, pitiful
astrut	prominent, protruding
bashy	gloomy, dirty
begrudge	envy
beholden	indebted, obliged
belegged	unable to keep up with someone
belike	probably
bishoped	confirmed
bodily back and edge	entirely
brackly	brittle, crumbly
brangled	confused, mixed up
chocky	rutted, uneven (roads)
churly	hard, dry
clagg'd	having wet, muddy petticoats(from dirty paths/lanes)
claggy	muddy, dirty (paths)
dannies	hands
clammer	parched with thirst
clapered	mud-spattered
clean	completely
clumpy	bulky
complin	impertinent
corned	drunk
cottering, croodling	(1) sitting close to a fire (2) reluctant to leave
cotting about	tied close to
cruel	excessive
crumpy	crisp

dark	blind
deadly (well, bad)	really
deep	crafty
doddy	marshy, waterlogged
drearisome	lonely (road, place)
drowking	drooping (from heat)
dwizy	sleepy
eyeable	pleasant to the eye
flaggy	large and thick
frem (ON)	(1) strange (person)
	(2) juicy (fruit, food)
frousty	filthy
googy	marshy
gravelled	mortified, vexed
great	familiar, intimate
hard on	nearly
hip and thigh	completely
hob-job	clumsy
hum-strum	unskilled
in the dismals	sad
kick, kicking	height of fashion
moozing	dozing
mated	confused, puzzled
moping	dreamy, vacant
muggy (ON)	mouldy
naish	tender, delicate
nuzzling	caressing, nestling
pranked	dressed up
puggy	damp
puling	whimpering, whining
punning	dreamy, inactive
pure	extremely, very
queachy, quaggy	marshy
randy	unruly, rowdy
rash	dry, over-ripe
rousing, roozing	great (roaring fire)
roiling	fidgety (child)
scraggling, tousy	disorderly, wild
shanny	shy
sloomy	gloomy
sprack	shrewd, intelligent (used around Whittlewood)
sqeauchy	waterlogged
starky	stiff, shrivelled up
swaly	cool and shady
tatered	worn out, tired
temporary	dilapidated
tight	clean, tidy

Threshing at Weldon in the 1890s.

trig (ON)	neat, trim
unkid, unked	dreary-looking (place), sinister (feeling)
waffling	non-stop barking
watchet	pale blue
work brittle	industrious

Agricultural

assil-tree	wheel axle
aum, awm (ON)	beard on head of barley
baffled	corn beaten down by the wind
bagpipes	flail
bait	worker's lunch
batting (south)	bundle of straw bound with bands after threshing
bolting, bottling (north)	bundle of straw bound with bands after threshing

beastings	first milk after a cow has calved
bells	ears of oats
binstead	a bay in a barn for storing the corn
bleed	good yield
blind	poor yield
blow	blossoms of fruit trees or flowers
bone, bun	to mark out land or timber for felling
bottle, costerel	small wooden barrel of beer for field workers
bout	ploughing once along a field and back again
brackle	break up soil or stone
brake	(1) narrow strips of shrub-covered land (2) field after reaping
brands	pitch used for sheep marking (busting)

brawn	a boar pig	fantome	poor quality or 'sickly' corn
broad cast	sow seed by hand		
bull-pated grass	a crop driven by wind and rain into an eddy	fezzle	pig litter
		fog	coarse grass avoided as food by cattle
cave	(1) separate wheat from chaff	goggy, boggy, soppy	heavy soil
	(2) break up large clods of earth	gratten	stubble
		to glean, lease	gather loose corn
cavings	chaff	grudgeons, sharps	coarse wheatmeal
cazzleby	sickly looking cattle	hain	lay a field for mowing (by taking out cattle)
clat	cow pat		
colly fleece	black wool	hog, teg, hoggard	a yearling sheep
cradging	mending river banks to prevent overflow of water into a field	to keel or raddle	use red stain for marking sheep
		Jinny	large shire horse
		keep	grass as food
dibbling	making holes in the soil to seed corn	lath (ON)	granary, loft in a barn
double couple	twin lambs	laughter	(1) roost (2) gather heaps of grain
drape	cow that can no longer give any milk	mag	penny
		mawkin	(1) scarecrow (2) hare
drug	heavy cart		
dudman	scarecrow	pie	a pit for storing root crops
eddish, aftermath	second crop of grass after mowing	piggle	root out potatoes by hand

A humorous sign recently seen along a quiet road near Southwick.

piling	breaking off beards of thrashed barley using a piling iron
poached	marks in pasture made by the feet of livestock
pollard cow	one without horns
puggens	barley husks
quail	to 'turn' or curdle milk
queach	unploughable land adjacent to arable land
raddle, ruddle	red sheep dye (red ochre with grease)
shorts	fine bran
screwing	mean, stingy
smut,	bunty, blunt stick, half, flail
thone	moist, damp (crop)
tig-rigs	pigs
yolk	grease on wool

People

Amy Florence	a shabbily dressed female
anointed rascal	a troublesome boy
avern, drab, fagot	coarse and uncouth in dress and manners
drotchell, flommax	coarse and uncouth in dress and manners
bab	baby
barley bump	sluggard
brother chip	fellow worker
cade	spoilt child (also a pet lamb)
cank	gossipmonger
chap	husband
come day, go day	a person who wastes money, spending and never saving
Cousin Betty	insane person
Bess o'Bedlam	insane person
crab stick	sour-tempered person
dawdle	a female slow in speech and manner

dilling	youngest in a family
dotkins	spitting image
emmot	a lively person
fiz-gig	a wild flirty girl
guttling	a voracious eater
half and halfer	a gay person
jingle brains	a wild, noisy male
lown	peasant
Joan/John Blunt	one who freely speaks her/his mind
John George	a person with little knowledge of grammar
molly-cot	a man tied to his wife's apron strings, especially in the kitchen
old-fashioned	a child quiet in manner
pigeon	young girl
raffling	wild, unsteady person
rattle cap or pate	a flirty, chatty girl
scribe	a skinny person
shackler	a dishonest or idle person
shiner	a clever person
splatherdab	a woman who goes from house to house spreading gossip
sprunny	lover, sweetheart
tool	a frail elderly person
trolley mog	a slovenly person
tyke (ON)	an annoying person
urk	small child or person
whopstraw	peasant (derogatory)
younker	youngster

General

appern	apron
ballet	ballad
barnacles	spectacles
bass	hassock (church)
beetle	heavy wooden mallet

Right: One of several pumps that once served the villagers of Middleton and Cottingham.

Below: A firehook for pulling burning thatch from cottage roofs; it is kept in the church of St John the Baptist, Harringworth.

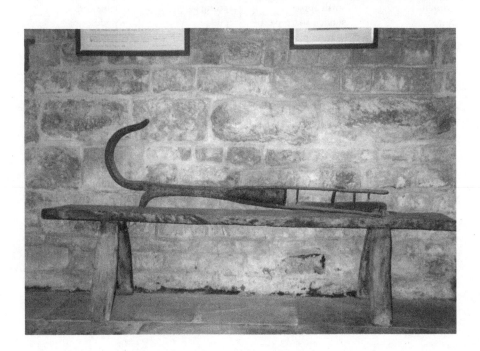

berrin	funeral	haulm	stubble for
besom	broom		thatching
bever	refreshment	holt	field
bib	pinafore	house	the best room
bob	bunch	hust (ON)	cough
buffle greens	Brussels sprouts	ing	water meadow
bummer	foreman	jessup	juice, syrup
budget	gossip, news	jitty	alleyway
blunt	money	jog	small load
breeze	row, quarrel	jorum, crag, crog	a lot, great quantity
butter pound	money	kelter	money
cabbage	leather offcuts	kids	pea or bean pods
cag–mag	tough meat	lather	ladder
chats	sticks to put on a	licker	puzzle, mystery
	fire	Lob's pound	bridewell, gaol
chump	a thick log for	lumping penn'orth	good bargain
	burning on the fire	masterpiece	wonder, marvel
cockers	gaiters, or legs of	muffle greens	Brussels sprouts
	old stockings to	nappy	ale
	keep snow out of	onkers	knees
	shoes	pad	path
colly	black soot from a	pass	state, condition
	pot	pen and ink	sound of footsteps
conger, congoes,	cucumber	penthouse	hen coop
conkers, cowcumber	cucumber	piccolo	shotgun
coshes, quashes	pea or bean pods	pother	dust
coverslut	a clean pinafore	pot house	low-class public
	over a dirty dress		house
creeses	watercress	pot wabbler	housekeeper
crinklin	small apple	prong	table fork
dag	sudden sharp pain	pudge	puddle
delf	gravel or old	rammel	building rubble
	stone pit	rig	joke, trick
disabil	working clothes	rounds	rungs on a ladder
doddle	cigarette end	rout	hearty welcome
eay	pond	runnel	small stream, brook
fad	feast, gathering	scrat,scrawk	scratch, mark
fashion	health	shin timber	small piece of
feather legs	Brussels sprouts		firewood
fletches	pea or bean pods	shiver (ON skive)	slice of bread or
gadabout	wild gossip		meat
goat, gout	drain, ditch	spring	young tree
gotty	wet, boggy field	spud	weeding spade
gravel	ford	sukey	tea kettle
grammer	dirt, mire	take away	good appetite
grimmer south	large shallow pool	tegs	teeth
grip	narrow ditch	tell post	fingerpost,
grouse	gravel		waymarker
gudgell, pudgell	stagnant, muddy	till	money
	water	thrall	stand for a beer
			barrel

The clapper bridge, a primitive way of crossing water using stone slabs resting on pillars, on the Wilbarston/Stoke Albany parish boundary, one of only three surviving in the county today.

tizzy	sixpence	trucks	trousers
Tom Hackett	a beating	twang	(1) pungent taste
tot	half-pint mug		(2) acute toothache
tray	wash tub	yelk	egg yolk
tree	spade handle	yep	heap

Weather Lore

FROSTS

black frost	with no rime
sniveling frost, white frost	hoar frost
duck frost	slight frost at night, thawing in the morning – which ducks like
snow bones	remnants of snow after a frost
greasy	slippery after a slight frost

ICE

daggers	icicles
a snipe	a hanging icicle
cat ice	ice from which water has receded and which cannot support any weight
clock ice	ice which has cracked and formed various imaginative patterns, caused by pressure such as ice-skating on the surface, or by the displacement of an area of water beneath the surface.
to fret, forgive	to thaw

RAIN

gaudy or glaudy day	showery with gleams of sunshine
a night for lost souls	howling wind and rain
water gall	a second rainbow, a sign of rainy weather to come.
watery sunshine	a halo around the sun – wet weather to come
to wet	to rain slightly
a payling	a driving heavy shower
falling in planets	rain falling heavily in a field while an adjoining one stays dry.
glut	a long continuous spell of wet weather
donk, donkey (ON)	wet, moist, damp
to rain heavens hard	to rain heavily
lambing storm	sudden squall of rain or snow around March and April, with bright sunshine afterwards

CLOUDS

Billy Mums	approaching dark clouds
woolpack clouds	a rack of high clouds
Noah's Ark	a long dark cloud stretching across the sky, with a broad centre and tapering at each end, symbolising that a flood is on the way. However, if it extends in a south–north direction, good weather is assured. There was also a saying: 'East and west the sign of a blaze, north and south the sign of drought'.

OTHER

hunch weather	damp, cold, foggy
rawk (north)	mist, fog (adj: rawky)
thony	moist, damp
creamy weather	when the sky is suffused with thick haziness (not cloudy)
sniving	raw and sleety
shuff	a sudden gust

shufty	changeable with a wind blowing strongly at times
whirlipuff	a sudden gust whipping up dust into an eddy
pothery	muggy
chaps, chops	cracks in the earth after a long period of hot, dry weather
Blindman's holiday	when it is too dark to see or work properly

Calling animals

Various calls were used to attract or repulse certain animals when carrying out tasks around the farm or fields:

chook! chook!	for attracting hens
coop! coop!	calling up a horse from the fold or common
coop, wench!	calling cows for milking
cup, cup!	calling chickens together, getting a horse ready for mounting, or making a draught horse approach the driver
hoo'e, hoo'e, hoo'e!	driving away pigs
shoo! shoo!	scattering hens
soo, soo, soo, my wench!	soothing cows when milking
suss! suss!	calling pigs
tig! tig! tig!	calling pigs

Expressions

about October	pregnant
a bag of moonshine	nonsense
as dry as a lime burner's hat	thirsty
I'll pay you at Tibbs Eve	never
It's Martin's masterpiece	it's a mystery
I've got a crow to pick with you	pick an argument
I was kept so long, I stood upon thorns	to become impatient
no pockets in shrouds	you can't take it with you
old Bushy's dead	old news
riding the pony	paying craftsmen for work not yet finished
the creaking gate hangs longer	an ailing person who outlives a healthier person.
them's at brings'll carry	used about gossips
to see a man, or my aunt, about a dog	to go to the toilet
to spin street webs	to walk around idly, gossiping house to house
when two Sundays meet	never (to express an impossibility)

FIELD NAMES

These are the original names that appear on maps and in deeds and records. Some of them still exist, though the vast majority have disappeared, many of the fields having been renamed or broken up during Parliamentary 'Inclosure'. More common names, such as those indicating direction (e.g. North Field), position (e.g. Upper Leys), size (e.g. Great Folds), the name of an occupant/tenant, and those of obvious meaning (e.g. Horse Close, Foxholes, Home Close, Kiln Close) have been omitted. Many names are intriguing, while others are deceptive to modern eyes. A separate list is given for woodland names. All are, or were, within the boundaries of the county.

Shape/pattern/size

Brown Cow Common (Woodford) – strips of land, from the OE 'brecchia'
Ell Edge (Lt Haughton) – L-shaped
Sauceridge (Little Houghton)
The Wrongs (Sibbertoft) – crooked
Spangle Row (Bozeat), Long Spong (Bradden), The Spung (Heyford) – a narrow strip of land
Damsel Meadow (Brixworth) – damask pattern (ridge and furrow)
Damask Gore (Woodford) – 'gore' means a triangular piece of land
Winkles (Litchborough) – many bends or angles, from the OE 'vinkel'
Pingle (Boddington) – OE for 'small enclosed piece of land'
Shakeldine (Little Oakley) – a wooded valley, from the OE 'sceaga'
Trinder (Hannington) – circular hill, from the OE 'trynde'
Cringleholme (The Bramptons) – circular meadow, from the ON 'kringla'
Worley (Overstone) – winding
Wounds (Cransley) – enclosed meadow or 'wong'
Starch Hill (Dallington) – tails of land, from the ME 'stertes'
Wranglands (Fotheringhay) – twisted strips
Wofurlong (Weedon Lois) – crooked
Slench (Addington) – curved boundaries, from 'sling'
Swing Slang (Grendon) – inverted 'L' shape

Poor fertility

Hell's Kitchen (Earls Barton)

Purgatory (Braybrooke)

Clem Vengeance (Charwelton) – from the OE 'clem' meaning 'to starve'

Scrawge or Scrooge Hill (Naseby)

Hunger Hill (Brigstock), Ungerull (Harpole), Hungry Hill Furlong (Deene), Hunger Hills
(Weldon)

Devil's Corner (Litchborough)

Pinchcut (Yardley Hastings)

Deadlands (Little Houghton)

Hard Hills (Guilsborough)

Sour Leys (Corby)

Sowrelands (Kingsthorpe)

Little Gains (near Grendon)

Belsen (Falcutt) – originally Long Meadow but later named after the Second World War
concentration camp, as a place where cows did not thrive very well

Good fertility

Silver Hill (Brigstock)

Gold Diggings (Woodnewton)

Honey Dole (Kislingbury), Honey Hill (Elkington)

Blithe Meadow (Kislingbuury)

Prospect (Braybrooke)

Gadshill (Harpole) – 'blessed by God', the provider of daily bread

Paradise (Litchborough) – the name can also be used sarcastically for land which requires a
lot of work!

Egglands (Brigstock)

Sweet Acre (Grendon)

Sunny Hill, Soilly Hill, Sweet Hill (Deenethorpe)

Martin's Gold (Harpole)

Garden of Eden (Wellingborough)

Nature of surface/soil

Clay Close (Great Oakley)

Cat's Brain (Little Houghton, Maidford) – mottled soil, rough clay with stones

Driffield (Cottingham) – dry field

Grimy (Harpole)

Red Ground (Greatworth) – the colour is due to ironstone deposits

Blackleys (Harpole) – dark soil

Featherbed (Maidford) – soggy soil

Moss Hall (Cottesbrooke) – boggy land, from the ON 'mos'

Rough Piece (Farthinghoe)

Smith Hill (Bozeat), Smith Meadow (Welton) – from 'smooth'

Callowell (Harpole) – bare hill

Calvey Close (Apethorpe) – bare enclosure

Row Dykes (Harpole) – rough ditches

Dungee (Bozeat) – covered with manure

Shotty Meadow (Yarwell) – covered with manure

Spanhoe (Laxton) – hill covered with wood chippings.

Rooty Hill (Moulton)

Cobra, Cogboro (East Farndon) – limestone hill', from the ON 'kalk'

Firmity (Evenley), Furmenty Slade (Brafield) – spongy soil, named after the popular wheat dish frumenty, either as a reference to its consistency when cooked or suggesting that the fields grew the wheat for it.

Topographical features

Bandy Slade (Corby) – from the OE 'beonet', meaning 'where bent grass grows', a type that is not good for grazing

Grymstone Slade (Geddington) – green stone, i.e. one covered in moss or lichen

The Hassocks (Geddington) – tufts of grass

The Twitch (Clipston), Twitch Common (Hollowell), Squitch (Badby), Squitch Field (Syresham), Switchley (Bugbrooke) – these five names refer to a particularly troublesome type of grass flourishing in loose soil, hated by farmers though much valued in folk medicine for the treatment of kidney and urinary problems. It has long, creeping underground stems which quickly spread just beneath the surface and it is harmful to crops. The name is derived from the OE 'civice' meaning 'vivacious' and it is difficult to eradicate, the only traditional remedy being to leave the ground as pasture for a few years, during which time other grasses, of a close-growing nature, will destroy its growth

Hob End (Milton Malsor) – land covered with tussocks of grass

Morehay (Blatherwycke) – enclosure on marshy land

Piper's Irons (Geddington) – shown on seventeenth-century maps of the Boughton House estate; it is believed that the 'irons' refer to a gibbet that stood there but this cannot be verified. An eponymous ballad tells the tale of one unfortunate who was chained up there for murdering his lover – dialect for 'hernes' (corners)

Sykiemore (Spratton) – from the OE 'sike', meaning 'land by a stream'

Brickle Meadow (Spratton) – from 'prickle'

Three Hills Field (Woodford) – refers to Bronze Age burial mounds

Everdon Stubbs (Everdon) – cleared land containing an ancient burial mound, now ploughed out

Worley (Overstone), Worledge (Brackley) – land by ancient burial mounds

Life (Holcot) – the hill, from the ME 'le lyth'

Ostor Hill (West Haddon) – eastern hill, an ancient tumulus, from the ON 'austr'

Warth/Wharf (Harrington) – fields with heaps of stones (cairns), from the ON 'vartha'

Wild Ho (Syresham) – wooded hill, from the OE weald

Dane Hole (Catesby) – the name is derived from 'dene' or valley and has nothing to do with the Danish invaders but an association was made long ago and has passed into folklore!

Hells Closes (Deenethorpe) – hills

Position/order/features

Angulls (Little Houghton) – from 'Hang Hills' meaning on a slope

Windesarse (Hanging Houghton) – this was later changed to Windhouse, another example of later fashionable sensibility!

Cold Croft Leys (Wadenhoe)

Cracknuts (Little Houghton) – a swing gateway into an angled enclosure, similar to a kissing or 'cuckoo' gate

Modley Gate (Green Norton) – communal meeting place in a clearing, from the OE 'mot'

Pudding Bag (Marston Trussell, Sibbertoft), Puddin' End (Braybrooke) – a dead end

Waypost Close (Wadenhoe, Weldon)

Drake Stones Furlong (Woodford) – a corruption of 'dragon' and a reference to the thin flat stones used by children at play.

Buffton (Deenethorpe) – a field above the township or village

Boundary/status

Cut Throat Field (Great Doddington) – dialect 'cut through' (short cut).

Flitlands (Yelvertoft), Flitwell (Clipston), Flitnill (Harpole), Flitnells (Gayton), Flitten Hills (Passenham), Flithills (Cottebrooke) – from the OE 'flit' meaning disputed land that is claimed by more than one parish or owner

Landymore (Spratton)

Bondage (Greatworth) – fields that have since lost their boundaries

Mere (Harpole) – from the OE for boundary

Jack Arthur (Great Oakley) – a piece of wasteland is a 'jack'

Scotland (Evenley) – land subject to taxation, from the ON 'skot', meaning 'tax'; a boundary field

Whorestone Furlong (Desborough) – from 'hoarstone' or greystone on a boundary

Studbough Hill (Staverton) – hill of contention, from the OE 'stint beorg'; the field lies on the boundary with Catesby

Distance from settlement

Van Diemen's Land (Brigstock)

Damons (Harpole) – a corruption of Van Diemen's Land

Botany Bay (Moulton, Eydon, Yardley Gobion)

New Zealand (Eydon)

Manitoba (Eydon)

Scarborough (Harpole)

Canada (Bozeat)

Klondike (Earls Barton)

Type of cultivation

Stubby Stiles (Brigstock) – former woodland that has been 'assarted' or cleared of trees and roots

Stockings (Brackley, Little Oakley), Long Stockings (Duddington), Stocker (Corby), Stokewood Leys (Brigstock), Stoken Hill (Bozeat), Great and Little Stocking (Geddington) Stocking (Hartwell) – former woodland that has been cleared, usually with some vestiges of tree stumps remaining

Dibbings (Deene) – a field where acorns were once planted

Vink Dibing Furlong (Corby) – a strip of land where acorns have been or once planted; 'vink' comes from the ON 'vengi', meaning 'field'

Winning Foot Hill (Lyveden area) – from the OE 'whin', meaning 'to cultivate' former woodland or marsh lying at the bottom of a slope

Specific crop grown

Lincroft (Brackley), Flaxlands (Gretton, Everdon, Grafton Underwood, Ecton), Flexland (Grendon) – flax

Wadcroft (Kettering), Wadells (Woad Hills), Wot Ground (Harlestone), Wodells (Spratton), Wad Ground (Culworth) – woad

Madcraft (Braybrooke) – madder

The Lusome (Piddington) – lucerne

Banhaw Closes (Benefield), Bangraves Close (Deene) Bandland (Brigstock, Brackley), Banlands (Brington), Bancroft, (Yelvertoft), Ballards (Ashby St Ledger), Ballands (Haselbech), Banlands (Brington), Bollands (Tiffield) – beans

Rugg Hole Field (Pipewell) – rye corner, from the ON 'rugr'

Berrel (Woodford Halse, Maidford) – barley hill

Pesshills (Ecton) – peas

Sanfion Field (Falcutt) – a natural habitat of the plant sainfoin, which made excellent fodder for cattle and was also a good honey plant

Association with animals

Easter Hill (Rushton) – from the OE 'eowestre' meaning 'sheepfolds', from where we get our word for female sheep, 'ewe'; no connection with Easter!

Dagmore Furlong (Woodford) – 'dags' were the mud and mire which accumulated on the wool of the sheep's undersides; 'dagging' was the removal of the dirty wool

Luscotes (near Brigstock) – where pigsties were kept

Excellent (Corby) – from 'exland', land where oxen were kept

'Ug 'Ill (Wellingborough) – a corruption of Hog Hill

Uddermuster (Wadenhoe) – cows

Conigeer (Stanion), Conny Geer (Hemington) – rabbits

Studfall (Corby) – enclosure where horses were kept

Wormstalls (Great Oakley) – cow shelters

Cockerhead (Brigstock) – frequented by woodcock; it was originally known as Cockerode, from 'roding' to denote the bird circling its territory

Tickidy Field (Geddington) – probably where goats (OE 'ticce') were kept; a later name was Cid Field

Haver Hill (Twywell) – male goats (ON 'haefer')

Woolspit (Ashby St Ledger) – wolf snares

Wolfage (Brixworth) – hedged enclosure to keep wolves out

Sharrag Hill (Castle Ashby) – where 'shearhogs' (sheep) were kept

Horsley Hill (Everdon) – horses

Cathanger (Woodend) – wild cat slope

Markers

Christmas Hill (Litchborough) – hill with a cross as a boundary marker

White Cross Field (near Pipewell) – there was probably a signpost here as the Cistercian abbey of Pipewell was close by and the field, which belonged to the abbey, adjoins the only road which led to it

Waypost Close (Wadenhoe, Weldon)

Association with owner or tenant

Gunhole (Ashton, near Roade) – a corner of land belonging to Gunhild
    (an OE female first name)
Gunsex (Higham Ferrers) – Gunni's land with streams
Grimble White (Deene) – Grimbold's clearing (ON 'thveit')
Sulehay (near Yarwell) – clearing belonging to Serfa (an OE male first name)
Tottenhoe (Southwick) – spur of land belonging to Totta (an OE male first name)
Snatch Hill (Corby) – hill belonging to Snota (an OE male first name; 'Nottingham' is also
    derived from this name)
Parrot's Ground (Falcutt) – surname of the nineteenth-century owner
Golden Slade (Armston) – Goldwine's strip of land

Association with tragedy or burial

(either as a result of battle, murder or natural causes; some burials were on parish boundaries)
Deadman's Grave (Kislingbury, Warmington), Deadman (Hollowell)
Dead Shells (Welton) – where a churl lay dead, from the ME 'dedechurl'

Owner's status

Hangman's Barn (Spratton)
Presgrave, Prestoe (Deene) – priest
Parson's Piece (Great Doddington), Parson's Close (Grendon)
Anchor Terrace (Milton Malsor) – habitation of an anchorite/hermit
Hermitage Meadow (Braybrooke)

Purpose of income from land

Poor's Lot (Weston by Weedon Lois), Poor Close (Sibbertoft), Poor's Close (Greatworth),
    Poormans Sale (Deene), Poor's Piece (Aynho)
Charity (Kislingbury)
Bellropes (Clipston) – church income from renting this field.
Lamp Acre (Little Oakley) – income from renting this field went towards the support of a
    light for the altar

Supernatural associations

Puckwell Hill Field (Glapthorn)
Harrow Hill (Brington) OE 'hears', heathen.
Grimsland (Benefield-Oundle), Grymsfielde (Glapthorn)
Scratland (near Deenethorpe) ON 'skratti', demon.
Ghostly Leys (Brigstock)
Devil's Hole (Wellingborough)

Seasonal or Festival use

The Merrymaking (Pury End)

Midsummer Meadow (Northampton)

Maze Green (Woodford)

Shewters Hill (Great Oakley), Shooters Hill (Great Addington, Easton Neston) – used for practice with the longbow

Lamas Ground (Deenethorpe) – a field used from Lammas Day (1 August) until the following spring specifically for the grazing of cattle or pasturing of sheep

Lamas Ground, Midsummer Holm, Whit Sunday Holm, Feast Day Holm (Woodford) – these four meadows were used seasonally in rotation; as one season finished, the animals were moved into the next designated field

The Tilting Ground (Rockingham) – a field belonging to the castle and used for jousting during a royal stay; the castle was a popular residence for medieval kings when hunting in Rockingham Forest

Ankers (Higham Ferrers) – the handcross carried during the 'beating the bounds' custom

Former use or association

Oven (Farthinghoe) – where a kiln or furnace once stood; it can also mean a rubbish tip

Irons Corner (Greatworth) – ironstone quarrying

Bloom Field (Southwick) – named after the vast scatterings of iron bloom from the former smelting site

Gallows Hill (Gretton), Gallows Hill (Rushden), Gallows Bank (Kilsby)

Gallow Field (Stuchbury) – originally the site of Anglo-Saxon moots for the Alboldstow hundred.

Gib Hill (Hollowell) – so-named after the execution of a murderer in 1764

Stunpit (Litchborough), Lung Stunny (Spratton) – stone quarrying

The Dale (Cottingham) – a former stone quarry

Halefield (Apethorpe) – site of a deserted medieval village called Hale

Milne Field (Gayton, Great Oakley) – mill

The Falls (Harrington) – earthworks of the former manor house, gardens and fishponds

Castle Hill (Wadenhoe) – site of a former Saxon manor house

Toot Hill Field (Barnwell), Tuthill (Towcester, Barnwell, Fineshade), Tootle (West Halse, Paulerspury), Tottenhoe (Southwick) – lookout hill

Swag Close (Weldon) – used by poachers

Spellow Close (Cottingham) – possibly from 'speech hill', a meeting place for important decisions

Commemorative

Spion Kop (Braybrooke) – named after a Boer War battle

Cromwell Corner (Sibbertoft) – near the site of the Battle of Naseby

Bunker's Hill (Spratton) – a battle during the American War of Independence

Canada (Moreton Pinkney) – named in the nineteenth century when Dr Oxendon, who was associated with the village, became Bishop of Montreal

Danes Moor (Edgcote) – the site of a 1467 battle during the Wars of the Roses; like other names in the county, it has no connection with the Danish invaders but the name has passed into folklore

Battle Green Pitt Meadow (Kingscliffe) – the supposed site of a battle between the forces of Ethelred, King of Northumbria, and Adelbald and Heardbert, who were in rebellion against him

WOOD NAMES

Bangrave (Deene) – grove by the beanfields

Banhaw Wood (Benefield) – wood adjoining a slope where beans are grown

Barrowdykes Wood (Wilbarston) – with mounds and ditches

Bearshank Wood (Lyveden) – the wood was owned by Robert de Bareschanke of Castor in the thirteenth century

Benty Coppice (Great Oakley) – contains bent grass

Bird's Grave (Biggin Hall, near Glapthorn/Oundle) – grove inhabited by many birds

Blackmore Thick (Kingscliffe area) – the name means 'dark pool thicket'

Bradshaw (Lyveden) – 'broad wood'

Britain Sale (Blatherwycke) – named after Ranulf Brito, who was granted the wood in 1277

Broil (Earls Barton) – from the Latin for 'a wood or park stocked with beasts of the chase'

Cadge Wood (Blatherwycke) – where falcons were sold

Catshead Wood (near Brigstock) – named after the original unique shape of the wood

Cattage Wood (near Middleton) – wood with a homestead or cottage

Chequer Hill Coppice (Titchmarsh) – refers to the pattern of the soil

Cherry Lap (Brigstock and Wadenhoe) – bright clearing in a wood

Cockborow (Brigstock) – frequented by woodcocks; 'borow' comes from the OE 'bearu', meaning 'wood'

Colsters (Kingscliffe area) – where charcoal was burned

Crayley (Blatherwycke) – the name means 'grey wood'

Cuckoo Pen Wood (Barnwell All Saints)

Cut Throat Spinney (Aynho)

Earlstrees (Corby) – belonging to the Earl (of Cardigan)

Ellens Bower (Little Oakley), Ellens (Hemington) – elder tree bower

Fougill Wood (Daventry) – bird wood, from the OE 'fugol'

Friar's Sale – belonging to the the monks of Fineshade Abbey

Hollow Wood (Deene) – wood at a corner of land

Horsehoes (Blatherwycke) – dirty wood, from the OE 'horsc'

Hornstocks (Duddington) – strangely shaped stumps

Hostage Wood (Blatherwycke) – hedges fastened with a hesp (lock), that is, a wood protected against intruders.

Laundimer Woods (Brigstock) – on a parish boundary, from the OE 'gemaere'

Linches (Achurch), Lynches (Church Brampton) – a slope formed by ancient ploughing; Linches is now covered in woodland

Mawkin Hedges (Geddington Woods) – frequented by hares, from the ME 'malkin'

Mazedale Spinney (Norton) – wooded valley on the boundary, from the OE 'maeresdael'; also called Marsdale

Pest House Wood (Aynho) – where a building for the isolation of those with a contagious disease once stood

Plum Cake Spinney (Wellingborough) – the name refers to the waterlogged soil

Presgrave (Corby) – priest's grove

Priors Haw (Weldon), Priors Hall (Woodnewton) – both connected with nearby Fineshade Abbey. The latter site should also read 'Haw' but it became 'Hall' after a clerical misreading or copying of a document, when two upward strokes of the handwritten 'w' were interpreted as 'll'. Consequently, for many years there was local speculation as to whether a building ever existed there. A similar situation happened with nearby Corby Haw, which appeared on some maps as Corby Hall

Ratling Irons Plantation (Achurch) – it was here that French prisoners were chained overnight on their way to Norman Cross

Rawhaw (Pipewell) – roe deer coppice, from the ON 'rå'

Ringhaw (Nassington) – from the ON 'dreng' meaning 'boy'; the name means 'coppice maintained by a young man'

Rising Wood (Little Oakley) – 'brushwood'

Salcey Forest – willow wood, from the old French 'salceia'

Sart Wood (Little Oakley) – land cleared (ME 'assart') of trees for farming; this has now reverted back to woodland

Scotland Wood (Maidwell) – subject to taxation, from the ON 'skot', meaning 'tax'

Silley Coppice (Churchfield Farm, near Lyveden/Oundle) – from the ON 'selja' for 'willow'

Skulking Dudley Coppice (Clopton) – named after a local ghost

Thoroughsale Wood (Corby) – from the ME 'thursall', an area of woodland under special management for fencing, marking and other purposes, for future sale

Thrift (Glapthorn), Thrift Close (Harringworth) – woodland, from the OE 'fyrhth'

Waterloo Gorse (near Ashley) – covert of the Pytchley Hunt a commemorative name (after the famous battle).

Yokewood (Great Oakley) – named after 'ye Oke', a spectacular oak tree shown and named on old maps of the area

BIBLIOGRAPHY

Primary sources

Baker, Anne Elizabeth, *Glossary of Northamptonshire Words & Phrases*, J.R. Smith, 1854

Gelling, Margaret, *Place Names in the Landscape*, Dent, 1984
Gover, J et al, *The Place Names of Northamptonshire*, CUP, 1933

Hill, Peter, *In Search of the Green Man in Northamptonshire*, Orman, 1997
   Rockingham Forest Then and Now, Orman, 1995
   Rockingham Forest Revisited, Orman, 1998

Markham, C.A. *The Proverbs of Northamptonshire*, Stanton, 1897

Sternberg, Thomas, *The Dialect & Folklore of Northamptonshire*, J.R. Smith, 1851

Turner, G.J. ed., *Select Pleas of the Forest*, Selden Society, 1899
The English Folk Dance and Song Society Journal No. 7, 1905
The Vaughan Williams Collection, Lucy Broadwood m/s

Secondary Sources

Alexander, M., *British Folklore, Myths & Legends*, Weidenfeld & Nicholson, 1982
Askham, John, *Sketches in Prose and Verse*, NMC, 1893

Bailey, H. *Archaic England*, Chapman & Hall, 1919
Baker, John, *History of the County of Northamptonshire*, 1822
Bayley, Thomas Haynes, *The Mistletoe Bough*, 1834
Bennett, Judith, *A Medieval Life*, McGraw-Hill College, 1999
Berger, J. *The Social Reality of Religion*, Penguin, 1971
Bishop, Peter, *The Greening of Psychology*, Spring Publications, 1990

Bord, Janet and Colin, *Earth Rites*, Paladin, 1983
Brand, J., *Observation on the Popular Antiquities of Great Britain* (three volumes), 1853

Chambers, R., *Book of Days*, London, 1860
Child, F.J., *English and Scottish Popular Ballad*, Houghton Mifflin, 1882
Clare, John, *Poems Descriptive of Rural Life and Scenery*, 1820
   Introduction to *The Village Minstrel*, 1821
   The Shepherd's Calendar, 1827
   The Rural Muse, 1835
   The Cottage Festival (unpublished writings)
   Letter to William Hone (unpublished writings)
Coales, Tony, *They Walked By Night*, privately published, 1995
Cooper, H., *Pastoral: Medieval into Renaissance*, D.S. Brewer, 1977
Cooper, Quentin, *Maypoles, Martyrs & Mayhem*, Bloomsbury, 1994

Deacon, George, *John Clare and the Folk Tradition*, Sinclair Brown, 1983
Dryden, Alice, *Memorials of Northamptonshire,* Bemrose 1903

Field, John, *English Field Names*, David & Charles, 1972
Forman, Joan, *Haunted East Anglia*, Jarrold, 1974
Fraser, James, *The Golden Bough*, Macmillan, 1922

Green, M., *A Harvest of Festivals*, Longman, 1980
Grimes, Dorothy, *Like Dew Before The Sun*, privately published, 1991

Hackwood, Frederick H., *Legends, Traditions, Myths & Symbols*, London
Hill, Peter, *Witch Beliefs in 16th & 17th Century England*, unpublished thesis, 1975
   Around Oundle and Thrapston, Tempus, 1998, reprinted 2002
   Corby, Tempus, 1996, reprinted 2004
   Corby: A Second Selection, Tempus, 1997
   Millennium, Herald & Post Publications, 1999
   Articles in *Northamptonshire Times*, July 1998, December 1998, July 1999
   Material from BBC Radio Northampton talks
Hole, Christina, *British Folk Customs*, Hutchinson, 1976
Hone, William, *Every-Day Book* (three volumes), London, 1824
   The Year Book, London, 1832
Hutton, Ronald, *Stations of the Sun*, Oxford University Press, 1996
   The Rise and Fall of Merry England, Oxford University Press, 1994

Jones, E.L., *Agriculture & Economic Growth,* London 1970

Lambeth, M., *A Golden Dolly*, John Baker, 1969

Markham, C.A., *Northamptonshire Villages*, 1921
Morton, John, *The Natural History of Northamptonshire*, 1712

NFWI (Northamptonshire Federation of Women's Institutes), *Northamptonshire Village Book*,
   NFWI Countryside Books

Pennick, Nigel, *Crossing the Borderlines*, Capall Bann, 1998
Pipe, Marion, *Northamptonshire Ghosts & Legends*, Countryside Books, 1993
Purkiss, Diane, *At The Bottom of the Garden*, New York University Press, 2000

Sammes, Aylett, *Britannia Antiqua Illustrata*, 1676

Scot, Reginald, *The Discoverie of Witchcraft*, 1584

Scott, C.H. Montagu-Douglas, *Northamptonshire Songs*, Chiswick Press, 1904-6
  Tales of Old Northamptonshire, 1924

Scott, Simon, *The Follies of Boughton Park*, Scott Publications, 1995

Sharp, C.J., *English Folk Songs* (two volumes), London, 1921

Simpson, Jacqueline, *A Dictionary of English Folklore*, OUP, 2000

Slade, Paddy, *Seasonal Magic*, Capall Bann, 1997

Spence, L., *The Fairy Tradition in Britain*, Rider, 1948
  Myth and Ritual in Dance, Game & Rhyme, Watts, 1947

Storey, Alfred, *The Historical Legends of Northamptonshire*, Taylor, 1880

Strutt, Joseph, *The Sports & Pastimes of the People of England*, Chatto & Windus, 1880

Stubbes, Philip, *An Anatomie of Abuses*, ed. New Shakespeare Society, 1882

Summers, Montagu, *The Geography of Witchcraft*, Keegan Paul, 1927

Swift, E., *Folk Tales of the East Midlands*, Nelson, 1954

Taylor, John, *Northamptonshire Witchcraft*, Northampton, 1867
  Bibliotheca Northantonensis, Northampton, 1869

Thomas, Keith, *Religion and the Decline of Magic*, Penguin, 1971

Thompson, Beeby, *The Brooks & Rivers in Northamptonshire*, 1929

Wise, Charles, *The Northamptonshire Legends*, Goss, 1905

Periodicals

Bailey, H., 'Plough Plays in the East Midlands', Journal of the English Folk Dance and Song Society (Vol VII, No. 2, 1953)

CPRE (Council for the Protection of Rural England) magazine

Northamptonshire Notes & Queries (Vols 1-6), 1889-1894

Northamptonshire County Magazine (various)

Weldon Local History Society Magazine

Brigstock Local History Society Magazine

Taking Stock, Gretton Local History Magazine

Aspects of Helmdon

Hindsight

Posthumous memoirs

Bagshaw, Gertrude

Bailey, Jack

Beaver, Annie

Bonney, Henry Key

Colyer, Flo

Ellis, Frank

Harrison, Elsie

Kimbell, Charles

Lock, Lance

Lock, Adèle

Palmer, Edith

Archives of local history societies

INDEX